A

GRAMMAR

OF THE

ANGLO-SAXON LANGUAGE.

BY

LOUIS F. KLIPSTEIN,

AA. LL.M. & PH.D.

OF THE UNIVERSITY OF GIESSEN; AUTHOR OF "ANALECTA ANGLO-SAXONICA," ETC.

REVISED AND ENLARGED EDITION.

NEW YORK:
GEO. P PUTNAM, 506 BROADWAY.

1859.

TO

ORVILLE HORWITZ, ESQ. M.A.

This Volume

IS SINCERELY INSCRIBED

BY ONE

WHO HAS EVER ADMIRED

HIS TALENTS AND SCHOLARSHIP,

AND

APPRECIATED A FRIENDSHIP,

WHICH A CLOSE INTIMACY OF YEARS HAS TENDED ONLY

TO STRENGTHEN.

PREFACE.

It has been asserted by some that the common people of Italy, Spain, and Portugal, speak the language of their respective countries mostly in accordance with what is written among them; while the same class in England, and we may add in our own country to a certain extent, are generally deficient with regard to the received principles of correct speech in the quality and use of words. Without saying how far the assertion holds good, we will only remark that the philologist and the attentive observer who understands the language of his forefathers, will at once perceive that what is supposed to be incorrect, is in the majority of cases the genuine Anglo-Saxon, which expresses itself through its natural channel. Above the class to which we have alluded, a superstructure has been raised in the various elements which have entered into the composition of our present English since the days of Gower and Chaucer, of Surrey and Spenser, and which took their rise, indeed, considerably anterior to that period, if not with the Norman Conquest. The languages of Italy, Spain, and Portugal, on the contrary, have remained comparatively stationary since their first formation, and, from their very nature, they must be spoken by all conditions of society with but little difference.

1*

If we are partly led to the study of the Latin and Greek languages from the light which they throw upon the structure of our own, the Anglo-Saxon, for the same reason, has claims upon us almost equally great, forming, as it does, the broad basis upon which the others rest. So true is this, that it can be safely affirmed that no one has a thorough knowledge of English, who is unacquainted with an element of so much importance.

It is from a desire of making American youth, who glory in their Anglo-Saxon descent, acquainted with the language of their ancestors, that the author has been induced to issue the following pages. He has long perceived the want of something of the kind from the press in this country, while the subject has of late years received so much attention in Great Britain, and trusts that he has at last met it in a certain measure. How far he has succeeded in his attempt, he leaves it to the literary portion of the community to judge.

The principal authorities consulted in preparing this work, have been the *Angelsaksisk Sprogloere* of the late distinguished philologist, Prof. Rask, of Copenhagen, the learned *Deutsche Grammatik* of Prof. Grimm, and the *Compendious Grammar of the Primitive English or Anglo-Saxon Language* and larger *Dictionary* of that eminent Saxon scholar, the Rev. J. Bosworth, LL. D., PH. D., etc., etc., etc. In the general order and arrangement of his matter the author has differed both from Prof. Rask and Dr. Bosworth, and likewise from them and the rest who have written upon the subject, in many of his views of the language. In some few instances he has used the expressions of others, either through inadvertence, or where he had found the same employed by more than one to such an extent as to become common property.

It was intended at first to introduce the Ablative, but upon mature reflection, deemed unnecessary, as however general and express that case may have been in earlier times, with the exception of a few peculiar forms, it evidently does not belong to the language as we now have it, distinct from the Dative. It would seem to have been gradually laid aside, while the Dative finally, in almost every instance, was used in its stead.

The accent has been employed in every case in which analogy would justify it. How much the proper pronunciation, as well as distinction, of words depends upon its adoption, will be easily seen.

Not only has the "monkish" character been rejected and the Roman substituted in its place, but the Þ, þ, has been represented by Ṯẖ, ṯẖ, and the Ð, ð, by Th, th. While nothing is lost by this further change, typographical uniformity has been gained.

St. James, Santee, S. C.,
April 1, 1848

PREFACE TO THE REVISED EDITION.

The disadvantageous circumstances under which the Author's *Grammar of the Anglo-Saxon Language* was originally prepared for the press, owing to his distance from the place of publication, and the accidental loss of matter designed for rendering the work more complete, having led to defects in its mechanical execution and general structure, a new and improved edition is herewith offered to the public. While therefore much that was unintentionally omitted, has been added to the pages which follow, nothing has been done to affect the arrangement and division previously adopted, in order that all confusion with regard to references might be avoided. In the work as it now stands, the peculiar views entertained by the author concerning the intimate structure of the tongue, will be found to correspond more nearly with the same as set forth by him in the *Analecta Anglo-Saxonica,* and still more fully in the copious *Glossary* intended to accompany the volumes which bear that title.

In giving the various forms of such words as are introduced in the evolution of the different parts of speech, those have generally been rejected which cannot be referred to the genius of the language as otherwise developed, or which evidently belong to its transition state. At the same time, there have been added many others which connect themselves with the tongue in its earlier stages, and which help to confirm the opinion elsewhere advanced concerning its highly original character.

The term "monkish," borrowed and applied to the peculiar form of the Anglo-Saxon characters, as modified from the Roman, we would reject from the foregoing Preface. It is no more applicable to the Anglo-Saxon than to the various forms of the Gothic once obtaining wherever the latter name was carried. All the modified forms of the Roman letter will be found indeed to correspond to the modifications of the Roman architecture, among whatever people they were both introduced.

Some observations by the same hand will be found to precede the Essay on the Study of the Anglo-Saxon as originally prepared, along with other additions.

The suggestions relative to the orthography of certain classes of words in English we must say deserve consideration. Attention to them as far as the removal of barbarisms from the language in that respect is concerned, will ultimately prevent complete radicalism. We want an orthography strictly *English* or *Anglican*, but one maintaining, not destroying analogies.

For the increased expense incurred, the author can expect to be repaid only through an increased interest in the study of the language, signs of which begin to show themselves in various sections of the country. Such signs should be hailed as the dawn of a day in American scholarship, in which to be acquainted with our mother tongue is not to be ignorant of the genius of its main element.

St. James, Santee, S. C.,
May 1, 1849.

CONTENTS.

CHAPTER IV.

CHAPTER V.

CHAPTER VI.

CHAPTER VII.

CHAPTER VIII.

CHAPTER IX.

CHAPTER X.

CHAPTER XI.

PART III.—SYNTAX.

PART IV.—PROSODY.

INTRODUCTION.

ON THE STUDY OF THE ANGLO-SAXON LANGUAGE.

The history of a language is in truth the history of a people. In seeking for the elements of which the one is composed, we are necessarily obliged to inquire into the vicissitudes that the other has undergone. Every change that has taken place in the condition of a people, and every revolution that has marked its existence, may as distinctly be traced in the structure of the language of that people, as the age of a tree may be known by the successive layers of which it is composed, or that of the earth itself deduced from the geological evidences in its crust. No better example could possibly be adduced of this philological truth, than an examination of the English tongue in connection with the history of Britain,—a history that might almost as clearly be derived, if we were deprived of every other source, from a careful, minute, and skilful analysis of the language itself, as the Indian hunter is said to derive the precise characteristics of the animal he is pursuing, from an accurate examination of the footprints it has left in the sand, or of the marks it has made in its progress.

The early history of the inhabitants of Britain, like that of all the ancient nations, is lost in the twilight of fable, and the imagination of their descendants has been, from time to time, exercised in accounting by fanciful and, often, supernatural causes for that origin which is either entirely unknown, or so wrapped in mystery as to deserve but little consideration. Unable to give any satisfactory account of their true origin, poetry was permitted to supply the place of history, and, veiling ignorance under myths and allegories, the Egyptians, the Greeks and the Romans, were not behind the Britons, the Celts or the Saxons, in supposing that they had sprung, like plants, from the ground, or were descended from the gods,* or had existed before the moon herself.† It is in vain, therefore, to attempt to penetrate those mysteries in which ancient history, beyond a certain period, is hopelessly involved, or to lift that veil by which, no doubt with some wise design, the unknown is separated from the known.

One truth seems, however, to be as firmly settled by those marks which the successive migrations of tribes and of nations have left behind them, in their advance westward, as by the Pentateuch itself; and that is, the fact recorded by Moses, that man originated in the eastern portions of the world, to which region the various inhabitants of the different parts of the earth, in successive centuries, may be referred with something like certainty. There first began those associations of men, which were the basis of states, kingdoms, and empires; and there were first cultivated the arts and the sciences. Civilization, in the course of time, began, as a necessary consequence, to grow up in that quarter, and in its train followed all those evils which flow from ease, luxury, and refinement. Increased wants on the part of the people, and habits of indolence and indulgence, gave rise to inventions and to crimes; and that spirit of generosity and of noble bearing which seems the natural offspring of freedom from control, gradually gave way to less honorable feelings, until, strange as it may seem,

---

* The story of Cadmus, of Mars and Rhea Sylvia, and the Grecian fables, are well known.

† See Potter's Antiquities, vol. i. p. 1

luxury, avarice, and ambition, "dissolved their social morality, and substituted a refined, but persevering and ever-calculating *selfishness,* for that natural benevolence which reason desires." The diffusion of this worst of passions served the important purpose of spreading mankind over the face of the earth, just as the sordid endeavor to convert all the metals into gold, gave rise to the noble science of chemistry. Intestine dissensions and civil broils, the desire of novelty, or the still stronger desire of gain, the love of conquest, disease, and accidental circumstances, from time to time separated a portion of the people from the great mass, who shook off the trammels by which they had been bound, and advanced towards that country now called Europe, clearing its primeval forests, draining its pestilential marshes, and peopling its wild territories. Hence arose those nomadic tribes, to which modern Europe, modern languages, and modern civilization, are so much indebted for their present condition. It is to them, *barbarians** as they were called, that we must look for the population and the language of England.

Passing over the long interval clouded in mist and obscurity, and bounded on the one side by the *general* knowledge derived to us from an investigation of the imperfect fragments which remain of the character, languages, institutions, and religious superstitions of whole nations that have long since passed away; and on the other, by the more *specific* information handed down to us by tradition and history, we find that the Kimmerians (a people whose name

* This word which at first was applied by the Greeks, as the word *Goyim* by the Hebrews, to all *foreign* nations, gradually became perverted in signification, and now carries with it the idea of ignorance and ferocity; as the word *villain,* that originally indicated simply the tenure by which an individual held his property, is now necessarily connected in our minds with wickedness and rascality.

is mentioned by Homer,* nine hundred years before Christ) were the first of those three distinct races which successively crossed the Bosphorus, and spread themselves over northern and western Europe. The earliest correct information we have in regard to this people, locates one of their tribes in the Cimbric Chersonesus, (the present Denmark,) and another, the Celts, (more properly Kelts,) or Gauls,† on the shores of the ocean;—both situations admirably adapted for the conquest and colonization of Britain. That they, a roving and restless people, passed over into the adjacent islands, the examination of the languages of Wales and of Ireland, when compared with the ancient Gaulish, abundantly testifies and corroborates the faint outlines of history left us, and the conclusions drawn from the relative position and habits of the people. It is to these tribes that we must trace those remnants of the ancient Celtic tongue to be found in our vernacular.

It is impossible to say how long it was before the Kimmerians, Kelts, and their kindred tribes, were obliged to yield to another race, that came in floods from Asia, sweeping over the continent of Europe and driving before them, with resistless force, every impediment. The Goths composed the second inundation that rolled from beyond the Bosphorus.‡ True it is, that the Romans had, in the meanwhile, planted a colony in Britain, and from the time of Cæsar to that of Honorius, had, with difficulty and subject to continued outbreaks, held a footing in the island; but they had never been able to impress their manners, or their language on the mass of the population, and have left fewer

* ἔνθα δὲ Κιμμερίων ἀνδρῶν δῆμος τε πόλις τε. Od. Λ, v. 14.

† Qui ipsorum linguâ Celtae, nostrâ Galli appellantur.—*Caes. de Bel. Gal.*, Liber I., ch. 1.

‡ Dr. Percy has so clearly established the distinction between the Celtic and Gothic tribes, that we look upon it as a settled question among historians and philologists.

traces of their possession of Britain than any of its ancient inhabitants. About the middle of the fifth century, the Sons of the Sacæ, or Saxons, the Angles, and the Jutes, (three Gothic tribes,) began to drive the Kelts and the Britons to the fastnesses and mountains of Wales, and, across the sea, into Ireland, and to establish themselves permanently in the country now called England. So complete was this conquest effected by the Anglo-Saxons, that they replaced the manners, religion, laws, and language of the conquered tribes by those which they had brought with them from the continent. Dwellings in caves yielded to more formal habitations, and the worship of the Brazen Bull and the Druids gave way to temples dedicated to Woden and to Thor.* Their language so entirely took the place of that of the former inhabitants, and so permanently fixed itself in the island, that, although the manners and laws of the people have completely changed, although the worship of idols has yielded to a purer and more rational religion, neither time nor subsequent invasion has been able to expel from Britain the language of the Anglo-Saxons, which to this day forms the bone and sinew of our glorious mother tongue. It is to the importance of the study of this ancient language that we desire to direct our attention.

Language itself may properly be defined to be "the expression of ideas either by sounds or signs." To the former we give the more specific name of *spoken*, and to the latter that of *written* language. It is the capacity of expressing ideas through language which confessedly raises man above the other works of the Creator, and which places him in the scale of being "but little lower than the angels." It is the different degrees in which this capacity is possessed, that draws the line of demarkation between the untutored

* The names of the deities from whom we derive Wednesday, or Woden's day, and Thursday, or Thor's day.

mind of the New Zealand savage, and the intellect that originates the beautiful periods of Macaulay—a line, too, that is continually becoming more and more defined; for, just in proportion as civilization advances, and as the arts and sciences progress and develope themselves, does language become more useful in itself and more admirable in its structure, until the nicest shades of meaning, and the finest and most hair-split distinctions in thought, may be set forth and conveyed to other minds with a precision truly wonderful. So far, indeed, is this true, that, whether existing as cause or effect, the curious inquirer may trace the wavy line of civilization, from the wild hordes of Tartary to the polished inhabitants of Berlin, by exactly following the progress and more elevated structure of the tongues of the divers countries through which he may pass, as he advances from the disjointed jargon of Beloochistan to the learned and philosophic language of Germany. It will be further found on inquiry and reflection, that the desire of becoming acquainted with the various languages used by the inhabitants, both ancient and modern, of different portions of the earth, has kept pace or rather increased with social and intellectual improvement among nations. The North American Indian, proud of his native forest and of his naked form, feels his unwritten gibberish adequate to all his wants, and never spends a thought on the mode in which neighboring nations differ from his own tribe in their forms of speech. The Turkish merchant or the Mohammedan dervis, but half-animated under the influence of his opium and his pipe, is satisfied if he can give vent to his few words in a dialect understood by his customer, or misunderstood by his votary, his dull intellect having never been taught to stray beyond the confines of his coffee or his sherbet. But pass within the borders of enlightened France, or cross the channel which separates the continent from the research of England, and you may behold men who, not content with studying the various languages that are now spoken throughout the different kingdoms of Europe; who, not satisfied with analyzing the Latinity of Lucan, the Greek of Aristophanes, or the Hebrew of Maimonides, are searching for the hidden mysteries contained in the hieroglyphics of Egypt, and in the still more curious and recondite inscriptions of Central America, or are loading their brains with the numerous dialects of the vast territory of Hindustan. One may there admire the labors of a Champollion or a Jomard, of a Clarke or a Porson, of a Sir William Jones or a Warren Hastings.

We have intimated that this desire has increased with the rise and progress of the arts and sciences, and the general diffusion of letters. Is not this true? Compare the condition of the European world from the fifth to the fifteenth century; from the time when the swarms of barbarians from the northern hive overspread Italy, till the period of the invention of printing, of the compass, and of gunpowder, with its present state. The general darkness that prevailed during the former period is proverbial, and the learning preserved in the cloisters, where alone the merest elements of cultivation were to be found, was extremely limited. A knowledge of Latin, (the language of the church,) and the study of Greek, in which tongue the New Testament had been written, were thought to be paramount even to the preservation and use of the language of the country in which those asylums of study were situated. The language of Rome became the universal medium of communication, and was looked upon as the only true garb in which the thoughts of philosophers should be dressed; and posterity must gratefully acknowledge that the invaluable monuments of Greek and Roman literature were multiplied through the indefatigable pens of the monks, and thus saved from utter loss. But beyond this their inquiries into language did not extend. Every tribe, and every feudal territory looked upon its neighbors as barbarians, whose dialects, or whose customs and laws, were unworthy of being known. Except when marching to conquest, or when protecting themselves against the aggressions of their enemies, they knew little and cared less about the people by whom they were surrounded. But this state of indifference and disregard gradually passed away. The consequences of those great discoveries which mark the fifteenth century, were soon felt in the general impetus that was given to the diffusion of information, to the cultivation of the sciences, and to the establishment of that *commercial* intercourse, which has tended more than any thing else to the civilization of the world. Constant interchange of products and of wares soon taught men that their own interests would be promoted by a knowledge of the languages of those nations with whom they were brought in contact. No more powerful stimulus could have been applied, as may be gathered from the fact that *now* the craving for foreign languages is without limit, and no European of the present day thinks himself educated, even in this eminently practical age, without a tolerable acquaintance with the classics and some knowledge of more than one modern language besides his vernacular.

And should not this increased and ever-increasing desire of becoming acquainted with the modes of thought and expression of those nations which are now numbered with the dead and belong only to history, as well as of those which are still in existence, but which are separated from us by territorial limits and by difference of language, be, within certain bounds, encouraged? We answer that it should—and we would endeavor, as far as we are capable, to give it a right direction. Can it be doubted that the present system of education is susceptible of improvement? Is not too much, by far, too much time spent, particularly in Europe, by youths in lumbering their heads with the languages of ancient Greece and Rome—in scanning hexameters and writing anapests? Years of exertion, when the mind is fresh and the memory strong, are to a great extent wasted in the acquirement of information, which can, comparatively speaking, be but of little practical advantage in future life. Can it be questioned for a moment, that all the boasted discipline of mind so fondly attributed to a study of the classics, and all the elegance of taste supposed to be derived from a familiarity with Cicero and Virgil, may be equally insured from a thorough knowledge of the language and writings of Mendelsohn, of Schiller, and of Goethe, at the same time that we are mastering a living tongue used by millions of the most enlightened of men, and of incalculable benefit in our intercourse with the world? Change of case by change of termination, declension of articles, prepositions governing genitives, datives, and accusatives, and inversion of sentences, may all be found, ready to tempt the ardor and puzzle the ingenuity of the student. These general considerations for the more extended study of the modern languages in early years, as filling up in part the time now nearly entirely devoted to Latin and Greek, apply with double force to the youth of America, from the very character and nature of the country. This is an age of energy and improvement, and a country peculiarly distinguished for its rapid advancement and for the restless and unwearied ambition of its inhabitants. We become men here at a time of life when tutelage has not yet ceased in other countries. We enter upon the duties and take part in the great concerns of life, mere striplings. At an age when the Cretan youth was still compelled to sit at the public tables under the eye of his parent or guardian, and when the modern European is looked upon as incapable of self-protection, we leave our early homes and friends, and engage in the most serious and important enterprises. The peculiar nature of our political institutions, and the rewards held out by them to practical talent, have had much influence in moulding into this form the character of our people and in giving to them an utilitarian tendency—in producing a population anxious to acquire only those elements of information that can be brought into immediate use. Profound erudition and deep scientific research are too long in yielding their returns to meet with much countenance in a country where fortunes are accumulated with almost incredible rapidity, and offices of trust and honor may be procured by a flippant speech or a little dexterous manœuvring. And hence there has never been a land that has given rise to so much improvement in the arts, without profound science; to so many orators, without extended learning; to so much legislation, without accomplished statesmen. We make a professional man as we make a journey—by steam; we select a congressman as we select a wife—by accident, or under the influence of feeling. In such a country, we confess, we do not expect to find men devoting their whole lives to the thorough and masterly comprehension of a dead dialect, secure, in this way, of a place among the scholars and the venerated men of learning of their country. We do not, in the present state of things, expect to find an American Porson or Schrevelius. Such men are too plodding, such learning is too solid for so energetic a country. We would endeavor, then, (but without taking away the means of acquisition from those desirous of emulating European scholarship and erudition,) we would endeavor to make education more practical and better adapted to the age and country in which we live. We would have more time bestowed in our colleges upon the modern languages, at the expense of Latin, and especially of Greek; and we would also extend the ordinary programmes of our schools so as to embrace the Anglo-Saxon, the full sister of the

German and English, the daughter of the same common parent, the Teutonic, for the reasons which we are about to assign.

It will scarcely be denied that the first object of all who have any pretensions to the outlines of an education, should be a thorough comprehension of their mother tongue—its power—its character—its elements. Nothing has ever appeared to us more ridiculous than the abundant and pedantic Latin and Greek quotations of a man ignorant of his vernacular—learned in Horace and Juvenal, but shamefully negligent of Murray and Webster—at home in all the wars of Cæsar, but to whom the splendid productions of our mighty Shakspeare are a sealed book. Such a man reminds us of a mathematician who can calculate the recurrence of an eclipse with accuracy, but who cannot work out the simplest question in discount; of a chemist who will furnish us with the most correct and minute analysis of the waters of a mineral spring, but who blunders in decomposing common chalk. We hope the day is not far distant when such men may be rarely met with; and we think it will depend in some degree on the introduction of the study of the Anglo-Saxon into our colleges.

The English, like all other languages of the present day, is a derivative language, and its great bulk comes to us from the Anglo-Saxon, the Latin, the Greek, and the French. Of these four, by far the greater number of words, and those of the most important, necessary, and forcible sorts, are derived immediately from the Anglo-Saxon.*

* Under the head of *William the Conqueror*, Hume, in his celebrated History, has the following sentence: "From the attention of William, and from the extensive foreign dominions long annexed to the crown of England, proceeded that mixture of French which is at present to be found in the English tongue, and which composes *the greatest and best part of our language.*" Our remarks will be found

From the information that we can collect on the subject, it may be set down as very nearly certain that about five-eighths of our language is Anglo-Saxon, three-sixteenths Latin, one-eighth Greek, and the remainder a compound of French, Spanish, and other tongues. It will thus be seen how important a part, even numerically considered, the Anglo-Saxon plays in the formation of the English. Sharon Turner, whose history of that ancient people is replete with learning, with industrious research, and with correct views, has, in his chapter on the language of the Anglo-Saxons, marked the number of words immediately derived from that language, in several passages selected from the Bible and from some of our most classic writers, such as Shakspeare, Milton, Thomson, Addison, Locke, Pope, Swift, Hume, Gibbon, and Johnson. On counting the number of Anglo-Saxon words, and comparing it with the number derived from other sources, it will be found that in no selection is more than one third not Saxon, and in some less than one tenth, the largest proportion of words of Saxon origin being contained in those authors who are confessedly the most forcible in their expressions, and the most admired as models of strength; the translation of the Bible by the bishops, commonly known as King James's Bible, standing at the head of the list for the number of Saxon words, as it unquestionably does for terseness and force of language. We should, therefore, be doing injustice to the services rendered us by the good old Saxons, were we to look merely to the *number* of words transplanted from this source into the vernacular. For although of the forty thousand forms, exclusive of inflections and participles, now comprising the English language, more than twenty thou-

---

to be in collision with those of the great historian, and yet we think there can be little doubt that in this instance Hume has fallen into error.

[1] See Appendix B.—*K.*

sand—which exceeds the number of words contained in Bosworth's Anglo-Saxon Lexicon[1]—are incorporated intc it from the Anglo-Saxon, yet we believe that we are far more indebted to our Saxon progenitors because of the *peculiar* kinds of words we have obtained from them, as well as from the influence which they have exerted on the grammatical construction and the idiomatic expressions of our language, than on account of the actual proportion of them. Sir Walter Scott, than whom no man knew better the power of our most forcible language, or has probed more deeply the sources of its strength and flexibility, has borne testimony to the value and energy of our Anglo-Saxon derivatives in that masterpiece—his *Ivanhoe.* In a conversation between Gurth the swineherd and Wamba the jester, in which Gurth is calling upon Wamba to "up and help him, an' he be a man," to get together the wandering swine, Wamba says: "Gurth, I advise thee to call off Fango, and leave the herd to their destiny, which, whether they meet with bands of traveling soldiers, or of outlaws, or of wandering pilgrims, can be little else than to be *converted into Normans* before morning to thy no small ease and comfort."

"The swine turned Norman to my comfort!" quoth Gurth; "expound that to me, Wamba, for my brain is too dull, and my mind too vexed to read riddles."

"Why, how call you these grunting brutes, running about on their four legs?" demanded Wamba.

"Swine, fool, swine," said the herd, "every fool knows that."

"*And swine is good Saxon,*" said the jester, "and how call you the sow when she is flayed and drawn and quartered, and hung up by the heels like a traitor."

---

[1] But see *Analecta Anglo-Saxonica, Introductory Ethnological Essay,* § 83, Note 2.—*K.*

"Pork," answered the swineherd.

"I am very glad every fool knows that, too," said Wamba, "and pork, I think, is good Norman French, and so when the brute lives, and is in the charge of a Saxon slave, she goes by her Saxon name; but becomes a Norman, and is called pork, when she is carried to the castle-hall to feast among the nobles; what dost thou think of this, friend Gurth, ha?"

"It is but too true doctrine, friend Wamba, however it got into thy fool's pate."

"Nay, I can tell you more," said Wamba in the same tone. "There is old alderman Ox continues to hold his Saxon epithet, while he is under the charge of serfs and bondmen, such as thou; but becomes Beef, a fiery French gallant, when he arrives before the worshipful jaws that are destined to consume him. Mynheer Calf, too, becomes Monsieur de Veau in the like manner; he is Saxon when he requires tendance, and takes a Norman name when he becomes matter of enjoyment."*

And again he adds, in speaking of the introduction of the language of William the Conqueror, "In short, French was the language of honor, of chivalry, and even of justice, while the *far more manly and expressive Anglo-Saxon* was abandoned to the use of rustics and hinds, who knew no other."[1]

---

* These remarks might be extended to other words of the same class—the Saxon sheep was converted into the Norman mutton, for the use of the feudal lords, and a young hen tasted more palatable and seemed better adapted to Norman stomachs, served up as a French pullet, &c., &c. It was the perusal of the above quotation from the admirable production of the Wizard of the North, many years since, that first turned the writer's attention to the study of the Anglo-Saxon.

[1] But see *Analecta Anglo-Saxonica, Introductory Ethnological Essay*, § 81, Note 1.—*K.*

To infer from this last remark, that the Anglo-Saxon was a barren tongue, or not adapted to the use of the refined and courtly, would be to do great injustice to the copiousness and richness of that ancient language. It is almost needless to say, that it was necessarily deficient in those scientific words that subsequent investigations and discoveries have given rise to, and that it would have been impossible in the days of Ealdhelm, to have written a modern treatise on astronomy or an essay on the magnetic telegraph; but, for all the purposes of philosophy, of poetry, and of metaphysics, the language was abundant and unusually copious. Their synonyms were very numerous. They had ten different words to express the ideas conveyed by the words "man" and "woman;" they had more than twenty synonyms for the name of the Supreme Being; and in their compound words (curiously and ingeniously put together) may be found evidences of a powerful, abundant, and expressive language. No lack of words interrupted the expression of those thoughts that Egbert and Bede, Alcuin and Erigena, Alfred* and Wilfrith, chose to imbody in the Anglo-Saxon. Poetry could find language to picture her richest imagery and to draw her finest metaphors. Philosophy, however mistaken, could teach in language not to be misunderstood, that "the heavens

---

* The following commendation of wisdom, from the pen of the great Alfred, best distinguished by his surname of the "Truth Teller," evinces neither paucity of thought nor of language:—

"Do you see any thing in your body greater than the elephant? or stronger than the lion or the bull? or swifter than the deer, the tiger? But if thou wert the fairest of all men in beauty, and shouldest diligently inquire after wisdom, until thou fully right understood it, then mightest thou clearly comprehend, that all the power and excellence which we have just mentioned, are not to be compared with the one virtue of the soul. Now *wisdom* is this one single virtue of the soul; and we all know that it is better than all the other excellencies that we have before spoken about."—*Sharon Turner*, vol. i., p. 408.

turned daily round." And metaphysics was at no loss for words to tell us of the theophanies of angelic intellects. But our design was not to inquire into the literature of the Anglo-Saxons, or to examine the state of their philosophy.

An elegant writer in the Edinburgh Review, of 1839, sums up thoroughly and beautifully, and more forcibly than we could, the items of the debt of gratitude we owe to the Anglo-Saxon, (as by far the most important and influential element of our language,) in the following words, which we are glad to adopt.

"In the first place," says the reviewer, "English Grammar is almost exclusively occupied with what is of Anglo-Saxon origin. Our chief peculiarities of structure and of idiom, are essentially Anglo-Saxon; while almost all the *classes* of words, which it is the office of Grammar to investigate, are derived from that language. And though these peculiarities of structure may occupy little space, and these words be very few compared with those to be found in Johnson's Dictionary, they enter most vitally into the constitution of the language, and bear a most important part in shaping and determining its character. Thus, *what few inflections we have, are all Anglo-Saxon.* The English genitive, the general modes of forming the plural of nouns, and the terminations by which we express the comparative and superlative of adjectives, -er and -est; the inflections of the pronouns; of the second and third persons present and imperfect of the verbs; of the preterits and participles of the verbs, whether regular or irregular, and the most frequent termination of our adverbs (ly) are all Anglo-Saxon. The nouns, too, derived from Latin and Greek, receive the Anglo-Saxon terminations of the genitive and the plural, while the preterits and participle of verbs derived from the same sources, take the Anglo-Saxon inflections. As to the parts of speech, those which occur most frequently, and are individually of most importance, are almost wholly Saxon. Such are our articles and definitives generally; as, *a, an, the, this, that, then, those, many, few, some, one, none;* the adjectives, whose comparatives and superlatives are irregularly formed, and which (for reasons on which it would be irrelevant to speculate here) are in every language among the most ancient, comprehensive in meaning, and extensively used; the separate words *more* and *most,* by which we as often express the forms of comparison as by distinct terminations; all our pronouns, personal, possessive, relative, and interrogative; nearly every one of our so-called irregular verbs, including all the auxiliaries, *have, be, shall, will, may, can, must,* by which we express the force of the principal varieties of mood and tense; all the adverbs most frequently employed, and the prepositions and conjunctions almost without exception.

"Secondly. The names of the greater part of the objects of sense, in other words, the terms which occur most frequently in discourse, or which recall the most vivid conceptions, are Anglo-Saxon. Thus, for example, the names of the most striking objects in visible nature, of the chief agencies at work there, and of the changes which pass over it, are Anglo-Saxon. This language has given names to the heavenly bodies, *sun, moon, stars;* to three out of the four elements, *earth, fire, water;* three out of the four seasons, *spring, summer, winter;* and, indeed, to all the natural divisions of time, except one, as *day, night, morning, evening, twilight, noon, midday, midnight, sunrise, sunset;* some of which are amongst the most poetical terms we have. To the same language we are indebted for the names of *light, heat, cold, frost, rain, snow, hail, sleep, thunder, lightning;* as well as of almost all those objects which form the component parts of the beautiful in external scenery, as *sea* and *land, hill* and *dale, wood* and *stream*, &c. The same may be said of all those productions of the animal and vegetable kingdoms which form the most frequent subjects of observation or discourse, or which are invested with the most pleasing or poetic associations; of the constituent parts or visible qualities of organized or unorganized beings, especially of the members of the human body, and of the larger animals. Anglo-Saxon has also furnished us with that numerous and always vivid class of words, which denote the cries, postures, and motions of animated existence. These are amongst the most energetic that any language can supply; for the same reason that words expressive of individual objects are always stronger than general terms. It is a sound and universal maxim of rhetoric, that the more abstract the term is, the less vivid—the more special, the more vivid. Now, almost all the words which are expressive of these specialities of posture and bodily action, are the purest Saxon; such as, *to sit, to stand, to lie, to run, to walk, to leap, to stagger, to slip, to slide, to stride, to glide, to yawn, to gape, to wink, to thrust, to fly, to swim, to creep, to crawl, to spring, to spurn*, &c. If all this be true, we need not be surprised at the fact, that in the descriptions of external nature, whether by prose writers or by poets, the most energetic and graphic terms are almost universally Anglo-Saxon. It is as little matter of wonder, that in those simple narratives in which genius and wisdom attempt the most difficult of all tasks—that of teaching philosophy without the forms of it, and of exhibiting general truths in facts and examples, leaving the inferences to be drawn by the instinctive sagacity of human nature—the terms are often almost without exception Anglo-Saxon. It is thus with the narratives of the Old Testament—the history of Joseph, for instance—and with the parables of the New; perhaps the only compositions in the world which can be translated without losing much in the process, and which, into whatever language translated, at once assumes a most idiomatic dress. The same remark holds good to a certain extent, of 'Robinson Crusoe,' the 'Vicar of Wakefield,' 'Gulliver's Travels,' and other works, in which the bulk of the words are pure Saxon.

"Thirdly. It is from this language we derive the words which are expressive of the earliest and dearest connections, and of the strongest and most powerful feelings of our nature; and which are consequently invested with our oldest and most complicated associations. Their very sound is often a spell for the orator and the poet to 'conjure withal.' It is this language which has given us names for *father, mother, husband, wife, brother, sister, son, daughter, child, home, kindred, friends.* It is this which has furnished us with the greater part of those metonymies, and other figurative expressions, by which we represent to the imagination, and that in a single word, the reciprocal duties and enjoyments of hospitality, friendship, or love. Such are, *hearth, roof, fireside.* The chief emotions, too, of which we are susceptible, are expressed in the same language, as *love, hope, fear, sorrow, shame;* and what is of more consequence to the orator and the poet, as well as in common life, the outward signs by which emotion is indicated are almost all Anglo-Saxon. Such are, *tear, smile, blush, to laugh, to weep, to sigh, to groan.* In short, the words generally expressive of the strongest emotions, or their outward signs, as well as of almost all the objects or events calculated to call forth either, in all the more stirring scenes of human life, from the cradle to the grave, are of Saxon origin. This class of words, therefore, both from the frequency with which they are used, and from the depth of meaning attached to them, must necessarily form one of the most important and energetic portions of the language.

"Fourthly. The words which have been *earliest* used,

and which are consequently invested with the strongest associations, are almost all of a similar origin. This, indeed, follows from what has been already said; for, if the words descriptive of the most ordinary objects of sense, and of the principal varieties and signs of emotion, are Anglo-Saxon, such, from the course of development which the human mind takes, must necessarily be the terms which first fall upon the ear of childhood. Still, the fact that they *are* the earliest, gives them additional power over the mind—a power quite independent of the meaning they convey. They are the words which fall from the lips most dear to us, and carry back the mind to the home of childhood and to the sports of youth. That vocabulary was scanty; but every word, from the earliest moment to which memory can turn back, has been the established sign of whatever has been most familiar or most curious to us.

"Fifthly. Most of those objects about which the practical reason of man is employed in common life, receive their names from the Anglo-Saxon. It is the language, for the most part, of business—of the counting-house, the shop, the market, the street, the farm—and however miserable the man who is fond of philosophy or abstract science might be, if he had no other vocabulary but this, we must recollect that language was made not for the few but the many, and that that portion of it which enables the bulk of a nation to express their wants and transact their affairs, must be considered of at least as much importance to general happiness as that which serves the purposes of philosophical science.

"Sixthly. Nearly all our national proverbs, in which it is truly said, so much of the practical wisdom of a nation resides, and which constitute the manual and vade-mecum of hob-nailed philosophy, are almost wholly Anglo-Saxon.

"Seventhly. A very large proportion (and that always

the strongest) of the language of invective, humor, satire, and colloquial pleasantry, is Anglo-Saxon. As to invective, the language of passion is always very ancient; for men were angry and out of temper long before they were philosophers or even merchants. The vocabulary of abuse amongst most nations is not only very copious, but always singularly hearty and idiomatic. Almost all the terms and phrases by which we most energetically express anger, contempt, and indignation, are of Anglo-Saxon origin. Nearly all the obnoxious words and phrases which cause duels and sudden pugilistic contests, are from this language; and a very large proportion of the prosecutions for 'assault and battery,' ought, in all fairness, to be charged on the inconvenient strength of the vernacular. The Latin, we apprehend, much to its credit, is very rarely implicated in these unpleasant broils, although it often has a sly way of insinuating the very same things without giving such deadly offence. Again, in giving expression to invective, we naturally seek the most energetic terms we can employ. These, as already said, are the terms which are the most special in their meaning, and the bulk of such words are Anglo-Saxon, particularly those which denote the outward modes of action and the personal peculiarities indicative of the qualities that serve either to excite or express our contempt and indignation. Once more, the passions often seek a more energetic expression in metaphor and other tropes; but then such figures are always sought—and necessarily, considering the purpose—in mean and vulgar objects, and the majority of the terms which denote such objects are Anglo-Saxon. The dialect of the scullery and kitchen alone furnishes our newspaper writers with a large portion of their figurative vituperation, and it is hard tc say what they would do without 'scum,' 'dregs,' 'offscouring,' 'filth,' and the thousand other varieties supplied from such sources. Similar observations apply to the lan guage of satire and humor. The little weaknesses, the foibles, the petty vices, the meannesses, the ludicrous peculiarities of character, with which these are chiefly concerned, as well as the modes of speech, dress, action, habit, etc., by which such peculiarities are externally indicated, are for the most part Anglo-Saxon. Here, too, as in giving expression to invective, the speaker or writer is anxious for the sake of energy to secure the utmost speciality of terms; while the metaphors and other forms of figurative expression, to which he is prompted by the very same reasons, are necessarily drawn from the most familiar, ordinary, and often vulgar objects. As to the language of familiar dialogue and colloquial pleasantry, we know it is always in a high degree idiomatic both in the terms and phrases employed, and in the construction, and this is a principal reason why the comic drama in every language—and we may say the same of satire—is so difficult to a foreigner.

"Lastly, it may be stated as a general truth, that while our most abstract and general terms are derived from the Latin, those which denote the special varieties of objects, qualities, and modes of action, are derived from the Anglo-Saxon. Thus, *move* and *motion* are very general terms, and of Latin origin; but all those terms for expressing nice varieties of bodily motion, enumerated some time since, as well as ten times the number which might be added to them, are Anglo-Saxon. *Sound* is perhaps Latin, though it may also be Anglo-Saxon, but *to buzz, to hum, to clash, to rattle,* and innumerable others, are Anglo-Saxon. *Color* is Latin, but *white, black, green, yellow, blue, red, brown,* are Anglo-Saxon. *Crime* is Latin, but *murder, theft, robbery—to lie, to steal,* are Anglo-Saxon. *Member* and *organ,* as applied to the body, are Latin and Greek, but *ear, eye, hand, foot, lip, mouth, teeth, hair, finger, nostril,* are Anglo-Saxon. *Animal* is Latin, but *man, cow, sheep, calf, cat,* are Anglo-Saxon. *Number* is immediately French, remotely Latin; but all our cardinal and ordinal numbers, as far as *million,* are Anglo-Saxon, and that would have been so too, if it had ever entered the heads of our barbarous ancestors to form a conception of such a number."

How, then, can it be doubted, after this beautiful summary of the words, inflections, grammatical influences, and advantages, that we have derived from the Anglo-Saxon, that the most certain and shortest method of arriving at a thorough and correct comprehension of the English is by the study of its most important and powerful element? What chemist would think himself acquainted with the properties and characteristics of water, who did not know the virtues of oxygen? What mineralogist could lay claim to a knowledge of the granite rock, who knew not the properties of mica, or feldspar, or quartz? His knowledge would extend no further than that of the daily laborer, whose life is spent in hewing the rock into shape—or of the South American water-carrier, whose estimate of the properties of his commodity is regulated by the supply and demand. How often has it been repeated that study of the classics is important, because it enables us to understand more thoroughly and employ more correctly English words! And yet we do not derive one half the number of words from the Latin and Greek together, that we do inherit from the Anglo-Saxon; and, as we have before shown, in the still more important influence on the construction and character of our tongue, the classical languages bear no comparison with the Anglo-Saxon. Indeed, with the exception of some synonyms, and some few more liquid and poetical derivatives, our Teuton brethren, the Germans, have acted more wisely in making their language all-sufficient for itself, and in forming their technical and scientific compound words from elements preexisting in their own vernacular. They have no occasion to resort to what are called the learned languages for their scientific and metaphysical expressions, and always avoid it; and yet no one will pretend to deny, that, as they are the deepest and finest thinkers, so also are they amply supplied with words expressive of the nicest distinctions in German transcendentalism, and of the most accurate definitions in science.* Instead of calling in the aid of the Greek to teach them *geography* and *astronomy*, they are given the same information under the far more expressive and idiomatic words *Erdbeschreibung* and *Sternkunde*; instead of relying on the Latin for *venesection* and *amputation*, they are equally skilful with the good old German compounds *Aderlassen* and *Abschneidung*—words which, compounded of elements already existing in the language, are far more forcible, because the components themselves bring to our minds ideas independently of their connection, just as *play-fellow*, *sweet-heart*, and *love-letter*, speak more directly to the feelings than *companion*, *mistress*, and *billet-doux*, and as *thunder-bolt*, *earth-quake*, and *whirl-pool*, carry destruction in their very sound.

We would not wish to be understood as denying that our tongue has derived greater variety, more elegance, and in some cases more aptness of expression, from the intermixture of Latin and Greek words. There can be no doubt that to these languages we are indebted for many invaluable synonyms, for many beautiful and sonorous words, and for some modes of expression that we would not willingly part with; but in most cases, their assistance has

---

* We are aware that some of the late German writers, hankering after foreign idioms, have adopted the French synonyms of scientific words derived from the Latin and Greek, instead of their own compounds, and, like Carlyle, have only marred the beautiful original by their unnecessary use of words coined from other languages.

been rendered at the expense of vigor and vividness. Strength has been sacrificed to beauty, earnestness to elegance. Still less would we wish to be understood by what we have said as inculcating an entire neglect of the study of the classics. No one can delight more in dwelling on "the linked sweetness long drawn out," of the incomparable Homer; no one can enjoy more keenly the beauties of Virgil, or laugh with more real heartiness over the comedies of Terence; no one can appreciate more fully, or feel more forcibly, the strength, the beauty, and the taste displayed in the immortal orations of Demosthenes and Cicero than we have ever done. We would not have them neglected or disparaged. But if they are to be read and studied for the purpose of acquiring a more correct and intimate knowledge of our own language, how much more does the Anglo-Saxon merit the attention of the English, or American, or German student! If they are not to be neglected, and if so much time is spent in their acquisition by our youth, how much more of the student's time ought to be devoted to the great fountain of his mother tongue! We would have every one of our youth make himself acquainted with the character, construction, and vocabulary of this language. Deep scholarship in Anglo-Saxon we do not expect. That must of course be a rare commodity in *any* country—rarer in ours for reasons already assigned; but a general acquaintance with the language we firmly expect and sincerely hope to see a very common and ordinary acquirement at no remote period—a period when, indeed, it will be considered disgraceful to a well-bred Englishman or American—"utterly disgraceful to a man who makes the slightest pretensions to scholarship, to be ignorant as multitudes—otherwise well informed—now are, of the history and structure of the English tongue; and above all, of the genuine relations of modern English to that ancient dialect of the great Teutonic family, which has ever been and still is incomparably the most important element in its composition."

But to those who aspire to be orators or poets, this study recommends itself with peculiar force. If the speaker is desirous of appealing to the passions—of arousing the inmost feelings, he must resort to those words which present most strongly and vividly to the mind the idea he is endeavoring to impress. And surely those words which are most specific—those expressions which are associated with our earliest and tenderest feelings—those phrases which bring to mind our closest ties, are such as are best calculated to rivet our attention and challenge our sympathy. And all *such* words are, as we have already said, native Saxons. If the poet would pour forth a song framed to draw the tear from the manly eye; if he would bind together stanzas that should fire us with feelings of indignation, or arouse us to deeds of valor, he must seek for tender associations, or for strong and energetic language, in the suggestive words derived from the Anglo-Saxon. Examine the speeches of those English or American orators who have been the most effective and powerful in addressing an assembly—who have been best able to play upon the feelings, "sive risus essent movendi, sive lachrymae;" analyze those English national songs which have electrified whole bodies of men, and stirred up to unparalleled exertion armies of soldiers, and see whether three-fourths of the words in both are not Saxon, as it were, "to the manner born." On the attention of the divine, the philosopher, and the philologist, it urges its strongest claims, in being an important and interesting link in the chain of ethnography. The latest and most astonishing discoveries in modern science—the most improved theories of light—the revelations of geology—the chronology of the Chinese—the city of Petra—all that at first seemed to wage war with the Mosaic cosmogony, has only tended to confirm the sacred account; and we do not doubt that the further inquiries and researches of such men as Wiseman, the Younger Adelung, and William von Humboldt, will place ethnography among the first of sciences, as showing conclusively that all the various languages, dead and living, were derived from one original common parent. The study of the Anglo-Saxon will further this result; and therefore must its introduction be acceptable to the friends of the Bible.

In the following pages, the Author of the Anglo-Saxon Grammar (so far as the writer of this Introduction is enabled to judge, or has had an opportunity of examining) has brought together all that is valuable and known in regard to the structure and grammatical accidents of the language. The sources from which he has had to draw, and the materials with which he was obliged to construct, are well known to all scholars, to be limited indeed; and we feel that we are but doing sheer justice, and not stepping aside from propriety, when we say thus in advance, that he has made the best and most advantageous structure possible out of such scanty materials, and has wisely and judiciously drawn from such limited sources. This is the only *complete* Grammar of the language with which we are acquainted, and certainly the *only* Anglo-Saxon Grammar published in this country. We hope, therefore, that it will not need to be stamped first with the seal of European approval, before it can be received into favor in our own country; but that it will at once, as it certainly deserves, meet with its proper reward, and be adopted as a text-book in our colleges and high-schools. To that purpose it will be found adapted, no less from its size and cheapness, than from its real worth. At the same time that it contains all that is necessary and valuable on the subject, it is not encumbered with labored references to collateral languages, which are thought to exhibit great research in the compiler, particularly in reference to a language but little known. From this, the author (with all the learning that we know him to possess) has judiciously abstained, even at the expense of not being considered so good a linguist as he actually is.

Taking an interest in the subject, with the permission of the author, we have written these pages, in the hope that they may serve, in some slight measure, to awaken the attention of the American public to the importance of the study of the Anglo-Saxon, and may aid by that means in increasing the admiration which we ought to entertain for our noble and sonorous language; so that every one may realize the praises bestowed upon it by old Camden, who, in his quaint "Remains," assures us that, "Whereas our tongue is mixed, it is no disgrace. The Italian is pleasant, but without sinews, as a still, floating water. The French, delicate, but even nice as a woman, scarce daring to open her lippes for fear of marring her countenance. The Spanish, majesticall, but fulsome, running too much on the *o*, and terrible as the devill in a play. The Dutch, manlike, but withal very harsh, as one ready to pick a quarrel. Now we, in borrowing from them, give the strength of consonants to the Italian; the full sound of words to the French; the variety of terminations to the Spanish, and the mollifying of more vowels to the Dutch: and so, like bees, we gather the honey of their good properties, and leave the dregs to themselves. And thus, when substantialnesse combineth with delightfulnesse, fullnesse with firmnesse, seemlinesse with portlinesse, and correctnesse with stay'dnesse, how can the language which consisteth of all these, sound other than full of all sweetnesse?"

O. H.

BALTIMORE, MD., *April* 1, 1849.

A GRAMMAR

OF THE

ANGLO-SAXON LANGUAGE.

ABBREVIATIONS.

Nom., N., Nominative.
Gen., G., Genitive.
Dat., D., Dative.
Acc., A., Accusative
Abl., Ablative.
m., Masculine.
f., Feminine.
n., Neuter.
Pron., Pronoun.
Inf., Infinitive.
Ind. Indicative.
Sub. Subjunctive.

Imp., Imperative.
Indef., *i.*, Indefinite.
Perf., *p.*, Perfect.
Part., Participle.
pp., Perfect Participle
Ger., Gerund.
Con., Conjugative.
Cl., Class.
Anom., Anomalous.
Irr., Irregular.
Eng., English.

PART 1.—ORTHOGRAPHY

CHAPTER I.

THE ALPHABET AND PRONUNCIATION.

§ 1. The Anglo-Saxon Alphabet contains twenty-three letters, which we give with their proper representatives in the Roman character, and with their correct sounds.[1]

FORM.		REPRESENTATIVE AND SOUND.			
A	a	a	*a*	as in	*fat.*
B	b	b	*be*	"	*bad.*
C	c[2]	c	*ke*	"	*cot.*
D	ꝺ	d	*de*	"	*did.*
E	e[3]	e	*e*	"	*met.*
F	ꝼ[4]	f	*fe*	"	*find.*
G	ᵹ[5]	g	*ghe*	"	*got.*
H	h[6]	h	*he*	"	*hat.*
I	i[7]	i	*i*	"	*pin.*
L	l	l	*le*	"	*lamb.*
M	m	m	*me*	"	*me.*
N	n	n	*ne*	"	*neat.*
O	o	o	*o*	"	*not.*
P	p	p	*pe*	"	*pence.*
R	ꞃ	r	*re*	"	*rise.*
S	ꞅ	s	*se*	"	*sir.*
T	ꞇ	t	*te*	"	*term.*
Þ	þ[8]	ṭḥ	*the*	"	*thing.*
Ð	ð	th	*edh*	"	*smooth.*
U	u[9]	u	*u*	"	*full.*
Ƿ	ƿ	w	*we*	"	*willow.*
X	x[10]	x	*ex*	"	*six.*
Y	ẏ[11]	y	*y*	"	*lyrical.*[12]

§ 2. *á* is pronounced like *a* in *fate;* *é*, like *e* in *mete*,

---

[1] See Appendix A.

[2] *C.* *Ch* and *tch* have in many instances succeeded to this letter, either single or double, in the formation of the English; thus, "cild," *a child;* "wrecca," *a wretch.* A similar transition has taken place in Swedish from the Old Norse, and in Italian from the Latin, but without a change of orthography. *K*, which expresses the peculiar sound of *c*, has also been adopted; as, "cyng," *a king.* *Sc* has very often passed into *sh;* as, "fisc," *a fish;* "biscop," or "bisceop," *a bishop*, naturalized from the Greek "ἐπίσκοπος."

It is probable that *c* was sometimes pronounced like *k* followed by *y* consonant, especially before the soft vowels, a sound still heard in *cart, carve*, and a few other words; as, "cealf," pronounced *kyalf. Sc* follows the same analogy, and was sounded like *sk*, as occasionally heard, in *sky.* See also Note 5.

[3] *E.* *E* before *a, o*, had the sound of *y* consonant; as in "eorl," "Eádward," "eow," pronounced *yorl, Yádward, yow*, whence it appears to be inserted after *c* and *g*. It is also omitted after these two letters, and sometimes interchanged with *i*.

[4] *F.* *F* at the end of a syllable, or between two vowels, had probably the sound of *v*, which is further evident from the substitution of *u* in its place in many instances.

[5] *G.* *G* follows the analogy of *c*, but it seems also to have had a third sound, that of *y*, when placed between two of the letters *e, i, y*, or *ae*, and not unlikely at the end of words. It had the sound of *y* in the Moeso-Gothic, a sister dialect of the Anglo-Saxon, and easily passed into that letter in English; as, "geár," *a year;* "daeg," *a day;* "taegl," *a tayl*, and by a further change, *tail.* *Cg* is usually written for *gg;* as, "licgan" for "liggan," *to lie down.*

It is probable that the liquid sound of *c* and *g* did not exist in the earlier period of the language. Subsequently other consonants acquired the same sound before *u*, as now heard in *pure, tune*, etc.

[6] *H.* The sound of *h* was very hard, as in "heord," *a herd.* At the end of a word or syllable, or united with another consonant in closing a syllable, it was guttural, as is plain from the later and stronger orthography, "thurh," *through;* "leoht," *light;* "dóhtor," *a daughter;* in which *gh* has taken the place of simple *h*.

We will here observe, that the *g* might very properly be rejected from such words as *through, light, might, right, daughter*, giving them the forms, *throuh*, or *thruh, liht, miht, riht, dauhter.* Their present or-

í, like *i* in *pine;* *ú*, like *oo* in *cool;* and *y*, like *y* in *lyre.*

---

thography is neither English nor Saxon, but belongs to the transition state of the latter language, and the barbarous period of the former.

It is to be regretted that in English there has been a transposition of the *h*, when naturally coming before the *w*, as, "hwít," *white;* "hwǽr," *where;* "hwá," *who.* The Moeso-Gothic contains a distinct character for this combination of sound, which is, indeed, one.

[7] *I.* *I* has the sound of *y* consonant before *e* or *u*, as in "iett," *yet;* "iúgoth," *youth.* Hence, it is said, the insertion of *g* in the present tense, and in the indefinite participle of all verbs in -ian; as, "ic lufige" for "ic lufie," *I love;* "lufigende" for "lufiende," *loving*, from "lufian," *to love.* But see further, § 408.

[8] Þ is the same as the Runic *thorn.* Ð is the Roman D with a small hyphen to make it distinctive. These two characters are often confounded by writers. See also Postscript, Note 1.

Þ represents the hard, and Ð the soft sound of *th.* The former is generally used at the beginning, and the latter at the end of words and syllables. Rather than retain these two characters, as is usually done in adopting the Roman, we have distinguished the *the* from the *edh* by two dots under the *th*, which represents it; as, ṭḥ.

The English sometimes has the soft sound of *th* where the Anglo-Saxon has the hard one, as in *this, there;* and *vice versa.*

[9] *U.* *U* before a vowel has the sound of *v*.

[10] *X.* This letter is but seldom used. Its constituents *cs* are preferred.

[11] *Y.* The sound of this letter originally approached nearer that of the French *u* or the German *ü*, than any which we have in English. The *i*-sound, however, must have taken its place at a very early period.

[12] Such are the *initial* sounds of the consonants. The *final*, or *medio-final* would severally be, *eb, ek, ed, ef, egh, eh,* or *ekh*, guttural, *el, em, en, ep, er, es, et, ew,* or *ev;* *edh* is strictly *th final.*

That this system should be carried into English as far as practicable, there can be no doubt. We would no longer then hear the teacher tell the child to say, *be a de*, but *be a ed, bad;* not, *de a be*, but *de a eb, dab;* nor what is still worse, *aitch a te*, but *he a et, hat;* nor, *double v* (which is pardonable, but what shall we say of *double-u?*) *i te*, but *we i et, wit;* nor *wi e es*, but *ye e es, yes.* It is evident that in such a case, *ch, ph, sh, th,* and even *wh*, would necessarily be considered distinct sounds, which they are in reality, while a proper expression would be given to *w* and *y* as vowels. We are well aware of the difficulties of such a system, as well as of the modifications with

Ae has the sound of *a* in *glad*, and with the accent, one somewhat broader and more diphthongal.[1]

§ 3. The letters *j*, *k*, *q*, *v*, and *z*, are not found in genuine Anglo-Saxon. *C* was used for *k*, as in Latin, and *cw*, or *cu*, for *q*. *V* was only employed as a "calligraphic variation of *u*,"[1] while the proper soft sound of *z* was never heard.

§ 4. The Anglo-Saxons used the following abbreviations: for "anꝺ," *and*, ⁊ and ꝼ; for "þaꞇ" and "þaeꞇ," *that*, ꝥ; and for "oððe," *or*, and "-lice," *-ly*, Ɨ. To denote the omission of *m* likewise, they made a short stroke over the preceding letter; as, "þā" for "þám," *to the*; "þónne," *then*, they wrote "þōn."

§ 5. The only signs or notes of distinction which they employed, were one dot at the end of each sentence, or of each line of a poem, and three at the close of a complete discourse.

§ 6. The Accentuation will be found wanting for the most part in the printed copies of Anglo-Saxon works, and in some it is altogether omitted. By the older transcribers it was generally either neglected or capriciously applied.[1] The student will perceive how necessary it is to the proper pronunciation of the language, as well as in fixing the signification of words. Comparison with the Friesic, Lower German, Dutch, Icelandic, and English, throws much light upon the subject.

---

which it should be attended, modifications which will readily suggest themselves to every mind.

[1] *Ae* is set down by some as a distinct letter, as the Anglo-Saxons never admitted diphthongs, and such it must always be considered. *Oe* is seldom met with. It was introduced by the Scandinavians, but never adopted to any extent. Its sound is that of *é*.

[1] Hence the peculiar form of our *w*, in Old Saxon written *uu*. But the Anglo-Saxon character is ***Runic*** in its origin.

[1] The grave, circumflex, and acute accents have all three been sometimes employed, but we think that the last alone is sufficient for all practical purposes. It is now impossible to determine the nice shades of pronunciation in the language.

CHAPTER II.

CHANGE OF LETTERS.

§ 7. The student will observe many irregularities in the Anglo-Saxon language. These proceeded from the variety of writers, their little acquaintance with each other, the inevitable changes introduced by the lapse of time, and other causes. Irregularities must obtain to a great extent in the early stage of every language.[1]

The Anglo-Saxon writers very often confounded some letters, and used them indifferently for each other. They transposed, substituted, and inserted or added both vowels and consonants. The following are some of the principal changes.[2]

1. *With regard to Consonants.*

§ 8. *B, f,* and *u,* before a vowel,[1] are often interchanged; as, "beofer," "beber," *a beaver;* "ifig," "iuig," *ivy;* "ofer," "ober," "ouer," *over.*

---

[1] Many of the various forms of words that we meet with evidently owe their existence to the carelessness of transcribers, while others belong to a difference of dialect. The Anglo-Saxon in its purest days, though in its early stage, was a highly cultivated tongue, with all the elements of indefinite improvement within itself.—See Appendix B.

[2] The changes or permutations which letters, especially the vowels, undergo in the derivation and inflection of words in Anglo-Saxon, are very numerous. These will be better learned as they appear in their proper places.

[1] Also *p.* "In all languages, and especially in the dialects of cognate languages, the letters employing the same organs of utterance are continually interchanged."

§ 9. *C* interchanges with *g*, *k*, and *q*;[1] as, "ṭhonces," "ṭhonges," *of thanks;* "cyth," "kyth," *kindred;* "cwén," "quén," *a woman, wife, queen.* It also, either single or double, frequently becomes *h* before *s* or *th*, and especially before *t;* as, "ahsian," for "acsian," or "axian," *to ask;* "(he) sehth," for "(he) secth," (*he*) *seeks,* from "secan," *to seek;* "(hí) strehton," for "(hí) strecton," (*they*) *stretched,* from "streccan," *to stretch.*

§ 10. *D* and *t* are often used indiscriminately for each other; as, "(he) mette," for "(he) metde," (*he*) *met,* from "métan," *to meet.*

§ 11. *G* is changed into *h* in many cases; as, "dahum," for "dagum," *with days;* "burh," for "burg," *a town.* It is added to words which end with *i;* as, "híg," for "hí," *they;* and omitted in those words which terminate in -ig; as, "drí," for "dríg," *dry.* It is also omitted before *d* and *th;* as, "maedn," for "maegdn," *a maiden;* "maeth," for "maegth," *power;* and before *n*, it is either left out, or *gn* becomes *gen*, or is transposed to *ng;* as, "waegn," "waen," *a wagon, wain;* "ṭhegn," "ṭhen," "ṭhaegen," "ṭheng," *a servant, thane;* "regn," "ren," "reng," *rain. Ng* is likewise changed into *nc* and *ngc*, or *ncg;* as, "sang," "sanc," *a song;* "ring," "ringc," "rincg," *a ring.*

§ 12. *H* is sometimes changed into *g;* as, "(he) ṭhág," for "(he) ṭháh," (*he*) *grew,* from "ṭheón," *to grow.* It is also found added to monosyllables ending in a vowel; as, "freóh," for "freó," *free.*

§ 13. *L* is written double or single indiscriminately at the end of monosyllables, but the reduplication ceases when, in lengthening the word, a consonant follows; as, "well," or "wel," *well;* N. "eall," A. "eal-ne," *all.* It is also frequently aspirated; as, "hlútan," for "lútan," *to bow.*

---

[1] *K* and *q* in later Saxon. *Q* combining one *u*-sound in itself, is followed by this letter instead of *w*, when substituted for *c*.

§ 14. *M* sometimes interchanges with *f;* as, "emne-theow," "efne-theow," *a fellow-servant.*

§ 15. *N* follows the same law in regard to reduplication as *l.*

§ 16. *R* is often transposed in words; as, "forst," for "frost," *frost;* "gaers," for "graes," *grass.* Like *l,* too, it is aspirated; as, "reód," "hreód," *a reed;* "reól," "hreól," *a reel.*

§ 17. *X* is frequently supplied by *cs;* as, "neorcsen," for "neorxen," *quiet;* or it is changed into *sc;* as, "tusc," for "tux," *a tusk* or *tuks.*

2. *With regard to the Vowels.*

§ 18. *A* and *ae* interchange as follows:—

A and *ae;* as, "apl," "aepl," *an apple;* "aecer," "acer," *a field.*

A', *aa,* *aé,* *ai,* *eá,* and *é;* as, "ác," "aac," "aéc," *an oak;* "ád," "aad," *a heap;* "aér," "ár," "ér," *ere, before;* "án," "aén," "eán," "ain," *one.*

A and *e;* as, "arc," "erc," *an ark;* "elne," "alne," *an ell.*

A and *o,* particularly before *n* in a short syllable; as, "mann," "monn," *a man;* "sand," "sond," *sand;* "ob," "ab," *a beam.*

Ae and *e;* as, "aeft," "eft," *again;* "egsa," "aegsa," *fear.*

Ae and *oe;* as, "aeghwaér," "oeghwaér," *everywhere.*

Ae and *y;* as, "aelc," "ylc," *each one.*

§ 19. *E,* *ea,* and *eo,* as follows:—

E, *ae,* and *ei;* as, "ege," "aege," "eige," *terror.*

Ea, *e,* *a,* *aé,* and *eo;* as, "ceaster," "cester," *a fortified town;* "eall," or "eal," "al," "ael," *all;* "eard," "eord," *earth.* *Eá,* *é,* and *aé;* as, "eác," "éc," "aéc," *also;* "eá," "aé," *water;* *eá* and *ý,* as, "eáthelic," "ýthelic," *easy;* *eá* and *eó;* as, "Eáster," "Eóster," *Easter.*

Eo, e, and *y;* as, "seolf," "self," "sylf," *self; eo, io, ea,* and *i;* as, "seoc," "sioc," "seac," "sic," *sick; eo* and *u,* especially after *w;* as, "sweord," "swurd," *a sword. Eó* and *eú;* as, "eówu," "eúwu," *a ewe.*

NOTE.—*E* is not unfrequently added at the end of words which do not require it, and omitted in many cases where it naturally belongs. Its omission, though, especially before another vowel, and when belonging to declension, should always be denoted by the apostrophe, if not supplied in the letter itself.

§ 20. *I* is interchanged with *e* and *y;* as, "igland," "egland," "ygland," (ígland, égland, ýgland?) *an island;* and likewise goes into *ie* and *ii;* as, "il," (íl?) "iel," "iil," *a hedge-hog. I'* and *ý* also interchange; as, "hí," "hý," *they.*

§ 21. *O* is changed into *e, i, u,* and *y,* besides *a;* as, "on," "an," "en," "in," *in;* "pearroc," "pearruc," *a park;* "ofer," "yfer," *a shore.*

§ 22. *U* is sometimes converted into *eo, o,* and *y;* as, "scucca," "sceocca," "scocca," *a demon;* "ufera," "yfera," *higher.*

§ 23. *Y* is changed into *e, o, ie,* and *i;* as, "ylp," "elp," *an elephant;* "yrf," "orf," "ierfe," "erfe," *cattle;* "ylc," "ilc," *same.* Also *ý,* into *eó* and *ú;* as, "ýrre," "eórre," *ire, anger;* "ýtra," "útra," *outer.*

§ 24. The forms which the same word often assumes, are various; as, "sǽe," "sé," "seó," "sǽew," "séwe," "siew," *a sea;* "hwom," "hwem," "hwaem," "hwamm," "huomm," "waem," *a corner;* "stare," "staer," "stearn," "staern," *a thrush;* "rinan," "renian," "regnan," "hregnan," *to rain;* "forod," "forad," "forud," "fród," *old, debilitated.*[1]

[1] The most of the forms coming under our notice in the inflection of words, will be given for the convenience of the student.

PART II.—ETYMOLOGY.

CHAPTER I.

PARTS OF SPEECH.

§ 25. There are nine Parts of Speech: the Article, Noun, Adjective, Pronoun, Verb, Adverb, Preposition, Conjunction, and Interjection.

§ 26. These are divided into declinable and indeclinable. The declinable Parts of Speech are, the Article, Noun, Adjective, Pronoun, and Verb: the Adverb, Preposition, Conjunction, and Interjection, are indeclinable.[1]

NUMBERS.

§ 27. There are two Numbers in Anglo-Saxon, the Singular and the Plural; as, "smith," *a smith*, "smithas," *smiths*. A Dual form, however, evidently exists in the pronoun of the First and Second Persons; as, "ic," *I*, "wit," *we two;* "ṭḥú," *thou*, "gyt," *ye two*.[1]

---

[1] All words in Anglo-Saxon were undoubtedly at one time declinable, and such a thing as an *indeclinable* Part of Speech was unknown to the grammar of the language, as will plainly appear from the sequel. See also *Analecta Anglo-Saxonica, Notes, passim*, with *Glossary*.

[1] "Wit" and "git," as Duals, are also found in the Moeso-Gothic. One might suppose them to be the remains of a Dual that obtained generally in an earlier stage of the Teutonic dialects than the one in which they first appear to us, although not required by their connection with the Indo-Germanic range of languages. Compare the Latin with the Greek in that respect. But is not "wit" contracted from

§ 28. Nouns follow the declension to which they belong with regard to the formation of their plurals. But some are the same in both numbers; as, "cild," *child*, or *children;* "wif," *a wife*, or *wives;* "word," *a word*, or *words.* Others are used only in the singular; as, "gold," *gold;* "seolfer," *silver;* while many names of nations are found in the plural alone; as, "Dene," *the Danes;* "Angle," *the Angles.* Irregular plurals also exist; as, "bóc," *a book*, "béc," *books;* "mús," *a mouse*, "mýs," *mice;* "aeg," *an egg*, "aegru," *eggs.*

CASES.

§ 29. The Cases are four, the Nominative,[1] Genitive, Dative, and Accusative.[2]

GENDERS.

§ 30. There are three, the Masculine, Feminine, and Neuter.

The Masculine and Feminine genders are often assigned to things without life. Hence there are two ways of discovering the gender of nouns: 1. By the Signification; 2. By the Termination.

"we," *we*, and "twégen, twá," *two*, and "gyt," from "ge," *ye*, and "twégen, twá?"

[1] The Anglo-Saxon is one of those languages which settle the question whether the Nominative should be considered a case, as we very often find it distinct from the mere name, or *expressed idea* in general; as, "sunne," *the sun*, "sun-beám," *a sun-beam;* "lágu," *law*, "láh-mann," or "lág-mann," *a law-man*, or *lawyer.* See *Gloss. to Anal. Anglo-Sax., Introduction*, § XV.

[2] The Ablative case evidently once obtained throughout the Anglo-Saxon, but its place at length became occupied by the Dative, with the exception of a few archaic forms preserved for the most part in the poetry of the language. What remains of it, therefore, may very properly be termed the *Old Ablative.*

1. *By the Signification.*

§ 31. The names of all animals of the male kind are masculine, and those of the female kind are feminine, whatever the final letter, or syllable may be.

2. *By the Termination.*[1]

§ 32. The Masculine terminations are:—

-a; -el, -ol, -ul, or -l; -els; -em; -end; -ere, or -er; -et, or -t; -ing; -nath, -noth, -ath, or -oth; -scipe, or -scype.

The Feminine are:—

-d, or -t; -en, or -yn; -esse, -isse, or -ysse; -estre, -istre, or -ystre; -ele; -nes, -nis, or -nys; -raeden; -u, or -o; -ung, or -ing; -uth, or -th.

The Neuter are:—

-ed, -od, or -et; -ern; -incle; -ling.[2]

NOTE 1.—"Sunne," *the sun*, is feminine, and "mona," *the moon*, is masculine.[3]

NOTE 2.—The gender of compound words may be ascertained by that of the last part.

DECLENSIONS.

§ 33. There are three Declensions, the First, Second, and Third, distinguished by the ending of the Genitive case singular.

---

[1] These rules for determining the gender of nouns from the final syllable can be only general. The best mode of ascertaining it, is by comparison with the Icelandic and the German.

[2] See further, § 75, Note 1.

[3] The same is the case in many other languages.

General Rules for the Declensions.

§ 34. The Dative case singular is either like the Genitive, or it is formed from it by rejecting the *s*, when the termination is -es.

The Accusative singular is always like the Nominative, except when the Genitive ends in -an; it then takes the same termination.

In all the declensions, the Genitive plural ends in -a;[1] the Dative in -um, or -on;[2] and the Accusative is like the Nominative.

CHAPTER II.

THE ARTICLES.

§ 35. The Anglo-Saxon has two Articles, both definite: "se, seó, thaet," and "the," *the.* The former is declinable, and put before proper as well as common names: the latter is indeclinable, and often used for all the cases of "se, seó, thaet," especially in adverbial and other like expressions, and in corrupt forms of the language in its declining stage.

§ 36. "Se, seó, thaet" comprises the three genders, and is thus declined:—

---

[1] Sometimes preceded by *en*, and again by *r* insertive.

[2] Sometimes -an, and -un, and even -en. But the two last are found mostly in adverbial and other expressions of the kind, dating from remote periods in the history of the language. Indeed -on and -an themselves are strictly archaic.

Singular.

	m.	*f.*	*n.*	
N.	se[1]	seó	ṭḥaet	*the.*
G.	ṭḥaes	ṭḥǽre	ṭḥaes	*of the.*
D.	ṭḥám	ṭḥǽre	ṭḥám[2]	*to, for, with the.*
A.	ṭḥone	ṭḥá	ṭḥaet	*the.*

Plural.

	m. f. n.	
N.	ṭḥá	*the.*
G.	ṭḥára	*of the.*
D.	ṭḥám	*to, for, with the.*
A.	ṭḥá	*the.*

For the origin of the Article, see § 119.

---

[1] The following forms are also found: *se,* seó;—*seó,* sió, ṭḥeó, ṭḥaeó;—*ṭḥaet,* both Nominative and Accusative, ṭḥat, ṭḥet;—*ṭḥaes,* ṭḥas;—*ṭḥǽre,* Genitive and Dative, ṭḥére;—*ṭḥám,* singular and plural, ṭḥǽm, and ṭḥón, ṭḥán, and ṭḥǽn, employed chiefly in adverbial expressions, and the like;—*ṭḥone,* ṭḥaene, ṭḥaenne, ṭḥene, ṭḥanne;—*ṭḥára,* ṭḥǽra.

[2] The peculiar form appearing for the Ablative singular is:—

m.	*f.*	*n.*
ṭḥý	ṭḥǽre	ṭḥý.

As, "mid ṭḥý áthe," *with the oath.* Express forms in most cases seem to be *instrumental.*

It will be observed that "ṭḥý" is very often used in other cases than the Ablative singular, and apparently then in the place of "ṭḥe."

CHAPTER III.

NOUNS

§ 37. Nouns are divided into Proper and Common, both declinable.

§ 38. *Synopsis of the Declensions.*

1.

	Singular.			*Plural.*		
	m.	*n.*	*n.*	*m.*	*n.*	*n.*
N.	-	-	-	-as	-	-u.
G.	-es	-es	-es.	-a	-a	-a (-ena.)
D.	-e	-e	-e.	-um	-um	-um (-on, -an.)
A.	-	-	-	-as	-	-u.

2.

	m.	*f.*	*n.*	*m.*	*f.*	*n.*
N.	-a	-e	-e.	-an	-an	-an.
G.	-an	-an	-an.	-ena	-ena	-ena.
D.	-an	-an	-an.	-um	-um	-um (-on, -an.)
A.	-an	-an	-e.	-an	-an	-an.

3.

	f.	*f.*	*f.*	*f.*
N.	-	-u	-a	-a.
G.	-e	-e.	-a	-ena.
D.	-e	-e.	-um	-um (-on, -an.)
A.	-e	-e.	-a	-a.

DECLENSION OF NOUNS.

First Declension.

§ 39. This Declension is characterized by the Genitive singular in -es. It includes a large part of the Anglo-Saxon nouns: almost all masculines ending in -dóm, -end, -ere, or -er, -els, -ing, -erd, -órd, -est, -nath, -noth, -ath, -oth, -eth, -scype, or -scipe, and generally those in -l, -m, -n, and -r; also neuters in -e and -incle, those ending in one consonant or more, dissyllables in -el, -ol, -ul, -en, and -er, and the terminations -ed, -od, -ud, -et.

§ 40. Nouns ending in a consonant, add -es to form the Genitive, while those in -e take -s alone, as:[1]—

"se smith," *the smith.*

Singular.

N.	se smith	*the smith.*
G.	thaes smith-es[2]	*of the smith.*
D.	thám smith-e	*to, for, with the smith.*
A.	thone smith	*the smith.*

Plural.

N.	thá smith-as[3]	*the smiths.*
G.	thára smith-a	*of the smiths.*
D.	thám smith-um	*to, for, with the smiths.*
A.	thá smith-as[3]	*the smiths.*

---

[1] The English Possessive or Genitive is derived from the Genitive singular of this declension, the *e* being omitted and the apostrophe taking its place; as, "Abráhames God," *Abraham's God*, or, *the God of Abraham.*

[2] -es: sometimes -as, and -ys

-as: occasionally -es; but in both cases only in that confusion of dialect styled Dano-Saxon. *V. Anal. Anglo-Sax., Introd.,* § 78.

"se ende,"[4] *the end.*

Singular.

N.	se end-e	*the end.*
G.	ṭḥaes end-es	*of the end.*
D.	ṭḥám end-e	*to, for, with the end.*
A.	ṭḥone end-e	*the end.*

Plural.

N.	ṭḥá end-as	*the ends.*
G.	ṭḥára end-a	*of the ends.*
D.	ṭḥám end-um	*to, for, with the ends.*
A.	ṭḥá end-as[5]	*the ends.*

§ 41. When monosyllables having *ae*[1] before a single consonant, or before *sc, st,* assume another syllable with *a, o,* or *u,* the *ae* is changed into *a,* as :—

"se staef,"[2] *the letter*

Singular.

N.	se staef	*the letter.*
G.	etc. staef-es	*of the letter.*
D.	staef-e	*to, for, with the letter.*
A.	staef	*the letter.*

With regard to the Nominative and Accusative plural of nouns in -ende, see also § 81, Note 1.

[4] *Ende*, aende, ge-ende.

[5] It will be observed that nouns in -e differ from those ending with a consonant as the foregoing, in the Nominative and Accusative singular only.

[1] Not *aé*, which remains unchanged, although the rule is not strictly observed by writers or transcribers.

[2] *Staef*, staf, stef.

Plural.

N.	ṭḥá staf-as	*the letters.*
G.	etc- staf-a	*of the letters.*
D.	staf-um	*to, for, with the letters.*
A.	staf-as	*the letters.*

§ 42. Neuters ending in a single or a double consonant, have the Nominative and Accusative singular and plural all alike, while those in -l, -n, and -t, preceded by a short vowel, and not falling under the rule in § 43, usually double these letters in the other cases, though they are sometimes found double in the Nominative singular, as:—

"ṭḥaet word,"[1] *the word.*

Singular.

N.	ṭḥaet word	*the word.*
G.	ṭḥaes word-es	*of the word.*
D.	ṭḥám word-e	*to, for, with the word.*
A.	ṭḥaet word	*the word.*

Plural.

N.	ṭḥá word	*the words.*
G.	ṭḥára word-a	*of the words.*
D.	ṭḥám word-um	*to, for, with the words.*
A.	ṭḥá word	*the words.*

"gewil," *or* "gewill," *a will.*

Singular.

N.	gewil, *or* gewill	*a will.*
G.	gewill-es	*of a will.*
D.	gewill-e	*to, for, with a will.*
A.	gewil, *or* gewill	*a will.*

---

[1] *Word,* wyrd.

Plural.

N.	gewil, *or* gewill	*wills.*
G.	gewill-a	*of wills.*
D.	gewill-um	*to, for, with wills.*
A.	gewil, *or* gewill	*wills.*

§ 43. But neuter monosyllables having *aé,* or *ae,* dissyllables of the same gender ending in -el, -ol, -ul, -l, -en, -n, -er, diminutives in -incle, and likewise neuters in -e, make the Nominative and Accusative plural in -u, (-o,)[1] as:—

"ṭḥaet faet,"[2] *the vat.*

Singular.

N.	ṭḥaet faet	*the vat.*
G.	etc. faet-es	*of the vat.*
D.	faet-e	*to, for, with the vat.*
A.	faet	*the vat.*

Plural.

N.	ṭḥá fat-u	*the vats.*
G.	etc. fat-a	*of the vats.*
D.	fat-um	*to, for, with the vats.*
A.	fat-u	*the vats.*

§ 44. Dissyllables in -el, -ol, -ul, -l, -en, -n, -er, -r, -ed, -od, -ud, -et, are often contracted when a vowel follows, as:—

---

[1] Sometimes -a instead of -u, (-o.)

[2] *Faet,* fat.

"ṭḥaet tungel,"[1] *the star.*

Singular.

N.	ṭḥaet tungel	*the star.*
G.	etc. tungl-es	*of the star.*
D.	tungl-e	*to, for, with the star.*
A.	tungel	*the star.*

Plural.

N.	ṭḥá tungl-u	*the stars.*
G.	etc. tungl-a	*of the stars.*
D.	tungl-um	*to, for, with the stars.*
A.	tungl-u	*the stars.*

§ 45. Proper names in -us, introduced into the language from the Latin, sometimes follow the general rule in forming the Genitive, and sometimes undergo no change; as, N. "Rémus," *Remus,* G. "Rémuses," *Remus's;* N. "Matthéus," *Matthew,* G. "Matthéus," *Matthew's.*[1] Others of

[1] *Tungel,* tungol, tungul, tuncgol.

Another happy change in English orthography would be the substitution of the analogical termination -el, or -ol, as the case may be, for that of -le, a barbarism superinduced upon the language in a period not far back, through a French influence; as, *cradel,* for *cradle; needel,* for *needle; apostol,* for *apostle.* The change of a similar barbarism, -re, to -er, has already become quite general. The forms -le and -re suit a language in which the *e,* and, in some measure, even the *l* and the *r* are clipped off in the enunciation, but do not answer for the manly-spoken English. Indeed, -ne for -en would be just as reasonable.

In adjectives ending in -le and -ile, derived from the Latin, those terminations might very properly give place to -il; as, *venerabil,* for *venerable; hostil,* for *hostile.* So also -ine would become -in; as, *infantin,* for *infantine.*

[1] The Anglo-Saxon writers seem to have observed no rule with regard to the inflection of proper names in -us of foreign origin, naturally coming under this declension. Thus we find, N. "Justus," *Justus,* G. "Justi," D. "Justo," the Latin inflection of the name; but N. "Pétrus," *Peter,* G. "Pétrus," D. "Pétre." Again, we have N. "Ptolo-

foreign origin conform to the inflection of common nouns, in every respect.

§ 46. Some nouns of this declension transpose their consonants in the plural; as, "disc," *a table*, "dixas," *tables*.

Second Declension.

§ 47. The Second Declension, which includes all masculines in -a, all feminines in -e, -estre, -istre, or -ystre, some neuters in -e, and proper names, especially those of men and women, in -a, has the Genitive case singular in -an, as:—

"witega,"[1] *a prophet.*

Singular.

N.	witeg-a	*a prophet.*
G.	witeg-an	*of a prophet.*
D.	witeg-an	*to, for, with a prophet.*
A.	witeg-an	*a prophet.*

Plural.

N.	witeg-an	*prophets.*
G.	witeg-ena	*of prophets.*
D.	witeg-um	*to, for, with prophets.*
A.	witeg-an	*prophets.*

"seó tunge," *the tongue.*

Singular.

N.	seó tung-e	*the tongue.*
G.	ṭhǽre tung-an	*of the tongue.*
D.	ṭhǽre tung-an	*to, for, with the tongue.*
A.	ṭhá tung-an	*the tongue.*

méus," *Ptolemy*, G. "Ptoloméuses," or "Ptoloméi," D. "Ptoloméuse," or "Ptoloméo."

[1] *Witega*, witga.

Plural.

N.	ṭḥá tung-an	*the tongues.*
G.	ṭḥára tung-ena	*of the tongues.*
D.	ṭḥám tung-um	*to, for, with the tongues.*
A.	ṭḥá tung-an	*the tongues.*

§ 48. Neuters of this declension, as all others, make the Accusative singular like the Nominative, as:—

"ṭḥaet eáre," *the ear.*

Singular.

N.	ṭḥaet eár-e	*the ear.*
G.	etc. eár-an	*of the ear.*
D.	eár-an	*to, for, with the ear.*
A.	eár-e	*the ear.*

Plural.

N.	ṭḥá eár-an	*the ears.*
G.	etc. eár-ena	*of the ears.*
D.	eár-um	*to, for, with the ears.*
A.	eár-an	*the ears.*

§ 49. Proper Names.

"Attila," *Attila.*

N.	Attil-a	*Attila.*
G.	Attil-an	*of Attila.*
D.	Attil-an	*to, for, with Attila.*
A.	Attil-an	*Attila.*

"seó Anna,"[1] *Anna.*

N.	seó Ann-a	*Anna.*
G.	etc. Ann-an	*of Anna.*
D.	Ann-an	*to, for, with Anna.*
A.	Ann-an	*Anna.*

§ 50. Names of countries and places in -a, naturally falling under this declension, are sometimes found undeclined; as, N. and A. "Sicilía," *Sicily.* Again, they are inflected as in Latin; as, N. "Európa," A. "Európam," *Europe,* the Gen. and Dat. being "Európe," for "Európae," like "Italíe," for "Italíae," and "Róme," for "Rómae," if the termination -e in such instances is not derivable from the same in the Nominative unchanged for the other cases.

§ 51. The Genitive plural is not unfrequently contracted; as, "Myrcna cyning," *king of the Mercians.*

Third Declension.

§ 52. The Third Declension is known by the Genitive singular in -e. It includes only feminine nouns, and those feminines which end in a consonant, or in -o, or -u, with the terminations -ung, or -ing, -nes, -nis, or -nys, and -uth.[1]

§ 53. Nouns ending in a consonant make the Genitive plural in -a alone, as:—

---

[1] *i. e.* the *woman* Anna, or the *said* Anna.

[1] The names of women terminating in -burh, and the like, and those generally which end in a consonant, come under this declension; as, N. "Eádburh," *Eádburh,* or *Eádburga,* G. "Eádburge;" N. "Mildred," *Mildred,* G. "Mildrede." Also those in -u; as, "Eádgifu," *Eádgifu,* or *Eádgifa,* G. "Eádgife"

"wyln,"[1] *a female servant.*

Singular.

N.	wyln	*a female servant.*
G.	wyln-e	*of a female servant.*
D.	wyln-e	*to for, with a female servant.*
A.	wyln-e	*a female servant.*

Plural.

N.	wyln-a	*female servants.*
G.	wyln-a	*of female servants.*
D.	wyln-um	*to, for, with female servants.*
A.	wyln-a	*female servants.*

§ 54. Those in -u, or -o, have the Genitive plural in -ena, and sometimes the Accusative singular in -u, as:—

"denu," *a den.*

Singular.

N.	den-u	*a den.*
G.	den-e	*of a den.*
D.	den-e	*to, for, with a den.*
A.	den-e (u)	*a den.*

Plural.

N.	den-a	*dens.*
G.	den-ena	*of dens.*
D.	den-um	*to, for, with dens.*
A.	den-a	*dens.*

§ 55. Those which end in a single consonant after a

[1] *Wyln;* wylen, the original, uncontracted form. Nouns of this declension in -el and -en are often contracted in the Nominative, and these with others in -er, almost always in the oblique cases.

short vowel, double the final letter in the Genitive, and in all the other cases formed according to it, as:—

"syn,"[1] *sin.*

Singular.

N.	syn	*sin.*
G.	syn-ne	*of sin.*
D.	syn-ne	*to, for, with sin.*
A.	syn-ne	*sin.*

Plural.

N.	syn-na	*sins.*
G.	syn-na	*of sins.*
D.	syn-num	*to, for, with sins.*
A.	syn-na	*sins.*

§ 56. Nouns in -ung and others sometimes make the Dative singular in -a;[1] as, "fortrúwunga," from "fortrúwung," *presumption.* A few also are usually found with the Accusative like the Nominative; as, "hand," *a hand;* "miht," *power;* "tíd," *time;* "woruld," *the world.*[2]

Irregular Nouns.

§ 57. The few names of nations which are used only in the plural and terminate in -e, are thus declined:[1]—

---

[1] *Syn,* sin, synn.

[1] This termination is archaic, and is met with as the Old Ablative, especially in words used in later times as adverbs, either singly, or in phrases. For this declension generally, see also Postscript.

[2] *Woruld* sometimes has the Genitive in -es, as if masculine and be'onging to the first declension.

[1] To which must be added all such terminations as end in -e; as, býre, -saéte, -ware, and the like. See also § 69, and § 75, Note 1.

"ṭḥá Rómane," *the Romans.*

N.	ṭḥá Róman-e	*the Romans.*
G.	etc. Róman-a	*of the Romans.*
D.	Róman-um	*to, for, with the Romans.*
A.	Róman-a	*the Romans.*

§ 58. Those masculines which end in -u, are declined in the following manner:—

"sunu," *a son.*

Singular.

N.	sun-u	*a son.*
G.	sun-a	*of a son.*
D.	sun-a	*to, for, with a son.*
A.	sun-u	*a son.*

Plural.

N.	sun-a	*sons.*
G.	sun-ena[1]	*of sons.*
D.	sun-um	*to, for, with sons.*
A.	sun-a	*sons.*

§ 59. Nouns terminating in -or, -er, or -ur, and denoting relationship, whether masculine or feminine, are declined for the most part as follows:—

"bróthor,"[1] *a brother.*

Singular.

N.	bróth-or	*a brother.*
G.	bróth-or	*of a brother.*
D.	bréth-er	*to, for, with a brother.*
A.	bróth-or	*a brother.*

[1] *Sunena*, suna.

[1] *Bróthor*, bróther, and bróthur

Plural.

N.	bróth-ra[2]	*brothers*, or *brethren.*
G.	bróth-ra	*of brothers*, etc.
D.	bróth-rum	*to, for, with brothers*, etc.
A.	bróth-ra[2]	*brothers*, etc.

§ 60. Some nouns, chiefly monoşyllables, containing the vowels *a*, *ó*, *ú*, and *u*, change these vowels in the Dative singular, and in the Nominative and Accusative plural, as :—

"mann,"[1] *a man.*

Singular.

N.	mann	*a man.*
G.	mann-es	*of a man.*
D.	men	*to, for, with a man.*
A.	mann	*a man.*

Plural.

N.	menn[2]	*men.*
G.	mann-a	*of men.*
D.	mann-um[3]	*to, for, with men.*
A.	menn[2]	*men.*

---

[2] *Bróthra*, bróthru, and gebróthra, gebróthru, gebróthro. These nouns are very irregular. "Sweoster," "swyster," *a sister*, analogically has "swyster" in the Dat. or Abl. with the Nom. and Acc. plur. 'sweostra," or "gesweostra," while the Dat. or Abl. of "modor," "moder," "modur," *a mother*, is "méder," with "modru," or "modra" in the other cases mentioned.

[1] *Mann*, monn, maenn, man, mon, maen, both Nom. and Acc.; but sometimes "mannan" and "monnan" in the latter, as if from "manna," "monna."

[2] *Menn*, men, gemenn.

[3] *Mannum*, manum, monnum.

"se tóth," *the tooth.*

Singular.

N.	se tóth	*the tooth.*
G.	etc. tóth-es	*of the tooth.*
D.	téth	*to, for, with the tooth.*
A.	tóth	*the tooth.*

Plural.

N.	ṭḥá téth	*the teeth.*
G.	etc. tóth-a	*of the teeth.*
D.	tóth-um	*to, for, with the teeth.*
A.	téth	*the teeth.*

"cú," *a cow.*

Singular.

N.	cú	*a cow.*
G.	cú-s[4]	*of a cow.*
D.	cý	*to, for, with a cow.*
A.	cú	*a cow.*

Plural.

N.	cý	*cows.*
G.	cú-na	*of cows.*
D.	cý-n (?)	*to, for, with cows.*
A.	cý	*cows.*

"seó burh," *the city.*

Singular.

N.	seó burh	*the city.*
G.	etc. burg-e	*of the city.*
D.	byrig[5]	*to, for, with the city.*
A.	burh	*the city.*

---

[4] *Cús*, cuus.

[5] *Byrig*, byrih, byrg, byrh, birg, berig.

Plural.

N.	ṭḥá byrig[5]	*the cities.*
G.	etc. burg-a	*of the cities.*
D.	burg-um	*to, for, with the cities.*
A.	byrig[5]	*the cities.*

§ 61. So also "bóc," *a book,* "bróc," *breeches,* "fót," *a foot,* "gós," *a goose,* "lús," *a louse,* "mús," *a mouse,* "turf," *a turf,* "sulh," *a plow,*[1] make in the Dative singular, and in the Nominative and Accusative plural, "béc," "bréc," "fét," "gés," "lýs," "mýs," "tyrf," "sylh."[2]

§ 62. "Faeder," *a father,* is indeclinable in the singular,[1] but the plural has the regular forms of the first declension.

§ 63. Nouns in -eó, or -eóh, preserve the *ó* through all the cases except the Genitive and Dative plural, being commonly found without the *h;* as, "feó," (feóh,) *cattle, money,* Gen. "feós," Dat. "feó," etc. But such as have -á, or -áh, while the Genitive usually has -hes, when the noun belongs to the first declension, appear either with or without the *h* in the other cases, both singular and plural; as, "fáh," *a foe,* Gen. "fáhes," Gen. plur. "fáhra," or "fára." Those in -ó, or -óh, have the Genitive in -ós; as, "hó," or "hóh," *the heel,* or *hough,* Gen. "hós."

§ 64. "Sáe," *a sea,* "áe," *law,* and "eá," *water,* are not declined in the singular, except in the Genitive, which, especially in composition, makes "sáees," "sáes," and "eás," in the case of those two nouns.[1]

§ 65. Some nouns in -u change this letter into *w,* or *ew,*

---

[1] *Sulh,* sul, sulg.

[2] *Sylh,* syl, sylg.

[1] "Faederes" is sometimes found as the Genitive.

[1] "Eá" has "eá" in the Nominative and Accusative plural, with "eán" in the Dative; "sáe," "sáes," with "sáem," in the same cases. "Ae" would seem to be undeclined even in the plural.

in the oblique cases; as, "searu,"[1] *a device,* Gen. "searewes," or "searwes," etc. "Eówu,"[2] *a ewe,* has "eówes" in the Genitive singular, and "eówa" in the Nominative and Accusative plural, with "eówena" in the Genitive.

§ 66. "Feld,"[1] *a field,* has -a in the Dative or Ablative, while the Genitive terminates in -es; and "sumer,"[2] *summer,* "winter," *winter,* and some other nouns, both -e and -a.

§ 67. The Dative, or Ablative, of "duru," *a door,* is "dura," and "duran," besides the regular form "dure." "Tá," *a toe,* has the Genitive, etc., "táan," or "tán;" and "beó," *a bee,* "beóan," "beán," or "beón," with the Genitive plural, "beóena," or "beóna."

§ 68. "Freónd,"[1] *a friend,* and "feónd,"[2] *an enemy,* have "frýnd" and "fýnd" in the Nominative and Accusative plural.

§ 69. The termination -waru, *the population of a place collectively,* has -a, (-e,) -as, or -an in the Nominative plural.

§ 70. The inflection of names of men formed from feminine substantives, is according to that of their primitives.

§ 71. Some nouns are indeclinable throughout; as, "aethelo," *nobility.*

ORIGIN AND FORMATION OF NOUNS.

§ 72. Nouns may be divided into Primitive and Secondary.

§ 73. All Primitive Nouns in Anglo-Saxon are mono-

---

[1] *Searu,* searo, syru.

[2] *Eówu,* eúwa, éwe, both which forms have -an in the Genitive singular, with the regular declension throughout

[1] *Feld,* feald, fild.

[2] *Sumer,* sumor.

[1] *Freónd,* frénd, frínd, friend.

[2] *Feónd,* fiónd, fiend.

syllabic in their nature; as, "wer," *a man,* "ác" *an oak,* "mód," *mind.*

§ 74. From these Primitive Nouns were originally formed many adjectives and verbs, which gave birth in turn to other nouns. It was also by combining two or more words that many were made. These either appear with their constituents in full, or they present one complete word or more, together with the fragment of another having a definite signification.

§ 75. The Secondary Nouns were formed:—

1. By the union of two or more primitive nouns; as, "ác-corn," *an acorn,* from "ác," *an oak,* and "corn," *a corn,* or *nut;* "wín-treow," *a vine,* from "wín," *wine,* and "treow," *a tree;* "eáland," *an island,* from "eá," *water,* and "land," *land;* but it will be observed that *island* owes its peculiar form to "eás," the Genitive of "eá," or rather to the Genitive of the corruption "ié," and "land."

NOTE.—Sometimes the first noun may be rendered as an adjective; as, "eorth-cyning," *an earthly king;* "morth-weorc," *deadly work.*

2. By adding significant terminations, which are in fact other nouns, to primitive nouns, and to words already compounded, or derived;[1] as, "cildhád," *childhood,* from "cild,"

---

[1] The following are the most of the terminations with definite meanings, which enter into the composition of common nouns:—

-a, denoting *a person, an agent,* or *actor,* and sometimes, *an inanimate object.* It would seem also to be, in many cases, merely *distinctive.*

-býre, from "býr," *a son,* signifying *descendants, sons.*

-dóm, expressive of *authority, property, right, office, quality, state,* or *condition: Eng.* -dom.

-e, denoting either *a person,* or *an inanimate object,* and sometimes merely *distinctive.*

-els, -yls, -ls, *causative.*

-end, denoting *the agent.*

-en, -an, -un, -en, with the idea of *possession,* or *subjection.*

-en, -yn, -in, -n, belonging to nouns which denote *females.*

a child, and the termination -hád; "saédere," *a sower* or *seeder,* from "saéd," *seed,* and -ere; "sangistre," *a songstress*

-ere, -er, from "wer," *a man,* and signifying *a person,* or *an agent: Eng.* -er., -yer.—Obs. that in -ere, the radical part of the termination is -er, with -e *distinctive,* added.

-ern, from "aern," *a house,* or *room,* denoting *place.*

-estre, -istre, -ystre, either a complete word or the fragment of a word, once probably signifying *a woman: Eng.* -stress, -ess.

-hád, which expresses *person, form, sex, quality, state,* or *condition: Eng.* -hood.

-ing, -ingc, -incg, -inc, -eng, -ng, -ngc, -ncg, -ig, -eg, -g, denoting, 1. *origin,* and as such forming *patronymics;* 2. *action,* in this case used for -ung, as in the sequel. NOTE.—The plural -ingas, -inga, -ingum, signifies *the inhabitants of a country, as descendants of those who preceded them on the soil: Eng.* -ing.

-esse, -isse, -ysse, softened from "ides," "idese," *a female: Eng* -ess.

-lac, -laec, -lac-u, expressive of *offering,* or *giving: Eng.* -lock.

-leást, -lýst, implying *inferiority,* or *deficiency.*

-ling, -lingc, denoting, 1. *a state* or *condition;* 2. *an image, example,* and forming diminutives, besides seeming very often to imply *contempt: Eng.* -ling.

-nes, -nis, -nys, -ness, -niss, -nyss, -es, -is, -ys, signifying *quality,* or *state,* and forming abstract nouns: *Eng.* -ness.

-raeden, denoting, 1. *a state* or *condition;* 2. *the manner, reason, law,* or *rule of action.*

-ric, as a termination, expressive of *dominion,* or *power: Eng.* -ric.

-saéte, -saétan, -saétas, *inhabitants, dwellers, settlers.*

-scipe, -scype, signifying *state, office,* or *dignity: Eng.* -ship.

-ster, denoting *guidance, direction,* from "steór-e," *id.*

-ung, -ungc, -uncg, -unc, -ong, denoting *action,* or *passion.* See further "-ing."

-waetha, denoting *a leader,* or *chief.*

-waru, from "wer," *a man.* See again § 69.

Besides these there are others, the signification of which cannot well be defined, but which seem to denote *action, condition, quality, endowment,* or the like. They are, -ed, -od, -ud, -ad, -yd, -d, -et, etc.; -el, -ol, -ul, -yl, -il, -l; -el-e; -em, -om, -um, -ym, -im, -m, -on, etc.; -er, -or, -ur, -yr, -ir, -r; -et, -ot, -yt, -it, -t; -d, -t, -th;

or *song-woman,* from "sang," *a song,* and -istre; "cárleásnys," *carelessness,* from "cárleás," *careless,* and -nys.

3. From verbs, or more correctly speaking, from the same root or formation as the verb in any case; as, "gitsung," *desire,* from "gitsian," *to desire;* "hálgung," *a hallowing, consecration,* from "hálgian," *to hallow, consecrate;* "swutelung," *a manifestation,* from "swutelian," *to manifest.*

4. By employing primitive nouns without any change in a variety of figurative senses; as, "cniht," *a youth,* and also *a boy, servant, attendant, disciple, client,* and *soldier, a* KNIGHT.

5. By the union of significant prefixes to primitive nouns, and to others already formed in any way; as, "sib," *peace, concord,* "unsib," *discord, enmity;* "rihtwísnes," *righteousness,* "onrihtwísnes," *unrighteousness;* "cenning," *birth,* "edcenning," *regeneration.*[2]

-nath, -noth, -nyth, -nith, -nieth, -ath, -oth, -yth, -eth, -th; -u, -o, -a, -eo, -io; -u, -o, -eo, -eu, -ew, -ow, -uw, -aw, -eow, -iow, -w, and -ew-u, -ew-e, -ow-e, -uw-e, -wu, -wa; -uth, -oth, -ath, -eth, -th.

[2] The prefixes being more or less common to different parts of speech, we deem it best to give them all in this place. They are:—

a-, ae-, *negative, deteriorative,* or *oppositional.* But *a* prefixed to verbs especially, in many cases either *does not alter the meaning,* or it *adds some little force or intensity* to the original signification: *Eng.* a-, sometimes in the latter sense.

aef-, af-, of-, implying *descent,* and also *deteriorative.*

aeg-, ag-, oeg-, ae-, a-, and sometimes ge-, from "aelc," *each, every,* and signifying *every,* united with pronouns and adverbs.

ael-, al-, all-, eal-, eall-, signifying *all: Eng.* all-, al-.

áer-, expressing *priority.*

and-, ant-, an-, a-, ond-, on-, denoting *opposition.*

be-, bi-; this prefix is used in various ways: 1. it is *privative;* 2. it denotes *nearness, intensity,* or *excess,* and perhaps should then have the accent; 3. it usually gives *an active signification* to verbs; 4. it seems *to add nothing* to the meaning: *Eng.* be- in some cases.

ed-, signifying *again.*

6. By the union of an adjective with one noun or more, in a modifying but not a qualifying sense; as, "eald-

efen-, efan-, efn-, efne-, emn-, emne-, em-, expressing *equality, evenness: Eng.* from the Latin, co-, con-, com-, cor-.

eft-, implying *back, back again: Eng.* from the Latin, re-, retro-.

ell-, el-, ele-, ael- aele-, denotes what is *foreign.*

for-, fore-, fer-, is either the preposition *for*, or it gives the idea of *privation*, or *deterioration*, and sometimes even implies *abundance;* the word in each case probably having a different origin: *Eng.* for-, fore-, *very*, which indeed is derived from "fore," as the Old Abl. of the *expressed idea* "for."

fóre-, fór-, implying *precession: Eng.* fore-.

fraé-, expressing *abundance*, or *excess: Eng.*, from the Latin pre-

ge-, ie-, is employed in different ways like be-: 1. it forms *a sort of collective;* 2. it often seems *void of meaning;* 3. it gives verbs *an active signification*, or changes them from *literal* to *figurative*, 4. it is *a mere augment.*

mid-, myd-, signifying *with: Eng.* from the Latin, co-, com-, con-, cor-.

mis-, mys-, denoting *a defect, an error, evil, unlikeness: Eng* mis-.

n-, *negative: Eng.* n-.

on-, in-, an-, either *privative*, or signifying *in, on, upon*, but sometimes, like be- and ge-, apparently *without meaning: Eng.* in-, un-, or *in, on, upon*, detached.

or-, *privative.*

ór-, órd-, denoting *what is original, chieftancy, superiority, excess.*

oth-, signifying *from, out, out of;* but sometimes like and-, and again *deteriorative.*

regen-, regn-, ren-, denoting *intensity*, or signifying *very, chief.*

sam-, either signifying *half*, or, when used as the first member of "sámod," *together*, implying *conjunction.*—In the latter case, it should have the accent.

sin-, expressing *continuance.*

to-, either *to* in English, or with the idea of *deterioration.* In the former case it should be written with the accent, in the latter, without it.

tír-, meaning *powerfully, superlatively, exceeding, very.*

un-, on-, an-, in-, denoting *privation, deterioration*, or *opposition* It is supposed either to be allied to the German "ohne," *without*, or faeder," *a patriarch, a grandfather,* from "eald," *old,* and "faeder," *a father;* "heáh-setl," *a throne,* from "heáh," *high,* and "setl," *a seat;* "heáh-setl-wealdend," *ruler of thrones,* from "heáh-setl," and "wealdend," *a ruler.*

7. Sometimes nouns, especially the names of countries and places, are really compounded, although the first may be in the Genitive either singular or plural; as, "cumena-hús," *a guest-house, an inn,* lit. *a house of comers,* or *strangers;* "Rómana-burh," *Rome,* lit. *the city of the Romans;* "Asían-land," *Asia,* lit. *the land of Asia.* Again, the first noun is only the radical portion of the word; as, "luf-tácen," *a love-token;* "Frýsland," *Friesland.*

PROPER NAMES.

§ 76. The names of men and women as well as of places among the Anglo-Saxons being significant, are frequently compound words. Those of individuals appear to have been mostly the effect of caprice or the effusions of vanity; but without doubt many were received from the illustrious in the early history of the race, and perpetuated from one generation to another.[1]

---

to be derived form the prefix which follows. It is very probable that on- *privative,* has the same origin: *Eng.* un-, in-.

uth-, wuth-, implying any thing *mystical.*

wan-, won-, from "wana," *wanting, lacking,* and implying *a deficiency.*

wither-, denoting *opposition.* *V. Anal. Anglo-Sax., Gloss., pass.*

[1] The Anglo-Saxons sometimes added distinctive appellations to their original names. These were taken either from some peculiarity of appearance, or from residence, office, trade, possession, or affinity. Not unfrequently, too, the addition expresses the name of the individual's father. Thus we find "Wulfsie, se bláca," *Wulfsie, the Blake,* or *Pale;* "Eádric, se hwíta," *Eadric, the White,* or perhaps, *the White-haired,* as also "se blaca," *the Black,* or *Black-haired;* "Aelfric aet Sealtwuda," *Aelfric living at Saltwood;* "Leófwyn, Ealderman," *Leofwyn, an Elderman* or *Senator;* "Sweigen, Scýld-

The following are examples of compound proper names.

1. Names of men; as,

Aethelwulf	*a noble wolf.*
Egbert	*bright eye.*
Dúnstán	*a mountain stone.*
Sigfred	*the peace of victory.*
Eádric[2]	*happy and rich.*

2. Names of women; as,

Eádgifu	*a blessed gift.*
Aelfgifu	*an elf-favor.*
Werburh	*a fortified city.*
Mildred[3]	*mild in counsel.*

3. Names of places;[4] as,

Cynges-tún	*the king's town, Kingston.*
Cyric-burh	*the church city, Chirbury.*
Waering-wic	*a fortress-dwelling, Warwick.*

---

wyrhta," or *Sweigen, a Shieldmaker;* "Aegelpig, Munuc," *Aegelpig, a Monk;* "Eádwíg, his maég," *Eadwig, his Friend* or *Kinsman;* "Aelmaér, Aelfrices sunu," *Aelmaer, Aelfric's Son;* "Wulfrig Madding," *Wulfrig, the Son of Madd,* or *Maddson.* Hence the names of the *Blakes, Whites, Blacks, Cliffords, Brightons, Aldermans, Cooks, Smiths, Canons, Friends, Johnsons, Eppings,* and the like, and those which owe their origin to ridicule or derision, and to other causes. But it was not until after the Norman conquest, that surnames became generally established in England.

[2] "Ric" is used in the composition of male names both as a prefix and as a termination.

[3] There are some words which are frequently met with as terminations in the names of men and women among the Anglo-Saxons: as, "bearn," *son, issue;* "beorht," *bright;* "burh," *a city, fortress,* which, very common in the names of the fair sex, is equally expressive, and gives us an insight into the Saxon estimate of the female character; "heort," *heart;* "nóth," *daring, bold;* "wald," *a ruler, lord;* "wulf," *a wolf,* besides the others adduced above, and the like.

[4] There are some terminations which are common to names of

CHAPTER IV.

ADJECTIVES.

§ 77. Adjectives in Anglo-Saxon have variable terminations, to correspond with the nouns which they describe.

§ 78. They have two forms of declension, the Indefinite, and the Definite.

§ 79. The Indefinite form is used when the adjective stands alone with its substantive: the Definite, when it is preceded by an article, or by a demonstrative, possessive, or personal pronoun, even when the last is governed in the Genitive.

§ 80. *Synopsis of the Declensions.*

Indefinite Terminations.

	Singular.			*Plural.*
	m.	*f.*	*n.*	*m. f. n.*
N.	-	-	-	-e
G.	-es	-re	-es.	-ra.
D.	-um	-re	-um.[1]	-um, (-on, -an.)
A.	-ne	-e	-	-e.

places, as, "burh," *a city;* "tún," *a town;* "ceaster," or "cester," from the Latin "castrum," *a fortified camp*, cities so called being on such sites; "-wic," the present -wich, as well as -wick, *a dwelling, station, village, castle*, or *bay*, according to the situation of the places; "burne," *a brook, stream, bourn*, used also as a prefix, and now appearing as -burn, or Burn-, -bourn, -braun, -brown, and -bran, or Brown- and Bran-; "den," *a valley;* "holm," *a holm*, or *river-island;* "hýth," *a shore;* "hám," "hóm," *a home*, likewise a prefix, and others

[1] The distinct terminations for the Ablative singular are:—

m.	*f.*	*n.*
-e	-re	-e.

Definite Terminations.

	Singular.			*Plural.*
	m.	*f.*	*n.*	*m. f. n.*
N.	-a	-e	-e.	-an.
G.	-an	-an	-an.	-ena.[2]
D.	-an	-an	-an.	-um, (-on, -an.)
A.	-an	-an	-e.	-an.

DECLENSION OF ADJECTIVES.

Indefinite Adjectives.

§ 81. All Adjectives of one syllable, except those which contain *ae* before a single consonant; also those ending in -e, participles in -ende,[1] -od, -ed; dissyllables in -el, etc., are declined in the following manner:—

"gód," *good.*

Singular.

	m.	*f.*	*n.*	
N.	gód	gód	gód	*good.*
G.	gód-es	gód-re	gód-es	*of good.*
D.	gód-um	gód-re	gód-um	*to, for, with good.*
A.	gód-ne	gód-e	gód	*good.*

[2] Indefinite Participles generally have -ra instead of this termination.

[1] Nouns in -end nearly related to Indefinite Participles, and denoting the agent, are declined, as before stated, according to the 1st declension, and should never be confounded with the participles themselves. The Anglo-Saxon writers always made the distinction.

It will be observed, however, that in many instances the Nominative and Accusative plural of such nouns take the participial ending -e, instead of -as, while in others, those cases are like the same cases singular; as, "wígend," *a warrior*, N. and A. plural, "wígende," or "wígend," or, as the latter form should very often be written, "wígend'."—See § 19, Note.

Plural.

	m. f. n.	
N.	gód-e	*good.*
G.	gód-ra	*of good.*
D.	gód-um	*to, for, with good.*
A.	gód-e	*good.*

§ 82. Monosyllables ending in a single consonant preceded by *ae*, whenever the same consonant is followed by *a*, *e*, *o*, or *u*, in the course of inflection change *ae* into *a*; and these, as well as polysyllabic adjectives formed by the derivative terminations, -ful, -ig, -isc, -leás, -lic, -sum, etc., and participles passive of the 2d and 3d conjugations in -en, make the Nominative singular feminine, and the Nominative and Accusative plural neuter in -u,[1] as:—

"laet,"[2] *late.*

Singular.

	m.	f.	n.	
N.	laet	lat-u	laet	*late.*
G.	lat-es	laet-re	lat-es	*of late.*
D.	lat-um	laet-re	lat-um	*to, for, with late.*
A.	laet-ne	lat-e	laet	*late.*

Plural.

	m. f.	n.	
N.	lat-e	lat-u	*late.*
G.	laet-ra	laet-ra	*of late.*
D.	lat-um	lat-um	*to, for, with late.*
A.	lat-e	lat-u	*late.*

§ 83. Adjectives ending in -e, drop the *e* in declining, as:—

[1] Adjectives formed by derivative terminations, and participles in -en, are found, however, without the feminine in -u, while the neuter plural terminates in -e. Uniformity as to the change of *ae* into *a* also must not be expected.

[2] *Laet*, lat.

"niwe," *new.*

Singular.

	m.	f.	n.	
N.	niw-e	niw-e	niw-e	*new.*
G.	niw-es	niw-re	niw-es	*of new.*
	etc.	etc.	etc.	*etc.*

Plural.

	m. f. n.	
N.	niw-e	*new.*
G.	niw-ra	*of new.*
	etc.	*etc.*

§ 84. Those which end in a single consonant after a short vowel, double the consonant in declining; but one consonant is omitted before -ne, -re, -ra, as:—

"grim," *severe.*

Singular.

	m.	f.	n.	
N.	grim	grim	grim	*severe.*
G.	grim-mes	grim-re	grim-mes	*of severe.*
	etc.	etc.	etc.	*etc.*

Plural.

	m. f. n.	
N.	grim-me	*severe.*
G.	grim-ra	*of severe.*
	etc.	*etc.*

§ 85. Dissyllables, when the inflection begins with a vowel, are often contracted, as:—

"hálig," *holy.*

Singular.

	m.	f.	n.	
N.	hálig	hálig	hálig	*holy.*
G.	hálg-es	hálig-re	hálg-es	*of holy.*
	etc.	etc.	etc.	*etc.*

Plural.

	m. f. n.	
N.	hálg-e	*holy.*
G.	hálig-ra	*of holy.*
	etc.	*etc.*

Definite Adjectives.

§ 86. The inflections of Definite Adjectives are the same as those of the second declension of nouns.

§ 87. The definite termination of the Nominative singular masculine, is always -a, and that of the feminine and neuter, -e, as:—

"se góda, seó góde, thaet góde," *tne goo*.

Singular.

	m.	*f.*	*n*
N.	se gód-a	seó gód-e	thaet gód-e.
G.	thaes gód-an	thaére gód-an	thaes god-an.
D.	thám gód-an	thaére gód-an	thám gód-an.
A.	thone gód-an	thá gód-an	thaet gód-e.

Plural.

	m. f. n.
N.	thá gód-an.
G.	thára gód-ena.
D.	thám gód-um.
A.	thá gód-an.

§ 88. In all cases, *ae* before a single consonant is changed into *a* in accordance with the rule given in § 82.

[1] The peculiar form met with for the Ablative singular, is made by "thý, thaére, thý," as:—

m.	*f.*	*n.*
thý gód-an	thaére gód-an	thý gód-an.

"se lata, seó late, thaet late," *the late.*

Singular.

	m.	f	n.
N.	se lat-a	seó lat-e	thaet lat-e.
G.	thaes lat-an	thaére lat-an	thaes lat-an.
D.	thám lat-an	thaére lat-an	thám lat-an.
A.	thone lat-an	thá lat-an	thaet lat-e.

Plural.

	m. f. n.
N.	thá lat-an.
G.	thára lat-ena.
D.	thám lat-um.
A.	thá lat-an.

§ 89. Some adjectives, as, "waedla," *poor,* "wana," *deficient, wanting,* "wraecca," *wretched,* have only the definite form of declension, even when used in an indefinite sense.[1]

COMPARISON OF ADJECTIVES.

§ 90. There are three degrees of comparison, the Positive, Comparative, and Superlative.

§ 91. The Positive becomes the Comparative both definite and indefinite by annexing the termination -ra for the masculine, and -re[1] for the feminine and neuter; as, "smael," *small,* "smael-ra, smael-re," *smaller,* indefinite, and "se smael-ra," "seó, thaet smael-re," *the smaller,* definite.

§ 92. The Superlative is formed from the Positive indefinitely, by adding the termination -ost or -est, and definitely, by adding -esta for the masculine, and -este[1] for the

[1] "Wana" sometimes appears undeclined.

[1] The termination -or, sometimes -ur and -ar, through which -ra, -re, are obtained, is never used but adverbially.

[1] Instead of -ost, or -est, we sometimes find -ust and -ast, and in

feminine and neuter; as, "smal-est," *smallest*, and "se smal-esta, seó, thaet smal-este," *the smallest*.

Irregular Comparisons.

§ 93. The following list contains the most of these:—

Pos.	*Comp.*	*Superl.*
áer, (*adv.*)[1]	áera	áerest.
formerly, ere	*earlier*	*first.*
eald	yldra	yldest.
old	*elder, older*	*eldest, oldest.*
feaw		feawost.
few		*fewest.*
feor, (*adv.*)	fyrra	fyrrest.
far	*farther*	*farthest.*
geong	gyngra	gyngest.
young	*younger*	*youngest.*

the place of -esta, -este, not unfrequently -osta, -oste, we meet with -ista or -ysta, -iste or -yste.

[1] Variations in this and the following comparisons:—

Aer, ár, aar, eár, ér; *áera*, áerra; *áerest*, áerost, érest.

eald, aeld.

feaw: properly a Definitive Pronoun. See § 107.

feor, feorr.

geong, geonc, ging, giung, gung; *gyngra*, geongra.

betera, betra; *betst*, betest,—both formed regularly from the old positive "bet," *good*.

heáh, heág, heách, heá; *hyrra*, hyra; *hyhst*, hehst.

lang, long.

laest; laesest, formed regularly from the old positive "laes," *little*, whence also the English *lesser*.

mycel, micel; *máest*, mést.

neáh, neáhg, náh; *nyhst*, neahst, necst.

sceort, scort.

strang, strong, streng, straeng.

wyrst; wyrrest, wyrest, formed originally from the old positive "weor," *bad*.

Pos.	*Comp.*	*Superl.*
gód	betera	betst.
good	*better*	*best.*
heáh	hyrra	hyhst.
high	*higher*	*highest.*
lang	lengra	lengest.
long	*longer*	*longest.*
lytel	laessa	laest.
little	*less*	*least.*
mycel	mára	maést.
much	*more*	*most.*
neáh	nearra	nyhst.
near	*nearer*	*nearest.*
sceort	scyrtra	scyrtest.
short	*shorter*	*shortest.*
strang	strengra	strengest.
strong	*stronger*	*strongest.*
yfel	wyrsa	wyrst.
evil or *bad*	*worse*	*worst.*

Some form the Superlative by -mest, -myst, from "maést," *most*, as:—

Pos.	*Comp.*	*Superl.*
aefter, (*adv.*)[1]	aefterra	aeftermest.
behind	*after*	*aftermost.*
forth, (*adv.*)	furthra	fyrmest.
forth	*further*	*foremost.*
inneweard	innera	innemest.
inward	*inner*	*inmost.*

[1] ***Aefter***, efter, aeft, eft, aefte; ***aefterra***, aeftera; ***aeftermest***, **aef**termyst, aeftmest, aeftemyst.

fyrmest, formest, fyrest, fyrst, first.

inneweard, inneward, inweard; ***innemest***, innemyst, innost.

laet, lat, as already given; ***laetmest***, laetmyst, laetemest.

Pos.	*Comp.*	*Superl.*
laet	laetra	laetmest.
late	*later*	*latest.*
midd		midmest.
middle		*middlemost.*
nitheweard	nythera	nithemest.
downward	*lower*	*nethermost.*
northeweard		northmest.
northward		*northernmost.*
uppeweard	ufera	ufemest.
upward	*upper*	*upmost.*
úteweard	útra	útemest
and ýte	*and* ýtera	*and* ýtemest.
outward	*outer*	*outmost.*
sith	sithra	sithmest.
late	*later*	*latest.*

ORIGIN AND FORMATION OF ADJECTIVES.

§ 94. Adjectives in Anglo-Saxon owe their origin either to nouns or verbs.

1. They are nouns used in a descriptive sense; as, "hige," *diligence* and *diligent;* "láth," *evil* and *pernicious.*[1]

2. They are nouns with meaning terminations added to them;[2] as, "gold," *gold,* "gold-en," *golden;* "blód,"

---

nitheweard, nytheweard, nythewerd; *nythera,* neothera, neothra; *nithemest,* nythmest.

sithmest, sithest.

uppeweard, upweard; *ufera,* ufora; *ufemest,* ufemyst.

úteweard, úteweard; *útra,* útera, úterra, úttera, úttra; and, *ýtera,* ýttra.

[1] In the course of time slight changes were made in many instances, for the purpose of distinguishing the adjective from the noun.

[2] The following are these terminations:—

-baer, -baere, -bor, having the signification of producing, and re-

blood, "blód-ig," *bloody;* "wer," *a man,* "wer-lic," *man-like, manly;* "waestm," *fruit,* "waestm-baer," *fruitful;* "faeder," *a father,* "faeder-leás," *fatherless;* "áe," *a law,* "áe-faest," *fixed in the law, religious.*

---

lated to the root of "beran," *to bear, produce,* which also probably comes from the Teutonic "bar," *fruit.* Observe that -baere itself is a compound, being formed from -baer with the -e *distinctive.* So also with regard to -ende below.

-cund, denoting *a kind, origin,* or *likeness,* from "cynd," *id.*

-e seems to be merely distinctive.

-ed, -ad, -od, -ud, -yd, -d, -t, probably the perfect participle of a lost verb, and signifying *furnished* or *provided with.* Adjectives and participles thus formed usually have ge- prefixed to them, and such words may be considered as belonging in every instance to the latter class. *Eng.* -ed, -d.

-en, -an, -yn, and -n, from "unnan," *to give, grant,* and denoting *addition.* See farther § 408. *Eng.* -en.

-ende, -ynde, possibly from the same verb, the termination of participles indefinite.

-ern, -aern, -en (?), -an (?), from "aern," *a place,* as in nouns, and denoting *towards a place.* *Eng.* -ern.

-faest, -fast, signifying *fast, very, perfectly, effectually.* It is also used as a prefix. *Eng.* -fast.

-full, -ful-, -fol, expressive of *fulness, completeness,* or *perfection.* It is also a prefix. *Eng.* -ful.

-ig, -eg, -g, -i. -ic, -ec, -ich, -ech, -ie, -ug, -og, -eog, signifying *addition,* probably from the radical part of "ícan," *to eke, add.* *Eng.* -y.

-iht, -eht, the same.

-isc, -esc, -sc, denoting *the external quality of a subject, like Eng.* -ish.

-leás, denoting *privation.* It is also used as a prefix. *Eng.* -less.

-lic, -líc, -lec, -laec, -lc, -li, expressive of *similitude,* or *likeness Eng.* -like, -ly.

-ol, -ul, -el, -al, usually denoting *a mental quality.*

-or, the same.

-sum, -som, signifying *diminution,* from the pronoun "sum," *some. Eng.* -some.

-weard, -ward, -werd, denoting *situation, direction.* *Eng.* -ward.

-wís, either *wise,* or the radical part of "wíse," *a wise, manner Eng.* -eous. *V. Anal. Anglo-Sax., Gloss., passim.*

3. They are formed from nouns as well as from other adjectives by significant prefixes;[3] as, "mód," *mind*, "ae-mód," *out of mind, mad;* "geleáflic," *credible*, "un-geleáflic," *incredible;* "mihtig,"[4] *powerful*, "tír-meahtig," *exceedingly powerful.*

4. They are formed by the union of nouns and numerals; as, "án-eáge," *one-eyed*, from "án," *one*, and "eáge," *an eye;* "twý-feald," *twofold, double*, from "twý," *two*, and "feald,"[5] *a fold.*

5. They are formed from participles; as, "bebeódend-lic," *imperative*, from the indefinite participle of the verb "bebeódan," *to command*, with the termination -lic; or they still present the participial form alone; as, "berende," *fruitful*, from "beran," *to bear.*

6. They present compound forms from simple adjectives, or from simple adjectives and participles; as, "ylpen-bǽnen," *made of ivory*, from "ylpen," *belonging to an elephant*, and "bǽnen," *formed of bone;* "ethel-boren," *noble-born*, from "ethel," *noble*, and "boren," *born.*

7. They are further formed from pronouns and adverbs with significant terminations; as, "úre-lendisc,"[6] *of our country;* "úte-weard," *outward, external.*

8. The increase of the same adjective from the Positive, is by means of significant endings.[7]

---

[3] See § 75, Note 2.

[4] *Mihtig*, from miht, meaht, maeht, meht, and -ig.

[5] An-feald, twý-feald, etc., are considered numerals by some. In that case, "feald" becomes a 'numeral termination.'

[6] -lendisc, -laendisc, -landisc, as a termination compounded of "land," *land, a country*, and -isc, signifies *belonging to a country.*

[7] The termination of the comparative is from "ǽr," *before*, first with respect to *time*, and then, to *quality:* that of the superlative, from "ǽst," "ést," *abundance. Eng.* -er, and -est.

CHAPTER V.

PRONOUNS.

§ 95. Pronouns in Anglo-Saxon are divided into Personal, Adjective, Definitive, Relative, and Interrogative.

1. *Personal Pronouns.*

§ 96. These are "ic," "ṭḥú," "he," "heó," "hit," with their plurals "we," "ge," "hí," and the duals "wit" and "git."

§ 97. Declension of the First Person "ic," *I.*

	Singular.			*Plural.*	
N.	ic	*I.*	N.	we	*we.*
G.	mín	*of me.*	G.	úre	*of us.*
D.	me	*to, for, with me.*	D.	us	*to, for, with us.*
A.	me	*me.*	A.	us	*us.*

Dual.

N.	wit	*we two.*
G.	uncer	*of us two.*
D.	unc	*to, for, with us two.*
A.	unc	*us two.*

---

[1] The following different forms are found under the declension of this pronoun:—

me, Dat. and Acc., mec, meh, mek, mech, meck, poetic;—*úre*, user, owre;—*us*, Dat. and Acc., usic, usig, usih, usich, but, like the preceding forms of "me," used chiefly by the poets;—*wit*, wyt;—*unc*, Dat and Acc., ungc.

§ 98. Declension of the Second Person "ṭḥú," *thou*

	Singular.			*Plural.*	
N.	ṭḥú	*thou.*	N.	ge	*ye* or *you.*
G.	ṭḥín	*of thee.*	G.	eower	*of you.*
D.	ṭḥé[1]	*to, for, with thee.*	D.	eow	*to, for, with you.*
A.	ṭḥé	*thee.*	A.	eow	*you.*

Dual.

N.	git	*ye* or *you two.*
G.	incer	*of you two.*
D.	inc	*to, for, with you two.*
A.	inc	*you two.*

§ 99. Declension of the Third Person "he, heó, hit," *he, she, it.*

	Singular.			*Plural.*	
N.	he	*he.*			
G.	his[1]	*of him.*			
D.	him	*to, for, with him.*			
A.	hine	*him.*			
N.	heó	*she.*	N.	hí	*they.*
G.	hire	*of her.*	G.	hira	*of them.*
D.	hire	*to, for, with her.*	D.	him	*to, for, with them.*
A.	hí	*her.*	A.	hí	*them.*
N.	hit	*it.*			
G.	his	*of it.*			
D.	him	*to, for, with it.*			
A.	hit	*it.*			

[1] *ṭḥé*, Dat. and Acc., ṭḥec, ṭḥeh, used by the poets;—*eower*, eowr, iower;—*eow*, Dat. and Acc., eowic, eowih, iowih, poetic, iow, iu, geow;—*git*, gyt;—*incer*, incere, inca;—*inc*, Dat., incg, incrum;—*inc*, Acc., incg, incit.

[1] *his*, hys;—*him*, hym, hion;—*hine*, hyne, hiene;—*heó*, hió, used

§ 100. "Sylf,"[1] *self,* is declined like "gód," and added to personal pronouns in the same gender and case, as follows:—

Singular.			*Plural.*		
N.	ic-sylf	*I myself.*	N.	we-sylfe	*we ourselves.*
G.	mín-sylfes	*of myself.*	G.	úre-sylfra	*of ourselves.*
	etc.	*etc.*		etc.	*etc.*
N.	ṭhú-sylf	*thyself.*	N.	ge-sylfe	*ye yourselves.*
G.	ṭhín-sylfes	*of thyself.*	G.	eower-sylfra	*of yourselves.*
	etc.	*etc.*		etc.	*etc.*
N.	he-sylf	*he himself.*	N.	hí-sylfe	*they themselves.*
G.	his-sylfes	*of himself.*	G.	hira-sylfra	*of themselves.*
	etc.	*etc.*		etc.	*etc.*
N.	heó-sylf	*she herself.*	N.	hí-sylfe	*they themselves.*
G.	hire-sylfre	*of herself.*	G.	heora-sylfra	*of themselves.*
	etc.	*etc.*		etc.	*etc.*
N.	hit-sylf	*itself.*	N.	hí-sylfe	*they themselves.*
G.	his-sylfes	*of itself.*	G.	hira-sylfra	*of themselves.*
	etc.	*etc.*		etc.	*etc.*

§ 101. "Sylf" sometimes takes the Dative, or perhaps more properly speaking, the Ablative, of the personal pronoun before it; as, "me-sylf," *myself,* "ṭhé-sylf," *thyself,*

---

also for "he" and "hí," especially in poetry, hiú, scáe;—*hire,* hyre, hiere;—*hit,* Nom. and Acc., hyt, it;—*his,* hys;—*him,* hym.

hí, Nom. and Acc., híg, híe, hý;—*hira,* hyra, heora, hiora, hiera, herra;—*him,* heom, hiom, eom.

NOTE.—"He" and "heó," when representing a masculine or feminine noun which denotes *an inanimate object,* are properly rendered by *it* in English.

[1] *Sylf,* silf, self, saelf, seolf.

"him-sylf,"[1] *himself.* It is also annexed to nouns; as, "Pétrus-sylf," *Peter's self,* "Críst-sylf," *Christ himself.* But when used definitely, it signifies *the same;* as, "se sylfa mann," *the same man.*[2]

2. *Adjective Pronouns.*

§ 102. The Adjective Pronouns are only the Genitive cases of personal pronouns taken and declined like the indefinite form of "gód." They are "mín," *my,* "ṭḥín," *thy,* "uncer," *our-two,* "incer," *your-two,* "úre," *our,* and "eower," *your.* The personal pronoun of the third person has no declinable adjective pronoun, but the sense of the same is always expressed by "his," "hire," "hira," the Genitive cases of the primitive forms.

§ 103. To define the reciprocal sense in "his," "hire," "hira," more accurately, the word "ágen,"[1] *own,* declined like "gód," is added; as, "Tó his ágenre ṭḥearfe," *to his own necessity.* This sense the poets also express by "sín;" as, "Ofslóh bróthor sínne," *slew his own brother.*

§ 104. Declension of "mín," *my.*

Singular.

	m.	*f.*	*n.*	
N.	mín	mín	mín	*my.*
G.	mín-es	mín-re	mín-es	*of my.*
D.	mín-um	mín-re	mín-um	*to, for, with my.*
A.	mín-ne	mín-e	mín	*my.*

---

[1] For the real nature of this idiom, see *Anal. Anglo-Sax.*, Part I., Section IV., § 50, Notes.

[2] In poetry we often find the definite form used for the indefinite with the personal pronouns proper; as, "ic sylfa," *I myself;* "heó sylfe," *she herself;* etc.

[1] *Agen,* ágan, ágn, aégn, ágien, aéwen.

Plural.

	m. f. n.	
N.	mín-e	*my.*
G.	mín-ra[1]	*of my.*
D.	mín-um	*to, for, with my.*
A.	mín-e	*my.*

§ 105. Declension of "uncer," *our-two.*

Singular.

	m.	f.	n.	
N.	unc-er	unc-er	unc-er	*our-two.*
G.	unc-res[1]	unc-re	unc-res	*of our-two.*
D.	unc-rum	unc-re	unc-rum	*to, for, with our-two.*
A.	unc-erne	unc-re	unc-er	*our-two.*

Plural.

	m. f. n.	
N.	unc-re	*our-two.*
G.	unc-ra	*of our-two.*
D.	unc-rum	*to, for, with our-two.*
A.	unc-re	*our-two.*

§ 106. Declension of "úre,"[1] *our.*

Singular.

	m.	f.	n.	
N.	úr-e	úr-e	úr-e	*our.*
G.	úr-es	úr-e	úr-es	*of our.*
D.	úr-um	úr-e	úr-um	*to, for, with our.*
A.	úr-ne	úr-e	úr-e	*our.*

---

[1] *Mínra,* ménra.

[1] The contraction of the Possessive Pronouns in -er, when the syllable of inflection begins with a vowel, is common.

[1] *Ure,* user, usser, but chiefly poetic. "User" has a distinct but irregular form of declension, as follows:—

Plural.

	m. f. n.	
N.	úr-e	*our.*
G.	úr-ra	*of our.*
D.	úr-um	*to, for, with our.*
A.	úr-e	*our.*

3. *Definitive Pronouns.*

§ 107. The Definitive Pronouns are those which define or point out either classes or individuals. The following are the most of them:[1]—

aegther[2] *either.* aelc *each.*

Singular.

	m.	*f.*	*n.*
N.	us-er	us-er	us-er.
G.	us-ses	us-se	us-ses.
D.	us-sum	us-se	us-sum.
A.	us-erne	us-se	us-er.

Plural.

	m. f. n.
N.	us-se *or* us-er
G.	us-sa.
D.	us-sum.
A.	us-se *or* us-er.

[1] Others are, "feaw," "few," "fea," *few*, with the Gen. "feawa," Dat. "feawum," and "fela," "faela," "feala," "feola," *much, many, many a one*, indeclinable, both in like manner agreeing with nouns, and being used as distributives with the Genitive plural; "man," "mon," *one, they*, employed only in the Nominative singular; and "thyslic." "thislic," like "thyllic," *such, of this sort, this like.*

[2] Other forms of these pronouns are: *aegther*, egther,—*aelc*, ealc, elc;—*aénig*, aéneg, aéni, aéng, aéniht, áni, énig, éneg;—*aénlypig*, aénlipig, aénlipug, aénlypic, aénlep;—*áht*, úht, auht, awht, contracted from "awiht," "awuht," augments of "wiht," "wuht," *a thing. creature;*—*án*, aén, ain;—*áthor*, auther, awther;—*bégen*, as under the declension of the word § 109;—*eall*, eal, ael, all, al, aeall, geall;—*genóh*, genóg, nóh;—*manig*, maneg, mani, maenig, maeneg,

ǽnig	*any.*	náht	*nothing.*
ǽnlypig	*each.*	nán	*no one.*
áht	*anything.*	náthor	*neither.*
án	*one.*	other	*other.*
áthor	*either.*	sum	*some.*
bégen	*both.*	swilc	*such.*
eall	*all.*	thes	*this.*
genóh	*enough.*	thyllic	*such.*
manig	*many.*	unmanig	*few.*
nǽnig	*none.*	ylc	*same.*

§ 108. All these, with the exception of "bégen" and "thes," follow the inflection of indefinite adjectives. "Bégen" and "thes" are declined as follows.

§ 109. Declension of "bégen," *both.*

	m.	*f. n.*	
N.	bégen[1]	bá	*both.*
G.	bég-ra	bég-ra	*of both.*
D.	bám	bám	*to, for, with both.*
A.	bá	bá	*both.*

---

maeni, monig, moneg, menig, meneg, meni;—*nǽnig*, nǽneg, nénig;—*náht*, neáht, nauht, nawht, nóht, contracted from "nánuht," "nánwuht;"—*nán*, nǽn nén;—*náthor*, nauther, nawther;—*other*, othyr;—*sum*, som;—*swilc*, swylc, swelc, and the compound "alsuic," *all such;*—*thes*, see § 110;—*thyllic*, thýlíc, thylc, thillic, thillec;—*unmanig*, unmaneg;—*ylc*, ilc.

[1] The following variations are met with in this pronoun: *bégen*, béggen, beágen, búgan;—*bá*, both Nom. and Acc., bú;—*bégra*, bégea, béga;—*bám*, bǽm. A compound form also appears; as, "bá-twá," "bú-tá," "bú-té," "bú-twú," "bú-twér," "bú-tér," literally, *both the two.* Thus we have "Bá-twá Adam and Eue," *Adam and Eve both together.*

"Bégen," *both*, and "sum," signifying *some, about*, as, "sume ten," *some* or *about ten*, are usually regarded as numerals, like "ánfeald," etc. Indeed "sum," "eall," and other pronouns of the kind, might very properly be styled *indefinite numerals.* The number combined

§ 110. Declension of "thes," *this.*

Singular.

	m.	*f.*	*n.*	
N.	thes	theós[1]	this	*this.*
G.	this-es	this-se	this-es	*of this.*
D.	this-um	this-se	this-um	*to, for, with this.*
A.	this-ne	thás	this	*this.*

Plural.

	m. f. n.	
N.	thás	*these.*
G.	this-sa	*of these.*
D.	this-um	*to, for, with these.*
A.	thás	*these.*

§ 111. The Definite *that* is expressed by "se, seo, thaet."

4. *Relative and Interrogative Pronouns.*

§ 112. The Articles "se, seó, thaet,"[1] and "the," are

---

with "sum," in most cases, is put in the Genitive plural. See further *Anal. Anglo-Sax.*, Part I., Sec. V., § 25, and § 28, Notes.

[1] The variations in this pronoun are: *theós,* thiós;—*this* Nom and Acc., thys;—*thises,* thisses, thysses, thesses;—*thisse,* thysse, thissere, thyssere, in the Gen. and Dat. both;—*thisum,* sing. and plur., thysum, thissum, thyssum, theossum, and the archaic forms thison, thyson;—*thisne,* thysne;—*thissa,* thissera.

The express form met with for the Ablative singular is:—

m.	*f.*	*n.*
thise	thisse	thise.

We will here observe that "thes, theós, this" may sometimes be properly and forcibly rendered by *this . . . . here,* or *this very,* and by *this . . . . now,* or *this very.* The neuter "this," too, is often used idiomatically for "thaet," and *vice versa.*

[1] "Thaet" is sometimes used idiomatically for "se" and "seó," and thus becomes the origin of *that* for *who* in English.

generally used for the Relatives, *who, which, that.* The Interrogatives "hwá," *who?* "hwaet," *what?* are thus declined:—

Singular.

	m. f.	*n.*
N.	hwá[2] *who.*	hwaet *what.*
G.	hwaes *whose.*	hwaes *of what.*
D.	hwám *to, for, with whom.*	hwám *to, for, with what.*
A.	hwone *whom.*	hwaet *what.*

§ 113. "Hwaet" is sometimes used idiomatically for "hwá;" as, "Hwaet is thes," *who is this?* "Hwaet is thes Mannes Sunu," *who is this Son of Man?* In all such cases, it may be rendered *what one?*

§ 114. Like "hwá, hwaet," are also declined:—

m. f.		*n.*	
aeghwá[1]	*whoever.*	aeghwaet	*whatever.*
elles-hwá	*who else?*	elles-hwaet	*what else?*
gehwá	*whoever.*	gehwaet	*whatever.*
swá-hwá-swá	*whosoever.*	swá-hwaet-swá	*whatsoever.*

§ 115. "Hwylc,"[1] *who? which?* or *what?* and "swá-hwylc-swá," *whosoever, whichsoever,* or *whatsoever,* are declined like indefinite adjectives.

§ 116. "Hwylc" and its compounds, except "sum-hwylc," *some one,* are often used in a definitive sense, signifying *each, every one,* etc.

---

[2] In this pronoun we find: *hwá,* huá, wuá; *hwám,* hwǽm; *hwone,* hwaene.

The distinct form appearing for the Ablative singular is:—

m. f. n.
hwý *or* hwí.

[1] *Aeghwá;* ahwá, *any one.*

[1] *Hwylc,* hwilc, hwelc.

§ 117. "Hwaether" and "swaether,"[1] *whether? which of the two?* and "swá-hwaether-swá," *which one soever that,* have the same declension as "hwylc," and its compounds.

§ 118. *He who* is expressed by "se-ṭḥe," "ṭḥe-ṭḥe," "se .... ṭḥe," "ṭḥe .... ṭḥe, and occasionally by "he .... ṭḥe."

ORIGIN AND FORMATION OF THE ARTICLES AND PRONOUNS.

§ 119. Pronouns, as well as the Articles in Anglo-Saxon, have been supposed to be derived from nouns and verbs.

1. "Se," "seó" are said by some to come either from "saegan," *to say,* or from "seón," *to see,* and "ṭḥaet" and "ṭḥe," from "ṭḥicgan," *to take.*

2. "He," "heó," "hit," have likewise been considered as owing their origin to "hátan," *to call, name.*

But what is the origin of "ic" and "ṭḥú?"

The derivation of the Articles and of the Pronouns of the third person from verbs we think not only very improbable and far-fetched, but unnatural.

"Se," which exchanges the *sibilant* for *th* out of the Nominative feminine, is in English, "the;" in German, "der;" in Dutch, "de;" in Danish and Swedish, "den;" while the initial of the kindred word in other cognate languages or dialects, with the exception of the Moeso-Gothic which has "sa," is either *th,* or *d.*[1] We therefore consider "ṭḥe" and "ṭḥeó" to be more ancient forms than "se" and "seó."[2]

Any one closely observing the sound of "ṭḥe," will per-

---

[1] *Swaether,* swaethor, swathor.

[1] 'ο, 'η, το, the definite article in Greek, was probably at one time το, τη, το, or more anciently θο, θη, θοτ.

[2] "Se" is evidently a softened form of "ṭḥe," and so with regard to the Moeso-Gothic "sa."

ceive that it is original and arbitrary, and in itself definite with regard to another person or thing.[3]

"Ic," in English, "I;" in Dutch and Moeso-Gothic, "ik;" in German, "ich;" in Danish, "jeg;" in Swedish, "jag;" in Icelandic, "eg," "jeg;"[4] in Latin, "eg-o;" in Greek, "ἐγ-ώ;" in Slavonic, "az;" in Lithuanian, "asz;" in Hebrew, as a postfix "ī;" in Zend, "az-ĕm;" in Samkrit,[5] "ah-am;"[6] in Malay, "ek-o," all indicate a common source and an original sound pointing to the individual speaking in his own person.

"Ṭḥú," in English, "thou;" in Dutch, German, Danish, and Swedish, "du;" in Moeso-Gothic and Icelandic, "ṭḥú;" in Latin and Hindustanee, "tu;" in Greek, "σύ," "τύ;" in Slavonic, "ty;" in Lithuanian," "tù;" in Hebrew, "ăt," "ăttā;" in Armenian, "te," "to;" in Persian, "tu," "tou;" in Zend, "tû-m;" in Samkrit, "tu-am;" and the like in other languages and dialects either nearly related, or far removed from each other, is arbitrary in its nature, and leads the mind to the person addressed and in proximity.

"He," from which "heó" and "hit" are formed by a slight modification, in English, "he;" in Dutch, "hy;" in German, "er;" in Danish and Swedish, "han;" in Icelandic, "hann;" in Hebrew, "hī," seems to be simple and primitive, and to have reference to the person spoken of as absent.[7]

---

[3] Observe the difference between "ṭḥǽr," *there*, and "hér," *here*, in the organs employed to express them: the former in its sound determinate with regard to another place; the latter, with regard to that where the person is speaking.

[4] J in Danish, Swedish, and Icelandic, is pronounced like *y* in English.

[5] *V. Anal. Anglo-Sax., Introd.*, § 4, Note 3.

[6] In the Yorkshire dialect of England, "ah."

[7] The same difference is perceptible in the plural of these pronouns in all the persons, as well as in the oblique cases.

This view may be fanciful, but it is at least very plausible.

3. "Sylf," *self*, is probably derived from "sawl," "saul," *the soul*, and "lif," *the life*, as pointing the most determinately to the individual. "Sjel," *soul*, was used in Old Swedish in the place of the modern "sjelf," *self*, and the Hebrew "něphěsh" was likewise employed to express either idea.

4. "Agen," *own*, appears to be no other than the perfect participle of the verb "ágan," *to have* or *possess*, to OWN; or in its form "ágan," it may be the infinitive of the same.

5. "Ṭḥes," *this*, in its sound, seems to be definite with respect to something near. Compare it with "ṭḥaet," *that*.

6. "Hwá," *who?* seems to be arbitrary, and to contain the interrogative within itself.

7. Some of the Pronouns are compounded; as, "maenig," *many*, from "man," *one*, *they*, and the termination -ig; "náenig," *no one*, from "ne," *not*, and "áenig," *any one*, and "áenig" itself, from "áen," *one*, and -ig; "hwylc," *which?* from "hwá," and "líc," *like;* "swylc," *such*, from "swá,"[8] *so*, and "líc." Other examples might be given.

[8] Or rather from the old pronoun of which "swá," sometimes found as "suáe," or, perhaps better, "suáe," belonging to one case, preserves the remains.

CHAPTER VI.

THE NUMERAL

§ 120. The Numeral combines the Substantive and the Adjective, and ought to be treated as a distinct part of speech. It is divided into Cardinal and Ordinal Numbers; as, "án," *one;* "se forma, seó, ṭḥaet forme," *the first.*

1. Cardinal Numbers. These are:—

1	án[1]	*one.*
2	twégen, twá, twá	*two.*
3	ṭḥrý, ṭḥreó, ṭḥreó	*three.*
4	feower	*four.*
5	fíf	*five.*
6	six	*six.*
7	seofon	*seven.*

[1] The following are some of the variations of the Cardinal Numbers. It is deemed unnecessary to give those of the Ordinals, as an idea may be formed of them from the others.

án, see under § 121;—*twégen* and *ṭḥrý*, under § 121, 1, and § 121, 2;—*feower*, feowr, fowr, fewer, feór, fiér, féther, féthyr;—*six*, syx, sex, seox, siex, sexo;—*seofon*, seofan, seofen, siofon, siofun, syfan, syfon, seofa, seouen, sibun;—*eahta*, ehta, aehta, ahta;—*nigon*, nygon, nigan, nigen, nyga;—*tyn*, ten, tin;—*endlufon*, endleofun, aendlefen;—*feowertyne*, feowertine, feowertene;—*fiftyne*, fiftene, fiften;—*sixtyne*, sixtene;—*seofontyne*, seofontine;—*nigontyne*, nigontine, nigantine, nygantyne;—*twentig*, tweontig, twenta;—*ṭḥrittig*, ṭḥritig;—*feowertig*, feowrtig;—*sixtig*, sixteg, sextig. "Seofa," "nyga," and "twenta" would seem to be Genitives of dialectic forms "seofe," which is indeed found, "nyge," and "twente." Compare § 122.

8	eahta	*eight.*
9	nigon	*nine.*
10	tyn	*ten.*
11	endlufon	*eleven*
12	twelf	*twelve.*
13	threottyne	*thirteen.*
14	feowertyne	*fourteen.*
15	fiftyne	*fifteen.*
16	sixtyne	*sixteen.*
17	seofontyne	*seventeen.*
18	eahtatyne	*eighteen.*
19	nigontyne	*nineteen.*
20	twentig	*twenty.*
21	án and twentig	*one and twenty.*
	etc. etc.	*etc. etc.*
30	thrittig	*thirty.*
40	feowertig	*forty.*
50	fiftig	*fifty.*
60	sixtig	*sixty.*
70	hund-seofontig	*seventy.*
80	hund-eahtatig	*eighty.*
90	hund-nigontig	*ninety.*
100	hund-teontig, *or* hund	*a hundred.*
110	hund-endlufontig	*a hundred and ten.*
120	hund-twelftig	*a hundred and twenty.*
200	twá-hund	*two hundred.*
1000	thúsend	*a thousand.*
	etc.	*etc.*

2. Ordinal Numbers. These are:—

1st	se forma	*the first.*
2d	se other	*the second.*
3d	se thridda	*the third.*
4th	se feórtha	*the fourth.*

5th	se fifta	*the fifth.*
6th	se sixta	*the sixth.*
7th	se seofotha	*the seventh.*
8th	se eahtotha	*the eighth.*
9th	se nigotha	*the ninth.*
10th	se teotha	*the tenth.*
11th	se endlyfta	*the eleventh.*
12th	se twelfta	*the twelfth.*
13th	se thrytteotha	*the thirteenth.*
14th	se feowerteotha	*the fourteenth.*
15th	se fifteotha	*the fifteenth.*
16th	se sixteotha	*the sixteenth.*
17th	se seofonteotha	*the seventeenth.*
18th	se eahtateotha	*the eighteenth.*
19th	se nigonteotha	*the nineteenth.*
20th	se twentugotha	*the twentieth.*
21st	se án and twentugotha	*the one and twentieth.*
	etc. etc.	*etc. etc.*
30th	se thrittigotha	*the thirtieth.*
40th	se feowertigotha	*the fortieth.*
50th	se fiftigotha	*the fiftieth.*
60th	se sixteogotha	*the sixtieth.*
70th	se hund-seofontigotha	*the seventieth.*
80th	se hund-eahtatigotha	*the eightieth.*
90th	se hund-nigontigotha	*the ninetieth.*
100th	se hund-teontigotha	*the hundredth.*
110th	se hund-endlufontigotha	*the hundred and tenth.*
120th	se hund-twelftigotha	*the hundred and twentieth.*

§ 121. "An," *one,* is declined like "gód."[1] "Twégen, twá," *two,* and "thrý, threó," *three,* are declined in the following manner:—

[1] When standing definitely as a pronoun, it signifies *alone*

1. "twégen," *two.*

	m.	*f. n.*	
N.	twégen	twá	*two.*
G.	twég-ra	twég-ra	*of two.*
D.	twám	twám	*to, for, with two.*
A.	twégen	twá[2]	*two.*

2. "ṭḥrý," *three.*

	m.	*f. n.*	
N.	ṭḥrý	ṭḥreó	*three.*
G.	ṭḥreó-ra	ṭḥreó-ra	*of three.*
D.	ṭḥrym	ṭḥrym	*to, for, with three.*
A.	ṭḥrý	ṭḥreó[3]	*three.*

§ 122. "Feower," *four,* makes the Genitive "feowera;" and we sometimes find "fífa," "sixa," "seofona," as the same case of "fíf," *five,* "six," *six,* "seofon," *seven.* When used absolutely, "tyn," *ten,* makes the Nominative and Accusative "tyne," and the Dative "tynum:" also "twelf," *twelve,* the Nominative "twelfe," the Genitive "twelfa," and the Dative "twelfum."

§ 123. "Twentig" and the other numerals in -tig, are thus inflected:—

	m. f. n.	
N.	twentig	*twenty.*
G.	twentig-ra	*of twenty.*
D.	twentig-um	*to, for, with twenty.*
A.	twentig	*twenty.*

[2] In the declension of "twégen," we have *twá,* tú, tuá, tuu, twíh, or twíg, tuíg, twý, either in the Nom. and Acc., or in both;—*twégra,* twégera, twéga;—*twám,* twǽm.

[3] In "ṭḥrý" likewise;—*ṭḥrý,* ṭḥrí, ṭḥríg, ṭḥrýae, ṭḥré;—*ṭḥreó,* ṭḥrió;—*ṭḥrym,* ṭḥrim.

§ 124. All these numerals in -tig, are used in the Nominative and Accusative, both as nouns which govern the Genitive plural, and as adjectives which agree with nouns in the same case.

§ 125. "Hund" and "hundred,"[1] *a hundred*, and "ṭhú-send," *a thousand*, are treated in their inflection as nouns of the first declension.

§ 126. All the Ordinal Numbers with the exception of "se other," *the second*, are declined definitely; as, "se forma, seó, ṭhaet forme," *the first.*

§ 127. "Healf,"[1] *half*, when used as a numeral, is generally placed after the cardinal, or the ordinal which agrees with it, and which it diminishes by the one-half of a unit; as, "six healf marc," *five marcs and a half;* "ṭhridde healf," *two and a half.*[2]

§ 128. Distributives are made by a repetition of the Cardinal Numbers; as, "six and six," *six and six, by sixes.*

§ 129. The Anglo-Saxons also expressed numbers by the different positions of the letters I, V, X, L, C, and M.[1]

ORIGIN AND FORMATION OF THE NUMERALS.

§ 130. 1. The Cardinals "án," "twégen," "ṭhrý,"

---

[1] "Hundred" is, properly speaking, a noun with the signification of *centuria* in Latin; it not only means the number *hundred*, but it is applied to *a division of a county;* as, "innan his hundrede," *within his hundred.* It is compounded of "hund," and "red," a word supposed to mean *a stroke* or *line*, "it being the ancient custom to count or number by strokes or lines."

[1] *Healf*, half.

[2] For the explanation of this idiom, see *Anal. Anglo-Sax.*, Part I., Sec. V., § 18, Notes.

[1] It would seem that the letters I, X, C, M, were first assumed to represent the decimal numbers 1, 10, 100, 1000, and then by bisecting the three last were given V (U) 5, L 50, and D 500. After that, nothing more was wanting in order to complete the system than to place the different letters in additive and subtractive positions.

"feower," "fíf," "six," "seofon," "eahta," "nigon," are more or less simple.

2. "Tyn" appears to be a contracted form from "twâ," *two,* and "hand," *a hand;* signifying *both the hands,* or *the ten fingers,* the common way of counting in the early stage of mankind, as always with children.

3. "Endlufon," and "twelf," are compounded from "án," and "twégen, twá," and "lífan," *to leave.*[1] "Ṭhreottyne," "feowertyne," "fiftyne," "sixtyne," "seofontyne," "eahtatyne," "nigontyne," owe their origin to "tyn," and the simple numbers "án," "twégen," etc.

4. "Twentig" is compounded of "twá," "tyn," and the termination -ig, and signifies *two tens,* or *twice two hands added together.* The same formation obtains in all the numerals which end in -tig. It is true that from seventy to a hundred and twenty inclusive, "hund" is prefixed, but more as a refinement than any thing else, since it is sometimes omitted when the same word, used to express *a hundred,* goes before. In ancient times "hund" signified only *ten,* but its meaning was afterwards extended to *ten times ten.*

5. The tens are increased by placing the units first with "and," *and,* but after "hund," *a hundred,* the smaller number is set last, while the noun is repeated. When the smaller number is placed before "hund," it denotes multiplication. Thus "án and twentig," *one and twenty;* "án hund wintra and ṭhrittig wintra," *one hundred and thirty years.*

6. "Ṭhúsend," *a thousand,* is thought to be no other than the more complete Moeso-Gothic "tigos hund," or "taihuns hund," *ten times a hundred.* But such derivation is doubtful.

7. Ordinals are formed from the Cardinal Numbers; as, "six," *six;* "se sixta, seó, ṭhaet sixte," *the sixth.*

---

[1] See Appendix C.

CHAPTER VII.

VERBS.

§ 131. Verbs in Anglo-Saxon may be divided into two orders, the Simple and the Complex;[1] and also subdivided into Conjugations and Classes. They are likewise Mixed and Anomalous.

CONJUGATIONS.

§ 132. There are three Conjugations, the 1st belonging to the Simple order of verbs, and the 2d and 3d to the Complex order. Under each of these are arranged three Classes.

MOODS.

§ 133. These are four, the Indicative, Subjunctive, Imperative, and Infinitive.

TENSES.

§ 134. The Tenses are only two, the Indefinite and the Perfect; the former being predicated either of the present time or of a future period, and the latter, of any past time, according to the relation in which the sentence containing the one or the other stands.[1]

---

[1] Complex verbs receive their appellation from the complex modifications which the vowels of their roots undergo in forming the Perfect tense.

[1] The Perfect tense in Anglo-Saxon may be rendered by the Imperfect, the Perfect, or the Pluperfect in English. Like the Latin Imperfect, it is also used to denote *what is in the habit of being done*

NUMBERS.

§ 135. There are two Numbers, the Singular and the Plural.

PERSONS.

§ 136. Each number contains three Persons, the 1st, 2d, and 3d.

PARTICIPLES.

§ 137. There are two Participles, the Indefinite and the Perfect.

GERUND.

§ 138. The Gerund, termed by some a *Second Infinitive*, is always preceded by the preposition "tó."[1] With the verb of existence, it has a passive signification, or expresses what ought to be done.[2]

CONJUGATION OF VERBS.

1. *The Simple Order.*

§ 139. This Order is distinguished by having the Perfect tense of two or more syllables, with the termination -ode, -ede, -de, or -te, while the Perfect participle ends in -od, -ed, -d, or -t,[1] as:—

1st Conjugation.

Cl.	*Inf.*		*Perf.*		*Perf. Part.*	
1	luf-ian,	*to love,*	luf-ode,	*loved,*	luf-od,	*loved.*
2	baern-an,	*to burn,*	baern-de,	*burned,*	baern-ed,	*burned.*
3	syll-an,	*to give,*	seal-de,	*gave,*	seal-d,	*given.*

[1] This particle is never found before the Infinitive in Anglo-Saxon, as in English.

[2] The Gerund combines the nature of the noun with that of the verb, just as the Participle unites the properties of the adjective and of the verb.

[1] The difference between the endings -de and -te, and -d and -t, depends altogether upon the hardness, or the softness of the preceding consonant.

§ 140. Inflection of the verb "lufian," *to love,* 1st Class.

INDICATIVE MOOD.

Indefinite Tense.

Singular.

1 ic luf-ige	*I love.*
2 ṭḥú luf-ast	*thou lovest.*
3 he, heó, hit luf-ath	*he, she, it loveth,* or *loves.*

Plural.

1 we luf-iath[1]	*we love.*
2 ge luf-iath	*ye,* or *you love.*
3 hí luf-iath	*they love.*

Perfect Tense.

Singular.

1 ic luf-ode[2]	*I loved.*
2 ṭḥú luf-odest	*thou lovedst.*
3 he, heó, hit luf-ode	*he, she, it loved.*

Plural.

1 we luf-odon[3]	*we loved.*
2 ge luf-odon	*ye,* or *you loved.*
3 hí luf-odon	*they loved.*

---

[1] *Lufiath,* lufige. The form of the first person singular is used for the plural whenever the pronoun follows the verb, as in asking a question; and in accordance with this rule, the second person plural of the Imperative, which is always like the plural of the Indefinite Indicative, assumes the same form; but never when the Nominative is omitted.

Sometimes, however, we find the peculiar termination of the plural euphonically retained; as, "magon ge," *are ye able?*

[2] *Lufode,* lufede, and so also with regard to the plural.

[3] *Lufodon,* lufode, upon the same principle as in Note 1, but very seldom occurring. For -on we also find -an, -en, and -un.

Subjunctive Mood.

Indefinite Tense.

Singular.

1	ic luf-ige	*I love.*[4]
2	ṭḥú luf-ige	*thou love.*
3	he, heó, hit luf-ige	*he, she, it love.*

Plural.

1	we luf-ion[5]	*we love.*
2	ge luf-ion	*ye,* or *you love.*
3	hí luf-ion	*they love.*

Perfect Tense.

Singular.

1	ic luf-ode[2]	*I loved.*
2	ṭḥú luf-ode	*thou loved.*
3	he, heó, hit luf-ode	*he, she, it loved.*

Plural.

1	we luf-odon	*we loved.*
2	ge luf-odon	*ye,* or *you loved.*
3	hí luf-odon	*they loved.*

Imperative Mood.

Singular.

2	luf-a ṭḥú	*love thou.*

Plural.

2	luf-iath (ge)	*love ye,* or *you.*

---

[4] A conjunction such as "gif," *if,* "ṭḥaet," *that,* "ṭḥeáh," *though* accompanies the Subjunctive mood.

[5] *Lufion,* lufian, lufien.

INFINITIVE MOOD.

Indefinite Tense.

luf-ian[6] *to love.*

PARTICIPLES.

Indef. luf-igende[7] *loving.*
Perf. luf-od[8] *loved.*

GERUND.

Indef. tó luf-igenne,[9] *to love, about to love; of, in,* and *to loving,* and *to be loved.*

§ 141. Inflection of the verb "baernan," *to burn,* 2d Class.

INDICATIVE MOOD.

Indefinite Tense.

Singular.

1	ic baern-e	*I burn.*
2	ṭḥú baern-st	*thou burnest.*
3	he, heó, hit baern-th	*he, she, it burneth,* or *burns.*

Plural.

1	we baern-ath[1]	*we burn.*
2	ge baern-ath	*ye,* or *you burn.*
3	hí baern-ath	*they burn.*

---

[6] *Lufian,* lufigean. For -an we sometimes find -en.

[7] *Lufigende,* lufiende.

[8] *Lufod,* gelufod, gelufad, gelufed.

[9] *Lufigenne,* lufienne.—For the insertion of the *g* in such cases as "lufige," "lufigende," "lufigenne," see again § 1, Note 7, with § 408.

[1] *Baernath,* baerne;—*baernon,* baernan;—*baernan,* forbaernan, onbaernan;—*baernanne,* baernenne.

Perfect Tense.

Singular.

1 ic baern-de *I burned.*
2 ṭḥú baern-dest *thou burnedst.*
3 he, heó, hit baern-de *he, she, it burned.*

Plural.

1 we baern-don *we burned.*
2 ge baern-don *ye,* or *you burned.*
3 hí baern-don *they burned.*

SUBJUNCTIVE MOOD.

Indefinite Tense.

Singular.

1 ic baern-e *I burn.*
2 ṭḥú baern-e *thou burn.*
3 he, heó, hit baern-e *he, she, it burn.*

Plural.

1 we baern-on *we burn.*
2 ge baern-on *ye,* or *you burn.*
3 hí baern-on *they burn.*

Perfect Tense.

Singular.

1 ic bearn-de *I burned.*
2 ṭḥú baern-de *thou burned.*
3. he, heó, hit baern-de *he, she, it burned.*

Plural.

1 we baern-don *we burned.*
2 ge baern-don *ye,* or *you burned.*
3 hí baern-don *they burned.*

IMPERATIVE MOOD.

Singular.

2 bearn ṭḥú — *burn thou.*

Plural.

2 baern-ath (ge) — *burn ye,* or *you.*

INFINITIVE MOOD.

Indefinite Tense.

baern-an — *to burn.*

PARTICIPLES.

Indef. baern-ende — *burning.*
Perf. baern-ed — *burned.*

GERUND.

Indef. tó baern-anne, *to burn, about to burn; of, in,* and *to burning,* and *to be burned.*

§ 142. Inflection of the verb "syllan," *to give,* 3d Class.

INDICATIVE MOOD.

Indefinite Tense.

Singular.

1 ic syll-e — *I give.*
2 ṭḥú syl-st — *thou givest.*
3 he, heó, hit syl-th[1] — *he, she, it giveth,* or *gives.*

---

[1] ***Sylth,*** silth;—***syllath,*** sylle;—***sealde,*** gesealde;—***syllan,*** sellan, selan, gesyllan;—***seald,*** geseald;—***syllanne,*** syllenne.

We will here observe that a-, be-, for-, ge-, and in some few instances, on-, and to-, are indifferently and interchangeably prefixed to verbs, especially to perfect tenses and perfect participles; ge- to the perfect tense is universal. Some verbs are not met with in their simple

Plural.

1	we syll-ath	*we give.*
2	ge syll-ath	*ye,* or *you give.*
3	hí syll-ath	*they give.*

Perfect Tense.

Singular.

1	ic seal-de	*I gave.*
2	ṭḥú seal-dest	*thou gavest.*
3	he, heó, hit seal-de	*he, she, it gave.*

Plural.

1	we seal-don	*we gave.*
2	ge seal-don	*ye,* or *you gave.*
3	hí seal-don	*they gave.*

SUBJUNCTIVE MOOD.

Indefinite Tense.

Singular.

1	ic syll-e	*I give.*
2	ṭḥú syll-e	*thou give.*
3	he, heó, hit syll-e	*he, she, it give.*

Plural.

1	we syll-on	*we give.*
2	ge syll-on	*ye,* or *you give.*
3	hí syll-on	*they give.*

---

state, but only occur with these prefixes. Very often indeed they affect the signification of the simple word.

It is evident that in the earlier stage of the language, the distinctive forces of the foregoing prefixes, naturally inherent in them, invariably obtained. At a later period, ge- especially, began to be used more for euphony than for any thing else, while the peculiar intensities of the others in many cases gradually disappeared. But see again § 75, Note 2, and also *Anal. Anglo-Sax., Gloss., sub vocibus.*

Perfect Tense.

Singular.

1 ic seal-de	*I gave.*
2 ṭḥú seal-dest	*thou gavest.*
3 he, heó, hit seal-de	*he, she, it gave.*

Plural.

1 we seal-don	*we gave.*
2 ge seal-don	*ye,* or *you gave.*
3 hí seal-don	*they gave.*

IMPERATIVE MOOD.

Singular.

2 syl-e ṭḥú	*give thou.*

Plural.

2 syll-ath (ge)	*give ye,* or *you.*

INFINITIVE MOOD.

Indefinite Tense.

syll-an	*to give.*

PARTICIPLES.

Indef. syll-ende	*giving.*
Perf. seal-d	*given.*

GERUND.

Indef. tó syll-anne, *to give, about to give; of, in,* and *to giving,* and *to be given.*

§ 143. *Remarks on the 1st Conjugation.*

1. The 1st Class contains all verbs in -ian.

2. The 2d Class comprises those which are derived from nouns, adjectives, and other verbs.

3. The 3d Class includes those which have the Perfect tense of more than one syllable like the rest, and which do not belong to the other two classes.

2. *The Complex Order.*

§ 144. This order makes the Perfect tense a monosyllable, with a change of vowel, and the Perfect participle in -en, or -n, as:—

2d *Conjugation.*

Cl.	*Inf.*		*Indef.*	*Perf.*	*Perf. Part.*
1	et-an,	*to eat,*	et-e	áet	et-en.
2	láet-an,	*to let,*	láet-e	let	láet-en.
3	far-an,	*to go,*	far-e	fór	far-en.

§ 145. Inflection of the verbs "etan," *to eat,* "láetan," *to let,* and "faran," *to go.*

Indicative Mood.

Indefinite Tense.

Singular.

1	ic et-e	láet-e	far-e.
2	ṭhú yt-st	láet-st	faer-st.
3	he, heó, hit yt[1]	láet	faer-th.

Plural.

1	we et-ath	láet-ath	far-ath.
2	ge et-ath	láet-ath	far-ath.
3	hí et-ath	láet-ath	far-ath.

[1] *yt,* ytt;—*etath,* ete;—*láetath,* láete;—*farath,* fare;—*láetan:* onláetan, *to continue;—faran,* fearran, gefaran, gefaeran: afaran afearrian, *to go out of:* on-faran, *to go on:* tó-faran, *to go to;—eten,* ge-eten;—*faren,* ge-faren.

Perfect Tense.

Singular.

1	ic ǽt	let	fór.
2	ṭḥú ǽt-e	let-e	fór-e.
3	he, heó, hit ǽt	let	fór.

Plural.

1	we ǽt-on	let-on	fór-on.
2	ge ǽt-on	let-on	fór-on.
3	hí ǽt-on	let-on	fór-on.

SUBJUNCTIVE MOOD.

Indefinite Tense.

Singular.

1	ic et-e	lǽt-e	far-e.
2	ṭḥú et-e	lǽt-e	far-e.
3	he, heó, hit et-e	lǽt-e	far-e.

Plural.

1	we et-on	lǽt-on	far-on.
2	ge et-on	lǽt-on	far-on.
3	hí et-on	lǽt-on	far-on.

Perfect Tense.

Singular.

1	ic ǽt-e	let-e	fór-e.
2	ṭḥú ǽt-e	let-e	fór-e.
3	he, heó, hit ǽt-e	let-e	fór-e.

Plural.

1	we ǽt-on	let-on	fór-on.
2	ge ǽt-on	let-on	fór-on.
3	hí ǽt-on	let-ou	fór-ou.

Imperative Mood.

Singular.

2 et	láet	far thú.

Plural.

2 et-ath	láet-ath	far-ath (ge.)

Infinitive Mood.

Indefinite Tense.

et-an	láet-an	far-an.

Participles.

Indef.	et-ende	láet-ende	far-ende.
Perf.	et-en	láet-en	far-en.

Gerund.

Indef.	tó et-anne	láet-anne	far-anne.

§ 146. *Remarks on the 2d Conjugation.*

1. The 1st Class contains those verbs which have a long *e* or *i* before a single characteristic.

2. The 2d Class includes those which have a short *e* and short *eo* in the Perfect.

3. The 3d Class comprises those which form the Perfect in *ó*.

3d Conjugation.

Cl.	*Inf.*		*Indef.*	*Perf.*	*Perf. Part.*
1	byrn-an,	*to burn,*	byrn-e	barn	burn-en.
2	wrít-an,	*to write,*	writ-e	wrát	writ en.
3	sceót-an,	*to shoot,*	sceót-e	sceát	scot-en.

§ 147. Inflection of the verbs "byrnan," *to burn,* "wrítan," *to write,* and "sceótan," *to shoot.*

INDICATIVE MOOD.

Indefinite Tense.

Singular.

1	ic	byrn-e	wrít-e	sceót-e.
2	ṭḥú	byrn-st	wrít-st.	scýt-st.
3	he, heó, hit	byrn-th	wrít	scýt.

Plural.

1	we	byrn-ath[1]	wrít-ath	sceót-ath.
2	ge	byrn-ath	wrít-ath	sceót-ath.
3	hí	byrn-ath	wrít-ath	sceót-ath.

Perfect Tense.

Singular.

1	ic	barn	wrát	sceát.
2	ṭḥú	burn-e	writ-e	scut-e.
3	he, heó, hit	barn	wrát	sceát.

Plural.

1	we	burn-on	writ-on	scut-on.
2	ge	burn-on	writ-on	scut-on.
3	hí	burn-on	writ-on	scut-on.

SUBJUNCTIVE MOOD.

Indefinite Tense.

Singular.

1	ic	byrn-e	wrít-e	sceót-e.
2	ṭḥú	byrn-e	wrít-e	sceót-e.
3	he, heó, hit	byrn-e	wrít-e	sceót-e.

[1] ***Byrnath***, byrne ;—***wrítath***, wríte ;—***sceótath***, sceóte ;—***barn***, born ;—***wrát***, gewrát ;—***byrnan***, gebyrnan, forbyrnan ;—***wrítan***, gewrítan : awrítan, *to write out* ;—***sceótan***, scótan, be-sceótan ;—***byrnen***, geburnen ;—***writen***, gewriten.

Plural.

1 we	byrn-on	wrít-on	sceót-on.
2 ge	byrn-on	wrít-on	sceót-on.
3 hí	byrn-on	wrít-on	sceót-on.

Perfect Tense.

Singular.

1 ic	burn-e	writ-e	scut-e.
2 ṭḥú	burn-e	writ-e	scut-e.
3 he, heó, hit	burn-e	writ-e	scut-e.

Plural.

1 we	burn-on	writ-on	scut-on.
2 ge	burn-on	writ-on	scut-on.
3 hí	burn-on	writ-on	scut-on.

IMPERATIVE MOOD.

Singular.

2 byrn	wrít	sceót ṭḥú.

Plural.

2 byrn-ath	wrít-ath	sceót-ath (ge.)

INFINITIVE MOOD.

Indefinite Tense.

byrn-an	wrít-an	sceót-an.

PARTICIPLES.

Indef.	byrn-ende	wrít-ende	sceót-ende.
Perf.	burn-en	writ-en	sceot-en.

GERUND.

Indef.	tó byrn-anne	wrít-anne	sceót-anne.

§ 148. *Remarks on the 3d Conjugation.*

1. The 1st Class contains those verbs which have a short *i* (*y*) before *mb, mm, mp, nc, nd, ng, nn, rn ;* a short *a* (*o*) in the Perfect, and *u* in the Perfect participle: also those which have a short *e* or *eo* before *gd ; ht ; ld, lf, lg, ll, lp, lt ; rc, rf, rg, rn, rp, rs ; sc, st ; ea* (*ae*) short in the Perfect, and *o* in the Perfect participle.

2. The 2d Class comprises those which have a hard *i* (*í*) in the Indefinite, and *a* in the Perfect.

3. The 3d Class bears a near resemblance to the 2d.

FORMATION OF THE DIFFERENT PARTS OF THE VERB

§ 149. *Imperative Mood.*—This part of the verb is formed from the Infinitive by rejecting the termination -an; but if the final consonant of the root be double, one of the consonants is also thrown away, and *e* put in its place. Verbs in -ian make the Imperative in -a. Thus, "baern-an," "baern;" "syll-an," "syl-e;" "luf-ian," "luf-a."

§ 150. *Indefinite Participle.*—This Participle is formed by rejecting the Infinitive ending -an, and adding the termination -ende; as, "baern-an," "baern-ende."

§ 151. *Gerund.*—The Gerund appears to be the Dative case of the Infinitive declined as a noun, the *a* of the termination -an being sometimes changed into *e ;* as, "wrít-an," "wrít-anne;" "baern-an," "baern-enne."

§ 152. The Perfect tense and Perfect participle, and, to some extent, the Persons, are formed differently in the Simple, and in the Complex Verbs.

1. *Simple Verbs.*

§ 153. *Perfect Tense.*—The Perfect tense rejects the -an or -ian, and adds -ode, -ede, or -de to the root; as, "luf-ian," "luf-ode;" "segl-ian," "segl-ode," or "segl-ede." The form -de, which is a contracted one, belongs mostly to verbs having *d, f, g, l, m, n, r, s, w,* and *th* before the Infinitive termination; as, "baern-an," "baern-de;" "alýs-an," "alýs-de."

§ 154. Verbs which end in -dan or -tan preceded by a consonant, do not take an additional *d* or *t;* and those having either *c* or *cc* before the termination -an, change the *c* or *cc* into *h* whenever *t* follows; as, "send-an," "send-e;" "pliht-an," "pliht-e;" "recc-an," "reh-te."

§ 155. In many cases the letters *t, p, c, h, x,* and *s,* after another consonant, and preceding the Infinitive -an, not only contract the Perfect tense, but also change the *d* into *t;* as, "dypp-an," "dypp-ede," "dyp-de," "dyp-te."

§ 156. *Perfect Participle.*—The Perfect participle is formed by changing the -an or -ian of the Infinitive into -ed or -od. It is also frequently contracted like the Perfect tense when *t, p, c, h, x,* or *s,* preceded by another consonant, terminates the root of the verb, while *d* passes into *t.* Sometimes the root itself is changed, and the *e* of the -ed rejected. Thus, "baern-an," "baern-ed;" "luf-ian," "luf-od;" "dypp-an," "dypp-ed," "dyppd," "dyppt," and "dypt;" "syll-an," "seald."

§ 157. The syllable ge- is not uncommonly prefixed to the Perfect participle in both orders of verbs; as, "lufod," "gelufod;" "faren," "gefaren." See also § 142, Note. 1.

§ 158. *Persons.*—The First person singular of the Indefinite Indicative is formed from the Infinitive by changing the termination into -e, the Second, by changing it into -st, -ast, or -est, and the Third, into -th, -ath, or -eth; as, "baern-an," "baern-e," "baern-st," "baern-th," etc. All the persons of the plural end in -ath, but -an with a vowel before it makes -iath; as, "baern-an," "we, ge, hí baern-ath;" "luf-ian," "we, ge, hí luf-iath."

§ 159. Verbs in -dan and -san have -t in the third person singular instead of the aspirate -th, while *d* before -an also makes the second person in -tst, though -dst is sometimes found. Verbs in -than and -tan do not receive *th* additional in the third person. Thus, "féd-an," "fét;" "ræ̍s-an," "ræ̍st;" "send-an," "sentst;" "cyth-an," "cyth;" "hát-an," "hæ̍t."

§ 160. Whenever a verb has a double consonant, one is always rejected in forming the persons in case another follows; and where it would make too harsh a sound to add *st* or *th* to the bare root, an *e* is usually inserted. Thus, "spill-an," "spil-st," "spil-th;" "nemn-an," "nemnest," "nemn-eth."

§ 161. In the Perfect tense the second person singular adds *st* to the first, and the third is like the first. The plural rejects the final *e* of the first person singular, and puts *on* in its place.

§ 162. In the Indefinite Subjunctive all the persons of the singular are like the first person of the same tense Indicative, while the plural adds -on, -an, or -ion, -ian, as the case may be, to the root of the verb.

§ 163. The Perfect tense is like the Perfect Indicative, except that it does not add *st* to the first person singular to form the second.

2. *Complex Verbs.*

§ 164. *Perfect Tense* and *Perfect Participle.*—The Perfect tense is formed by rejecting the Infinitive termination, with various changes of the radical vowel: the Perfect participle usually modifies the root in the same way, and converts its verbal ending into -en.

§ 165. Verbs, the roots of which present a monosyllabic form with *a* or *ea* after the rejection of the Infinitive ending, frequently change the *a* into *o*, and sometimes into *eo*, and the *ea* generally into *eo*, to form the Perfect tense, while in forming the Perfect participle no other change takes place than that of the termination; as, "stand-an," "stód," "gestand-en;" "beát-an," "beot," "beát-en."

§ 166. Verbs having *e* or *eo* before *ll, lf, lg, lt, rf, rg, rp,* and the like, make *ea,* and in some cases *ae,* in the Perfect tense, and *o* in the Perfect participle; as, "delf-an," "dealf," "dolf-en."

§ 167. Verbs having *i* before *gn, nn, nc, nd, ng, mb, mp,* etc., often change this vowel into *a* in the Perfect tense, and into *u* in the Perfect participle; as, "sinc-an," "sanc," "sunc-en." The same change of vowel takes place when *i* occurs before a single consonant; as, "nim-an," "nam," "numen;" but *í* becomes *á* in the tense, and *i* in the participle; as, "slit-an," "slát," "slit-en."

§ 168. Those verbs which have either *ú* or *eó* in the Infinitive, make the Perfect tense in *eá,* and the Perfect participle in *o;* as, "clúf-an," "cleáf," "clof-en;" "hreów-an," "hreáw," "hrow-en."

§ 169. *Persons.*—The Personal terminations are usually like those in verbs of the Simple Order; but while in the Indefinite Indicative the persons of the plural retain the vowel of the first person singular, the same is not unfrequently changed in the second and third. Thus, *a* becomes *ae,* and occasionally, *e,* or *y; e, ea,* and *u,* are converted into *y,* or *i; ó,* into *é;* and *ú,* or *eó,* into *ý;* as, "Ic bac-e, ṭḥú baec-st, he, &c., baec-th," "we, ge, hí bac-ath;" "Ic stand-e, ṭḥú stent-st, he, &c., stent," "we, ge, hí stand-ath;" "Ic et-e, ṭḥú yt-st, he, &c., yt," "we, ge, hí et-ath;" "Ic sceót-e, ṭḥú scýt-st, he, &c., scýt," "we, ge, hí sceót-ath."

§ 170. The termination of the third person singular in verbs ending in -dan, -san, -tan, etc., follows the same rules as those given in § 159; as, "ríd-an," "ic ríd-e, he, &c., rít, *or* ríd-eth;" "et-an," "ic et-e, he, &c., yt;" etc.

§ 171. In the Perfect Indicative, the second person singular commonly ends in -e, and gives form to all the persons of the same number in the Perfect Subjunctive; as, "Ic stód, ṭḥú stód-e;" "ic, ṭḥú, he, &c., stód-e."

§ 172. Verbs taking either *u* or *o* in the stem of the Perfect participle, in most cases have *u* in that of the second person singular and of all the persons of the plural in the Perfect tense, while the third person singular is like the first; as, "crung-en," &c., "ic crang, ṭḥú crung-e, he, &c., crang," "we, ge, hí crung-on."

§ 173. Verbs having *í* in the radical part of the Infinitive, and *i* in the Perfect participle, with *á* in the first and third persons singular of the Perfect tense, make *i* in the second, and in all the persons of the plural; as, "arís-an," "aris-en," "ic, he, &c., arás," "ṭḥú aris-e," "we, ge, hí aris-on."

§ 174. Contracted verbs of one syllable having the Perfect participle in -gen, terminate the first and third persons singular of the Perfect tense, and the second person singular of the Imperative mood, in -h, besides always inserting this letter before -st, and -th; as, "ṭḥweán," "ṭḥweg-en," "ic, he, &c., ṭḥwóh," "ṭḥweáh ṭḥú," "ṭḥú ṭḥwýh-st," "he, &c., ṭḥwíh-th." Those which terminate the root of the Infinitive in *g*, in general follow the same rule, converting the *g* into *h*; as, "stíg-an," "ṭḥú stíh-st," "ic, he, &c., stáh."

AUXILIARY VERBS.

§ 175. There are, properly speaking, no verbs in Anglo-Saxon which can lay claim to this peculiar character, as those which have been regarded as such, do not convey the idea of *time*, especially *future time*, except seemingly and in rare instances, but rather of *possession; affirmation*, or *existence; volition, obligation, command*, and *necessity*. They are, "habban;" "wesan," "beón," and "weorthan;" "willan," "sceal," "magan," "cunnan," and "mót."

§ 176. Conjugation of the verb "habban," *to have,* (1 Con. 2 Cl. Irr.[1])

INDICATIVE MOOD.

Indefinite Tense.

Singular.

1	ic habb-e[2]	*I have.*
2	ṭḥú haef-st	*thou hast.*
3	he, heó, hit haef-th	*he, she, it hath,* or *has.*

Plural.

1	we habb-ath	*we have.*
2	ge habb-ath	*ye,* or *you have.*
3	hí habb-ath	*they have.*

Perfect Tense.

Singular.

1	ic haef-de	*I had.*
2	ṭḥú haef-dest	*thou hadst.*
3	he, heó, hit haef-de	*he, she, it had.*

Plural.

1	we haef-don	*we had.*
2	ge haef-don	*ye,* or *you had.*
3	hí haef-don	*they had.*

---

[1] This verb, strictly speaking, unites two classes of the first Conjugation, the 1st and 2d, from the infinitives "habban" and "hafian," different formations from the same root, as will clearly appear. The same may be said of "lybban" and "leofian," *to live;* "hycgan" and "hogian," *to think;* "fyligan" or "fyligean" and "folgian," *to follow;* and some others. Such are usually considered *irregular.*

There is also a class of verbs which evidently form their different parts from two or more distinct roots. These will appear in the sequel.

[2] *Habbe,* haebbe;—*haefst,* hafast;—*haefth,* hafath;—*habbath,* hafiath;—*habbe,* hafie;—*habbe,* haebbe;—*habbon,* habban;—*habban,*

Subjunctive Mood.

Indefinite Tense.

Singular.

1	ic habb-e	*I have.*
2	ṭḥú habb-e	*thou have.*
3	he, heó, hit habb-e	*he, she, it have.*

Plural.

1	we habb-on	*we have.*
2	ge habb-on	*ye,* or *you have.*
3	hí habb-on	*they have.*

Perfect Tense.

Singular.

1	ic haef-de	*I had.*
2	ṭḥú haef-de	*thou had.*
3	he, heó, hit haef-de	*he, she, it had.*

Plural.

1	we haef-don	*we had.*
2	ge haef-don	*ye,* or *you had.*
3	hí haef-don	*they had.*

Imperative Mood.

Singular.

2	haf-a ṭḥú	*have thou.*

Plural.

2	habb-ath (ge)	*have ye,* or *you.*

---

haebban ;—*habbende,* haebbende ;—*haefd,* haefed ;—*habbanne,* haebbanne, habbenne, haebbenne.

Infinitive Mood.

Indefinite Tense.

habb-an *to have.*

Participles.

Indef. habb-ende *having.*
Perf. haef-d *had.*

Gerund.

Indef. tó habb-anne, *to have, about to have; of, in,* and *to having,* and *to be had.*

§ 177. Conjugation of the verbs "wesan" and "beón," *to be,* (2 Con. 2 Cl. Irr.,) and "weorthan," *to become, be,* (3 Con. 1 Cl. Irr.)

Indicative Mood.

Indefinite Tense.

Singular.

1 ic	eom[1]	beó	weorth-e.
2 thú	eart	bý-st	wyr-st.
3 he, heó, hit	ys	bý-th	wyrth.

[1] *Eom,* eam, am;—*eart,* earth;—*ys,* is;—*synd,* sind, synt, syndon, sindon;—*wáes,* wás;—*wáeron,* wáeren;—*sý,* sí, síg, seó;—*sýn,* sín;—*wesath,* wese;—*wesan,* wisan, wosan;—*wesen,* gewesen.

Beó, bió, bióm, bén;—*býst,* bíst;—*býth,* bíth:—*beóth,* bióth, beó, bió;—*beón,* bión;—*beónde,* biónde;—*beónne,* biónne.

Weorthe, wurthe, wyrthe;—*wyrth,* wirth, weorth, weortheth, wyrtheth;—*weorthath,* wurthath, wyrthath, weorthe, wurthe, wyrthe;—*weorthe,* weorth, weortheth, weordeth;—*weorthan,* wurthan, wyrthan;—*weorthende,* wurthende, wyrthende;—*worden,* geworden;—*weorthanne,* wurthanne, wyrthanne.

Plural.

1	we synd	beó-th	weorth-ath.
2	ge synd	beó-th	weorth-ath.
3	hí synd	beó-th	weorth-ath.

Perfect Tense.

Singular.

1	ic wǽs	wearth.
2	ṭḥú wǽr-e	wurd-e.
3	he, heó, hit wǽs	wearth.

Plural.

1	we wǽr-on	wurd-on.
2	ge wǽr-on	wurd-on.
3	hí wǽr-on	wurd-on.

Subjunctive Mood.

Indefinite Tense.

Singular.

1	ic sý̌	beó	weorth-e.
2	ṭḥú sý̌	beó	weorth-e.
3	he, heó, hit sý̌	beó	weorth-e.

Plural.

1	we sýn	beó-n	weorth-on.
2	ge sýn	beó-n	weorth-on.
3	hí sýn	beó-n	weorth-on.

Perfect Tense.

Singular.

1	ic wǽr-e	wurd-e.
2	ṭḥú wǽr-e	wurd-e.
3	he, heó, hit wǽr-e	wurd-e.

Plural.

1	we wáer-on	wurd-on.
2	ge wáer-on	wurd-on.
3	hí wáer-on	wurd-on.

IMPERATIVE MOOD.

Singular.

2	wes	beó	weorth thú.

Plural.

2	wes-ath	beó-th	weorth-ath (ge.)

INFINITIVE MOOD.

Indef.	wes-an	beó-n	weorth-an.

PARTICIPLES.

Indef.	wes-ende	beó-nde	weorth-ende.
Perf.	wes-en		word-en.

GERUND.

Indef.	wes-anne	beó-nne	weorth-anne.

§ 178. Inflection of the verbs "willan," *to will*, or *be willing*, (1 Con. 3 Cl. Irr.,) and "sceal," *shall*, "magan," *to be able*, "cunnan," *to know*, *know how*, and "mót," *must*, (Anom.)

INDICATIVE MOOD.

Indefinite Tense.

Singular.

1	ic wyll-e[1]	sceal	maeg	can	mót.
2	thú wyl-t	sceal-t	mih-t	can-st	mó-st.
3	he, &c., wyl-e	sceal	maeg	can	mót.

---

[1] *Wylle*, wille ;—*wylt*, wilt, wylst ,—*wyle*, wile ;—*wyllath*, willath.

Plural.

1	we	wyll-ath	sceal-on	mag-on	cunn-on	mót-on.
2	ge	wyll-ath	sceal-on	mag-on	cunn-on	mót-on.
3	hí	wyll-ath	sceal-on	mag-on	cunn-on	mót-on.

Perfect Tense.

Singular.

1	ic	wol-de	sceol-de	mih-te	cuth-e	mós-te.
2	ṭḥú	wol-dest	sceol-dest	mih-test	cuth-est	mós-test.
3	he, &c.	wol-de	sceol-de	mih-te	cuth-e	mós-te.

Plural.

1	we	wol-don	sceol-don	mih-ton	cuth-on	mós-ton.
2	ge	wol-don	sceol-don	mih-ton	cuth-on	mós-ton.
3	hí	wol-don	sceol-don	mih-ton	cuth-on	mós-ton.

SUBJUNCTIVE MOOD.

Indefinite Tense.

Singular.

1	ic	wyll-e	scyl-e	mag-e.
2	ṭḥú	wyll-e	scyl-e	mag-e.
3	he, heó, hit	wyll-e	scyl-e	mag-e.

Plural.

1	we	wyll-on	scyl-on	mag-on.
2	ge	wyll-on	scyl-on	mag-on.
3	hí	wyll-on	scyl-on	mag-on.

---

wylle, wille ;—*wylle*, wille ;—*wyllon*, willon, wyllen, willen ;—*wyllan*, willan ;—*wyllende*, willende.

Sceal, sceol, scal ;—*scealon*, sceolan, sculon ;—*scyle*, scile ;—*scylon*, scylan, scylen.

Can, cann, conn ;—*cuthe*, evidently contracted and modified from "cun-de ;"—*cunnan*, connan ;—*cuth*, i. e. "cun-ed," or "cun-d."

Perfect Tense.

Singular.

1	ic	wol-de	sceol-de	mih-te.
2	ṭhú	wol-de	sceol-de	mih-te.
3	he, heó, hit	wol-de	sceol-de	mih-te.

Plural.

1	we	wol-don	sceol-don	mih-ton.
2	ge	wol-don	sceol-don	mih-ton.
3	hí	wol-don	sceol-don	mih-ton.

IMPERATIVE MOOD.

Singular.

2 wyl-e ṭhú.

Plural.

2 wyll-ath (ge.)

INFINITIVE MOOD.

Indef.	wyll-an	mag-an	cunn-an.

PARTICIPLES.

Indef.	wyll-ende.		
Perf.			cuth.

COMPOUND TENSES.

§ 179. Hence, in strict terms, there can be neither Compound tenses, nor a Passive voice in Anglo-Saxon. Thus, in parsing forms like the following, "Ic haebbe geset," *I have set;* "ic maeg beón lufod," *I may be loved,* the Part. "geset" agrees with the Pron. "ic;" "beón" is the Inf. governed by "maeg," and "lufod" agrees with "ic," as before.[1]

[1] "Habban," there can be no doubt, is not unfrequently employed

§ 180. A participial form of tense exists as in English: thus, "ic eom baernende," *I am burning;* "ic waés lufigende," *I was loving.* It denotes *continuance of action.*

IMPERSONAL VERBS.

§ 181. These are used only in the third person singular with the pronoun "hit," *it,* either expressed or understood, while in other respects they are like regular verbs; as, "hit sniwth," *it snows;* "me ṭhúhte," *it seemed to me,* or *I thought.*

§ 182. "Man" corresponding to *one* and *they* in English, often gives the verb an impersonal sense; as, "man dyde," *one,* or *they did, it was done.*[1]

MIXED VERBS.

§ 183. Verbs in Anglo-Saxon may be termed Mixed when they combine both Orders in a greater or less degree. A large number will be found to possess this character; as, "adrencan;"[1] *p.* "adrenc-te;" *pp.* "adrenc-ed," "adrunc-en," *to immerge, drown;* "bringan;"[2] *p.* "bróhte," "brang;" *pp.* "gebróh-t," "brung-en," *to bring, pro-*

---

as an auxiliary; as, "hí haefdon lufod," *they had loved,* though some grammarians would consider the participle in such cases as "an unchangeable supine." But is it the nature of the supine *to agree?*

Sometimes we have the participle with "habban" agreeing with the governed word; as, "hine haefde he gesetenne," *him had he set,* which construction was probably at one time very general in the language, being more natural than any other, and therefore more ancient.

[1] Perhaps we ought to have introduced Reflexive verbs as a distinct class; as, "hí hí reston," *they rested themselves,* but such may not improperly be looked upon as active-transitive, for although from their nature, the subject and the object are the same in every case in which they are employed, still there is a *quasi* transition, or, so to speak, a transition from the outer to the inner person always implied.

[1] ***Adrencan;*** adrincan, also *to quench, p.* adranc;—***adrenced, adruncen,*** adraenct, adronct, adroncen, adronc.

[2] ***Bringan,*** brengan;—***gebróht,*** bróht.

duce; "acwencan;"[3] *p.* "acwanc;" *pp.* "acwenc-ed," "acwin-en," *to quench, extinguish.*

ANOMALOUS VERBS.

§ 184. Anomalous verbs in Anglo-Saxon are such as cannot be reduced to either of the two Orders. Besides those already inflected, we have the following:—

§ 185. "ágan,"[1] *to own, deliver, restore.*

Perf.	*Part.*	ág-en.		
Ind.	*Indef.*	ic ág-e	he áh	we ág-on.
—	*Perf.*	ic áh-te		we áh-ton.

§ 186. "búan,"[1] *to inhabit, to cultivate.*

Perf.	*Part.*	gebú-n.		
Ind.	*Indef.*	ic bú-e	he bý-th,	we bú-n.
—	*Perf.*	ic bú-de		we bú-don.

§ 187. "dear," *dare, presume.*

Perf. Part. —
Ind. Indef. ic dear,[1] ṭẖú dear-st, he dear, we durr-on.
— *Perf.* ic dors-te, ṭẖú dors-test, he dors-te, we dors-ton.
Sub. Indef. ic durr-e.
— *Perf.* ic dors-te we dors-ton.

§ 188. "dón," *to do, make, cause.*

Perf. Part. gedó-n.
Ind. Indef. ic dó, ṭẖú dé-st, he dé-th, we dó-th.

---

[3] *Acwencan,* cwencan, acwinan;—*acwenced, acwinen,* acwenct, acwent, acwan.

[1] *Agan,* ǽgan;—*ágon,* ágan;—*áhte,* ǽhte.

[1] *Búan,* býan, búgian.

[1] *Dear,* deor; *dearst,* durre;—*dorste,* durste

Ind. *Perf.* ic dy-de,[1] ṭḥú dy-dest, he did, we dy-don.
Imp. dó ṭḥú.

§ 189. "dugan,"[1] *to profit, care for, help, be good.*

Indef. *Part.* dug-ende.
Ind. *Indef.* ic deáh, ṭḥú dug-e, he deáh, we dug-on.
— *Perf.* ic dóh-te, ṭḥú dóh-test, we dóh-ton.

§ 190. "gán,"[1] *to go, walk, happen.*

Perf. *Part.* gá-n.
Ind. *Indef.* ic gá he gǽ-th, we gá-th.
— *Perf.* ic eó-de we eó-don.
Imp. gá ṭḥú.

§ 191. "geman,"[1] *remember.*

Perf. *Part.* —
Ind. *Indef.* ic geman ṭḥú geman-st we gemun-on.
— *Perf.* ic gemun-de we gemun-don.

§ 192. "ṭḥearfan,"[1] *to need, behoove.*

Indef. *Part.* ṭḥearf-ende.
Ind. *Indef.* ic ṭḥearf, ṭḥú ṭḥearf-t, he ṭḥearf, we ṭḥurf-on.
— *Perf.* ic ṭḥorf-te we ṭḥorf-ton.

---

[1] *Dyde*, dide;—*dydest*, didest;—*did*, dyde, dide;—*dydon*, didon.

[1] *Dugan*, digian;—*deáh*, dég, and from "digian," dige, dyge;—*dóhte*, dúhte.

[1] *Gán*, gangan;—*gán*, gangen;—*gá*, gange;—*gáth*, gǽth;—*gá*, gang.

[1] *Geman;* "gemunan," "munan," *to remember, reflect*, has p "gemunde," *pp.* "gemunen," being a mixed verb.

Geman, gemon;—*gemunon*, gemunan.

We also find, "ṭḥú gemyst," for "ṭḥú gemyndest," *thou rememberedst.*

[1] *Ṭḥearfan*, ṭḥurfan, ṭḥyrfan;—*ṭḥurfon*, ṭḥyrfon, ṭḥyrfen.

§ 193. "witan," *to know, wit,* WOT, *p.* WIST.

Indef.	*Part.*	wit-ende.			
Perf.	—	wit-en.[1]			
Ind.	*Indef.*	ic wat	ṭḥú wa-st	he wat	we wit-on.
—	*Perf.*	ic wis-te			we wis-ton.
Imp.		wit-e ṭḥú; wit-ath (ge.)			

§ 194. "unnan;"[1] *to grant, give, bestow.*

Perf.	*Part.*	ge-unn-en.		
Ind.	*Indef.*	ic an	ṭḥú unn-e	we unn-on.
—	*Perf.*	ic uth-e		we uth-on.

§ 195. "yrnan,"[1] *to run.*

Perf.	*Part.*	urn-en.		
Ind.	*Indef.*		he yrn-th.	
—	*Perf.*	ic arn		we urn-on.

NEGATIVE VERBS.

§ 196. The Anglo-Saxon has a few such forms, made by contracting the negative "ne," *not,* with the verb. They are as follows:—

---

[1] *Witen,* witod;—*wast,* probably contracted from "watst;"—*witon,* witan;—*wiste,* wisste, wisse;—*wiston,* wisston, wisson.

[1] *Unnan:* we have given this form in preference to the fuller one "ge-unnan," though contrary to the principle which we have adopted, as will appear in other cases.

Unnon, unnan, unnen;—*uthe,* formed in the same way as "cuthe," § 178, from "un-de."

[1] *Yrnan:* we have placed this among the anomalous verbs, although it is considered as differing from "rinnan," "rennan," "reonnan," only by the transposition of the *r.* The form "aernan," signifies *to let run.*

§ 197. "nabban,"[1] *not to have.*

Perf.	*Part.* —				
Ind.	*Indef.*	ic nabb-e,	ṭḥú naef-st,	he naef-th,	we nabb-ath.
—	*Perf.*	ic naef-de			we naef-don.
Sub.	*Indef.*	ic naebb-e			we naebb-on.
—	*Perf.*	ic naef-de			we naef-don.
Imp.		naf-a ṭḥú		nabb-ath (ge.)	

§ 198. "neom,"[1] *am not.*

Perf.	*Part.* —				
Ind.	*Indef.*	ic neom		he nis.	
—	*Perf.*	ic nǽs	ṭḥú nǽr-e	he nǽs	we nǽr-on.
Sub.	—	ic nǽr-e			we nǽr-on.

§ 199. "nágan,"[1] *not to own,* or *possess.*

Perf.	*Part.* —				
Ind.	*Indef.*			he náh	we nág-on.
—	*Perf.*	ic náh-te,	ṭḥú náh-test		we náh-ton.
Sub.	*Indef.*	ic nág-e.			

§ 200. "nitan,"[1] *not to know.*

Indef.	*Part.*	nit-ende.			
Ind.	*Indef.*	ic nát	ṭḥú ná-st	he nát	we nyt-on.
—	*Perf.*	ic nys-te,	ṭḥú nys-test		we nys-ton.

---

[1] *Nabban,* for "ne habban;"—*naefth,* nafath;—*nabbath,* nabbo, naebbe;—*naebbon,* naebben.

[1] *Neom,* for "ne eom;"—*nis,* nys.

[1] *Nágan,* for "ne ágan."

[1] *Nitan,* for "ne witan:" also nytan;—*nitende,* netende;—*nyton,* nytan, nuton;—*nyste,* nysse;—*nystest,* nysstest, nestest.

§ 201. "nyllan,"[1] *to be unwilling, to* NILL.

Perf. Part.	—			
Ind. Indef.	ic nell-e,	ṭḥú nel-t,	he nel-e,	we nell-ath.
— *Perf.*	ic nol-de			we nol-don.
Sub. Indef.	ic nell-e			we nyll-on.
Imp.	nel-e ṭḥú.			

A LIST OF COMPLEX VERBS.

§ 202. The following are the Complex Verbs in Anglo-Saxon, in addition to those already given, with the inflection and orthographic variations of the principal parts.[1]

§ 203. "Arísan,"[1] *to arise, rise.*

3 Con. 2 Cl.

Perf. Part.	aris-en.		
Ind. Indef.	ic arís-e	he arís-t.	
— *Perf.*	ic arás		we aris-on.

§ 204. "aslídan,"[1] *to slide.*

3 Con. 2 Cl.

Perf. Part.	aslid-en.		
Ind. Indef.	ic aslíd-e	he aslíd-eth.	
— *Perf.*	ic aslád		we aslid-on.

[1] *Nyllan,* for "ne wyllan;" also nillan;—*nele,* nyle;—*nellath,* nyllath;—*nelle,* nylle;—*nyllon,* nyllan.

[1] All the verbs in this list about the classification of which we have had any doubt, will be found marked with an asterisk. It is evident that any change in that respect would be predicated upon the removal, or the imposition of the accent.

[1] *Arísan,* rísan.

[1] *Aslídan,* aslýdan, slídan.

§ 205. "Bacan," *to bake.*

2 Con. 3 Cl.

Perf. Part. bac-en.
Ind. Indef. ic bac-e, ṭḥú baec-st, he baec-th.
— *Perf.* ic bóc we bóc-on.

§ 206. "beátan," *to beat.*

2 Con. 2 Cl.

Perf. Part. beát-en.
Ind. Indef. ic beát-e he beát-eth.[1]
— *Perf.* ic beot we beot-on.

§ 207. "belgan," *to enrage, be angry.*

3 Con. 1 Cl.

Perf. Part. bolg-en.
Ind. Indef. ic belg-e, ṭḥú bilh-st, he bylg-th.[1]
— *Perf.* ic bealg we bulg-on.

§ 208. "belífan,"[1] *to remain.*

3 Con. 2 Cl.

Perf. Part. belif-en.
Ind. Indef. ic belíf-e he belíf-th.
— *Perf.* ic beláf we belif-on.

§ 209. "bellan," *to bellow, roar, bark.*

2 Con. 2 Cl.

Perf. Part. bell-an.
Ind. Indef. ic bell-e.
— *Perf.* ic bell we bell-on.

---

[1] *Beáteth,* bét.
[1] *Bylgth,* bilhth ;—*bealg,* bealh.
[1] *Belífan,* bilífan, lífan, læfan ;—*beláf,* beleáf.

§ 210. "belúcan,"[1] *to shut up, lock up.*

3 Con. 3 Cl.

Perf. Part. beloc-en.
Ind. Indef. ic belúc-e he belýc-th.
— *Perf.* ic beleác we beluc-on.

§ 211. "beódan,"[1] *to command, offer.*

3 Con. 3 Cl.

Perf. Part. bod-en.
Ind. Indef. ic beód-e he bebýt.
— *Perf.* ic beád we bud-on.

§ 212. "beorgan," *to protect, avoid.*

3 Con. 1 Cl.

Perf. Part. borg-en.
Ind. Indef. ic beorg-e, thú birh-st, he byrg-th.[1]
— *Perf.* ic bearh we burg-on.
Imp. beorh thú.

§ 213. "beran,"[1] *to bear, suffer, excel.*

2 Con. 1 Cl.

Perf. Part. bor-en.
Ind. Indef. ic ber-e he byr-th.
— *Perf.* ic baér we baér-on.

---

[1] ***Belúcan***, bilúcan, lúcan, lócan ;—***belocen***, belocyn, bilocen.

[1] ***Beódan***, bédan, and bódian ;—***beád***, bád.

[1] ***Byrgth***, birhth ;—***bearh***, berh.

[1] ***Beran***, beoran ;—***boren***, boran, born ;—***byrth***, bireth: also "thú birest," for "thú berest ;"—***baér***, beár.

§ 214. "berstan," *to burst, fail, fall.*

3 Con. 1 Cl.

Perf. Part. borst-en.
Ind. Indef. ic berst-e he byrst.
— *Perf.* ic baerst we burst-on.

§ 215. "bídan," *to stay, bide, expect.*

3 Con. 2 Cl.

Perf. Part. bid-en.
Ind. Indef. ic bíd-e he bíd-eth.[1]
— *Perf.* ic bád we bid-on.

§ 216. "biddan," *to bid, beg.*

2 Con. 1 Cl.

Perf. Part. bed-en.
Ind. Indef. ic bidd-e ṭḥú bit-st he bit.[1]
— *Perf.* ic baéd we baéd-on.

§ 217. "bindan,"[1] *to bind, pretend.*

3 Con. 1 Cl.

Perf. Part. bund-en.
Ind. Indef. ic bind-e, ṭḥú bind-st, he bint.
— *Perf.* ic band we bund-on.

§ 218. "bítan," *to bite.*

3 Con. 2 Cl.

Perf. Part. bit-en.
Ind. Indef. ic bít-e he bít.
— *Perf.* ic bát we bit-on.

---

[1] *Bideth,* bít;—*bád,* béd.
[1] *Bit,* bitt, byt;—*baéd,* baédt, býd;—*baédon,* beádon.
[1] *Bindan,* baendan;—*band,* bend.

§ 219. "bláwan,"[1] *to blow, breathe.*

2 Con. 2 Cl.

Perf. Part. bláw-en.
Ind. Indef. ic bláw-e he blǽw-th.
— *Perf.* ic bleow we bleow-on.

§ 220. "blícan," *to shine, dazzle, amaze.*

3 Con. 2 Cl.

Perf. Part. blic-en.
Ind. Indef. ic blíc-e he blíc-th.
— *Perf.* ic blác we blic-on.

§ 221. "blinnan," *to cease, rest,* BLIN.

3 Con. 1 Cl.

Perf. Part. blunn-en.
Ind. Indef. ic blinn-e he blin-th.
— *Perf.* ic blan[1] we blunn-on.

§ 222. "blótan," *to sacrifice.*

2 Con. 2 Cl.

Perf. Part. blót-en.
Ind. Indef. ic blót-e he blét.
— *Perf.* ic bleot we bleot-on.

§ 223. "brecan,"[1] *to break, vanquish, excite.*

2 Con. 1 Cl.

Perf. Part. broc-en.
Ind. Indef. ic brec-e ṯẖú bric-st.
— *Perf.* ic brǽc we brǽc-on.

---

[1] "'Blówan,' *to blossom,* is sometimes used in Saxon instead of 'bláwan,' *to blow;* and thus, 'blówan' was occasionally used by the Saxons as the present English, *to blow.* We say, *to blow as the wind,* and *to blow,* or *blossom as a flower.*"—Bosworth.

[1] *Blan,* blon, blonn.

[1] *Brecan,* breacan, bracan

§ 224. "bredan,"[1] *to braid, seize, draw out, bend.*

3 Con. 1 Cl.*

Perf. Part. brod-en.
Ind. Indef. ic bred-e he brit.
— *Perf.* ic braed we brud-on.

§ 225. "breótan," *to bruise.*

3 Con. 3 Cl.

Perf. Part. brot-en.
Ind. Indef. ic breót-e.
— *Perf.* ic breát we brut-on.

§ 226. "breówan,"[1] *to brew.*

3 Con. 3 Cl.

Perf. Part. brow-en.
Ind. Indef. ic breów-e.
— *Perf.* ic breáw we bruw-on.

§ 227. "brúcan," *to use, eat, discharge.*

3 Con. 3 Cl.

Perf. Part. broc-en.
Ind. Indef. ṭẖú bríc-st, he brýc-th, we brúc-ath.
— *Perf.* ic breác we bruc-on.

§ 228. "búgan,"[1] *to bow.*

3 Con. 3 Cl.

Perf. Part. bog-en.
Ind. Indef. ic búg-e he býh-th.

---

[1] ***Bredan***, bregdan;—***broden***, brogden, bregden, braegd;—***braed***, braegd;—***brudon***, brugdon.

[1] ***Breówan***, bríwan.

[1] ***Brúcath***, brýcath.

[1] ***Búgan***, béngean, beógan, gebúgan;—***bogen***, bugen, bigen;—***býhth***, búhth;—***beáh***, beág;—***búg***, búh.

Ind. Perf. ic beáh we bug-on.
Imp. búg ṭḥú.

§ 229. "Ceorfan,"[1] *to cut, carve.*

3 Con. 1 Cl.

Perf. Part. corf-en.
Ind. Indef. ic ceorf-e he cyrf-th.
— *Perf.* ic cearf we curf-on.

§ 230. "ceósan," *to choose.*

3 Con. 3 Cl. Irr.

Perf. Part. cor-en.
Ind. Indef. ic ceós-e ṭḥú cýs-t he cýs-t.[1]
— *Perf.* ic ceás ṭḥú cur-e we cur-on.

§ 231. "ceówan," *to chew.*

3 Con. 3 Cl.

Perf. Part. cow-en.
Ind. Indef. ic ceów-e he cýw-th.
— *Perf.* ic ceáw we cuw-on.

§ 232. "cídan," *to chide.*

3 Con. 2 Cl.

Perf. Part. cid-en.
Ind. Indef. ic cíd-e.
— *Perf.* ic cád we cid-on.[1]

---

[1] ***Ceorfan,*** cearfan.
[1] ***Cýst,*** císt;—***ceás,*** caés.
[1] ***Cidon,*** cedun; we also have ***p*** cidde; ***pp.*** cidd.

§ 233. "climban,"[1] *to climb.*

3 Con. 1 Cl.

Perf. Part. clumb-en.
Ind. Indef. ic climb-e.
— *Perf.* ic clamb we clumb-on.

§ 234. "clúfan,"[1] *to cleave.*

3 Con. 3 Cl.

Perf. Part. clof-en.
Ind. Indef. ic clúf-e he clýf-th.
— *Perf.* ic cleáf we cluf-on.

§ 235. "cnáwan," *to know.*

2 Con. 2 Cl.

Perf. Part. cnáw-en.
Ind. Indef. ic cnáw-e he cnǽw-th.
— *Perf.* ic cneow we cneow-on.

§ 236. "cráwan," *to crow.*

2 Con. 2 Cl.

Perf. Part. cráw-en.
Ind. Indef. ic cráw-e he crǽw-th.
— *Perf.* ic creow we creow-on.

§ 237. "creópan,"[1] *to creep.*

3 Con. 3 Cl.

Perf. Part. crop-en.
Ind. Indef. he crýp-th.
— *Perf.* ic creáp we crup-on

---

[1] *Climban,* climan;—*clamb,* clomm.
[1] *Clúfan,* cleófan, cleáfan;—*clýfth,* clýth
[1] *Creópan,* crýpan.

§ 238. "cringan,"[1] *to die, submit, cringe.*

3 Con. 1 Cl.

Perf. Part. crung-en.
Ind. Indef. ic cring-e.
— *Perf.* ic crang   we crung-on.

§ 239. "cuman," *to come, happen.*

2 Con. 3 Cl.

Perf. Part. cum-en.
Ind. Indef. ic cum-e   he cym-th.
— *Perf.* ic cóm[1]   we cóm-on.

§ 240. "cwaethan,"[1] *to say, provoke by speaking,* QUOTH.

2 Con. 1 Cl. Irr.

Perf. Part. cwaed-en.
Ind. Indef. ic cweth-e, ṭḥú cwy-st, he cwy-th.
— *Perf.* ic cwaéth, ṭḥú cwaéd-e, he cwaéth, we cwaéd-on.
Imp. cwaéth ṭḥú   cweth-ath (ge.)

§ 241. "cwelan,"[1] *to die, be killed.*

2 Con. 1 Cl.

Perf. Part. cwel-en.
Ind. Indef. ic cwel-e   he cwil-th.
— *Perf.* ic cwaél   we cwaél-on.

---

[1] *Cringan,* crincan, crangan.

[1] *Cóm,* cwóm, cúm.

[1] *Cwaethan,* cwethan;—*cwaeden,* cweden, gecweden, cwaed;—*cwaéth,* cwaéthe, cwaéde.

[1] *Cwelan,* cwylan;—acwelan, perhaps the more common form.

§ 242. "Delfan,' *to dig,* DELVE.

3 Con. 1 Cl.

Perf. Part. delf-en.
Ind. Indef. ic delf-e he dylf-th.
— *Perf.* ic dealf[1] we dulf-on.

§ 243. "deófan,"[1] *to sink, dive.*

3 Con. 3 Cl.

Perf. Part. dof-en.
Ind. Indef. ic deóf-e.
— *Perf.* ic deáf we duf-on.

§ 244. "dragan," *to drag, draw.*

2 Con. 3 Cl.

Perf. Part. drag-en.[1]
Ind. Indef. ic drag-e he draeg-th.
— *Perf.* ic drég we drég-on.

§ 245. "dreógan," *to do, work, drudge, bear, live.*

3 Con. 3 Cl.

Perf. Part. drog-en.
Ind. Indef. ic dreóg-e, ṭḥú drýg-ast,[1] he drýh-th.
— *Perf.* ic dreáh we drug-on.

§ 246. "drepan," *to strike.*

2 Con. 1 Cl.

Perf. Part. drep-en.
Ind. Indef. ic drep-e.
— *Perf.* ic draép we draép-on.

---

[1] *Dealf,* dielf, dalf, dulf.
[1] *Deófan,* dúfan, gedúfan, dúfian
Dragen, draegen ;—*drég,* dróh.
Drýgast, drígast ;—*drýhth,* dríhth ;—*drugon,* drogon.

§ 247. "drífan,"[1] *to drive.*

3 Con. 2 Cl.

Perf. Part. drif-en.
Ind. Indef. ic dríf-e he dríf-th.
— *Perf.* ic dráf we drif-on.

§ 248. "drincan,"[1] *to drink, be drunk.*

3 Con. 1 Cl.

Perf. Part. drunc-en.
Ind. Indef. ic drinc-e he drinc-th.
— *Perf.* ic dranc we drunc-on.

§ 249. "dwínan," *to pine, fade, dwindle.*

3 Con. 2 Cl.

Perf. Part. dwin-en.
Ind. Indef. ic dwín-e he dwín-th.
— *Perf.* ic dwán we dwin-on.

§ 250. "Fealdan," *to fold, wrap up.*

2 Con. 2 Cl.

Perf. Part. gefeald-en.
Ind. Indef. ic feald-e he fylt.
— *Perf.* ic feold we feold-on.

§ 251. "feallan," *to fall, fail.*

2 Con. 2 Cl.

Perf. Part. gefeall-en.
Ind. Indef. ic feall-e he fyl-th.
— *Perf.* ic feoll we feoll-on.

---

[1] ***Drífan,*** drýfan ;—*dráf,* drǽf.
[1] ***Drincan,*** drican ;—*druncen,* druncn ;—*drincth,* dryncth.
[1] ***Fylth,*** fealth ;—*feoll,* feol.

§ 252. "feohtan," *to fight.*

3 Con. 1 Cl.

Perf. Part. foht-en.
Ind. Indef. ic feoht-e   he fyht.[1]
— *Perf.* ic feaht   fuht-on.

§ 253. "findan," *to find, devise, determine.*

3 Con. 1 Cl.

Perf. Part. fund-en.
Ind. Indef. ic find-e, ṭḥú fin-st, he find-eth.
— *Perf.* ic fand,[1] ṭḥú fund-e   we fund-on.

§ 254. "fleógan,"[1] *to fly, flee.*

3 Con. 3 Cl.

Perf. Part. flog-en.
Ind. Indef. ic fleóg-e   he flýh-th.
— *Perf.* ic fleáh   we flug-on.

§ 255. "fleótan,"[1] *to float.*

3 Con. 3 Cl.

Perf. Part. flot-en.
Ind. Indef. ic fleót-e   he flýt.
— *Perf.* ic fleát   we flut-on.

§ 256. "flítan," *to contend.*

3 Con. 2 Cl.

Perf. Part. flit-en.
Ind. Indef. ic flít-e   he flít.
— *Perf.* ic flát   we flit-on.

---

[1] ***Fyht***, fiht;—*feaht*, faht.

[1] ***Fand***, fond.

[1] ***Fleógan***, flíógan, flígan;—***Indef. Part.*** fleógendo, flégende;—*fleóge*, fleóhe;—*flýth*, flýcth. "Fleón, flíón," *to* FLEE, *escape*, and actively, *to rout*, has "ic fleó, flió,"—"we fleóth, flióth," in the *Indef*

[1] ***Fleótan***, flótan: also flótian. ***Indef. Part.*** flótigende.

§ 257. "flówan,"[1] *to flow.*

2 Con. 2 Cl.

Perf. Part. —
Ind. Indef. ic flów-e he fléw-th.
— *Perf.* ic fleow we fleow-on.

§ 258. "fón,"[1] *to take, undertake.*

2 Con. 2 Cl.

Perf. Part. fang-en.
Ind. Indef. ic fó ṭḥú féh-st he féh-th, we fó-th.
— *Perf.* ic feng we feng-on.
Imp. fóh ṭḥú.

§ 259. "forhelan;"[1] *to conceal, oppose.*

2 Con. 1 Cl.

Perf. Part. forhol-en.
Ind. Indef. ic forhel-e he forhil-th.
— *Perf.* ic forhǽl we forhǽl-on.

§ 260. "forleósan,"[1] *to lose, let go.*

3 Con. 3 Cl. Irr.

Perf. Part. forlos-en.
Ind. Indef. ic forleós-e he forlýs-t.
— *Perf.* ic forleás ṭḥú forlur-e we forlur-on.

§ 261. "forscrincan,"[1] *to shrink, wither.*

3 Con. 1 Cl.

Perf. Part. forscrunc-en.
Ind. Indef. ic forscrinc-e he forscrinc-th.
— *Perf.* ic forscranc we forscrunc-on.

---

[1] *Flówan,* fleówan.
[1] *Fón,* onfón, afón, gefón;—*fangen,* gefangen, gefongen;—*fó,* fóh
[1] *Forhelan;* helan, *to cover.*
[1] *Forleósan,* forlósan, forleóran;—*forlosen,* forloren, ferloren.
[1] *Forscrincan,* scrincan.

§ 262. "fretan," *to fret, gnaw, devour.*

2 Con. 1 Cl.

Perf. Part. fret-en.
Ind. Indef. ic fret-e he frit.[1]
— *Perf.* ic frǽt we frǽt-on.

§ 263. "frinan,"[1] *to ask.*

3 Con. 1 Cl.

Perf. Part. gefrun-en.
Ind. Indef. ic frin-e he frin-th.
— *Perf.* ic fran we frun-on.

§ 264. "Galan," *to enchant, sing.*

2 Con. 3 Cl.

Perf. Part. gal-en.
Ind. Indef. ic gal-e he gael-th.
— *Perf.* ic gól we gól-on.

§ 265. "gefeón,"[1] *to rejoice.*

3 Con. 3 Cl.

Perf. Part. gefag-en.
Ind. Indef. ic gefeó.
— *Perf.* ic gefeáh.

§ 266. "gelimpan,"[1] *to happen.*

3 Con. 1 Cl.

Perf. Part. gelump-en.
Ind. Indef. ic gelimp-e he gelimp-th.
— *Perf.* ic gelamp we gelump-on.

---

[1] *Frit,* fryt;—*frǽton,* fréton.

[1] *Frinan;* the proper form of this verb, the form which more correctly assigns it to the 3 Con. 1 Cl., is fregnan; *p.* fraegn, fraegin, fraeng; *pp.* frugnen. See also "bredan," § 224.

[1] *Gefeón,* gefeóhan;—*gefagen,* gefaegen. We also find, gefíhan; *p.* gefeáh, or gefáh;—*pp.* gefehen.

[1] *Gelimpan,* alimpan, limpan;—*gelamp,* gelomp.

§ 267. "gelpan,"[1] *to boast, desire earnestly.*

3 Con. 1 Cl.

Perf. Part. golp-en.
Ind. Indef. ic gelp-e he gylp-th.
— *Perf.* ic gealp we gulp-on.

§ 268. "genesan," *to heal, be saved.*

2 Con. 1 Cl.

Perf. Part. genes-en.
Ind. Indef. ic genes-e he genis-t.
— *Perf.* ic genǽs we genǽs-on.

§ 269. "geótan," *to pour.*

3 Con. 3 Cl.

Perf. Part. got-en.
Ind. Indef. ic geót-e he gýt.
— *Perf.* ic geát[1] we gut-on.

§ 270. "gesceátan," *to fall to.*

2 Con. 2 Cl.

Perf. Part. gesceát-en.
Ind. Indef. ic gesceát-e he gescýt-t.
— *Perf.* ic gesceot we gesceot-on.

§ 271. "gescrífan,"[1] *to shrive, enjoin penance, assign.*

3 Con. 2 Cl.

Perf. Part. gescrif-en.
Ind. Indef. ic gescríf-e.
— *Perf.* ic gescráf we gescrif-on.

---

[1] *Gelpan*, gilpan ;—*gylpth*, gelpth.
[1] *Geát*, gét.
[1] *Gescrífan*, scrífan ;—*gescrifen*, gescryfen.

§ 272. "geseón,"[1] *to see, behold.*

3 Con. 3 Cl. Irr.

Perf. Part. gesaw-en.
Ind. Indef. ic geseó, ṭḥú gesíh-st, he gesíh-th.
— *Perf.* ic geseáh, ṭḥú gesaw-e we gesaw-on.
Imp. geseóh ṭḥú.

§ 273. "geṭḥeón,"[1] *to flourish, perfect, gain.*

3 Con. 3 Cl.

Perf. Part. geṭḥog-en.
Ind. Indef. ic geṭḥeó he geṭḥýh-th.
— *Perf.* ic geṭḥeáh.

§ 274. "gewítan,"[1] *to depart, retreat, die.*

3 Con. 2 Cl.

Perf. Part. gewit-en.
Ind. Indef. ic gewít-e he gewít.
— *Perf.* ic gewát we gewit-on.

§ 275. "gifan,"[1] *to give.*

2 Con. 1 Cl.

Perf. Part. gif-en.
Ind. Indef. ic gif-e he gif-th.
— *Perf.* ic geáf we geáf-on.

---

[1] *Geseón*, gesión, seón, seán ;—*gesawen*, gesewen, gesaene, gesyne, gesegen, geseogen, geseowen ;—*gesíhth*, gesýhth ;—*geseáh*, geséh ; —*gesawe*, gesaege ;—*gesawon*, gesewen, gesegen, segun, seagon ;— *geseóh*, gesýh.

[1] *Geṭḥeón*, ṭḥeón ;—*geṭḥýhth*, geṭḥíth.

[1] *Gewítan*, wítan.

[1] *Gifan*, gyfan, geofian ;—*geáf*, gǽf, gáf.

§ 276. "glídan," *to glide, slip.*

3 Con. 2 Cl.

Perf. Part. glid-en.
Ind. Indef. ic glíd-e he glíd-eth.[1]
— *Perf.* ic glád we glid-on.

§ 277. "gnagan,"[1] *to gnaw.*

2 Con. 3 Cl.

Perf. Part. gnag-en.
Ind. Indef. ic gnag-e he gnaeg-th.
— *Perf.* ic gnóh we gnóg-on.

§ 278. "gnídan," *to rub.*

3 Con. 2 Cl.

Perf. Part. gnid-en.
Ind. Indef. ic gníd-e he gnít.
— *Perf.* ic gnád we gnid-on.

§ 279. "grafan," *to dig, grave, carve.*

2 Con. 3 Cl.

Perf. Part. graf-en.
Ind. Indef. ic graf-e he graef-th.
— *Perf.* ic gróf we gróf-on.

§ 280. "grindan,"[1] *to grind.*

3 Con. 1 Cl.

Perf. Part. grund-en.
Ind. Indef. ic grind-e he grint.
— *Perf.* ic grand we grund-on.

---

[1] *Glídeth,* glít.
[1] *Gnagan,* gnafan.
[1] *Grindan,* gryndan.

§ 281. "grípan," *to seize, gripe.*

3 Con. 2 Cl.

Perf. Part. grip-en.
Ind. Indef. ic gríp-e he gríp-th.
— *Perf.* ic gráp we grip-on.

§ 282. "grówan," *to grow.*

2 Con. 2 Cl.

Perf. Part. grów-en.
Ind. Indef. ic grów-e he gréw-th.
— *Perf.* ic greow we greow-un.

§ 283. "gyldan,"[1] *to pay, restore, yield, worship.*

3 Con. 1 Cl.

Perf. Part. gold-en.
Ind. Indef. ic gyld-e he gylt.
— *Perf.* ic geald we guld-on.

§ 284. "Hátan," *to call, be named, command.*

2 Con. 2 Cl.

Perf. Part. hát-en.
Ind. Indef. ic hát-e he háet.
— *Perf.* ic het[1] we het-on.

§ 285. "healdan,"[1] *to hold, regard, tend.*

2 Con. 2 Cl.

Perf. Part. heald-en.
Ind. Indef. ic heald-e he hylt.
— *Perf.* ic heold we heold-on.

---

[1] *Gyldan*, gildan, geldan.

[1] *Het*, heht.

NOTE.—*Hátte* appears to be used for the singular, and *hátton* for the plural of the Perfect tense, when the verb signifies *to be called.*

[1] *Healdan*, haldan, heldan;—*hylt*, healt, helt.

§ 286. "heáwan," *to hew, cut off, thrust.*

2 Con. 2 Cl.

Perf. Part. heáw-en.
Ind. Indef. ic heáw-e he heáw-eth.
— *Perf.* ic heow we heow-un

§ 287. "hebban," *to heave, raise.*

2 Con. 3 Cl.

Perf. Part. hef-en.[1]
Ind. Indef. ic hebb-e, ṭḥú hef-est, he hef-th.
— *Perf.* ic hóf we hóf-on.
Imp. hef-e ṭḥú.

§ 288. "helpan," *to help, preserve.*

3 Con. 1 Cl.

Perf. Part. holp-en.
Ind. Indef. ic help-e he hylp-th.
— *Perf.* ic healp we hulp-on.

§ 289. "hladan,"[1] *to load, lade,* or *draw out.*

2 Con. 3 Cl.

Perf. Part. hlaed-en.
Ind. Indef. ic hlad-e, ṭḥú hlaed-st, he hlaet.
— *Perf.* ic hlód we hlód-on.

§ 290. "hleápan," *to leap.*

2 Con. 2 Cl.

Perf. Part. gehleáp-en.
Ind. Indef. ic hleáp-e he hlýp-th.
— *Perf.* ic hleop we hleop-on.

---

[1] *Hefen,* hafen, heafen.
[1] *Hladan,* ladan, lodan

§ 291. "hleótan,"[1] *to cast lots.*

3 Con. 3 Cl.*

Perf. Part. hlot-en.
Ind. Indef. ic hleót-e he hlýt.
— *Perf.* ic hleát we hlut-on.

§ 292. "hlihhan,"[1] *to laugh, deride.*

2 Con. 3 Cl.

Perf. Part. hlaeg-en.
Ind. Indef. ic hlih-e he hlih-th we hli-ath.
— *Perf.* ic hlóh ṭḥú hlóg-e we hlóg-on.

§ 293. "hlimman,"[1] *to sound, resound.*

3 Con. 1 Cl.

Perf. Part. —
Ind. Indef. ic hlimm-e.
— *Perf.* ic hlam we hlumm-on.

§ 294. "hlówan,"[1] *to low.*

2 Con. 2 Cl.

Perf. Part. hlów-en.
Ind. Indef. ic hlów-e.
— *Perf.* ic hleow.

§ 295. "hnígan," *to bow, sink.*

3 Con. 2 Cl.

Perf. Part. hnig-en.
Ind. Indef. ic hníg-e he hníh-th.
— *Perf.* ic hnáh we hnig-on.

---

[1] *Hleótan,* hlótan.
[1] *Hlihhan,* hlihan, hleahhan, hlehan, hlichan.
[1] *Hilmman,* hlemman.
Hlówan, hlówan.

§ 296. "hón,"[1] *to hang, crucify.*

2 Con. 2 Cl.

Perf. Part. hang-en.
Ind. Indef. ic hó he héh-th, we hó-th.
— *Perf.* ic heng we heng-on.
Imp. hóh ṭhú.

§ 297. "hreósan,"[1] *to rush, waver, fall.*

3 Con. 3 Cl. Irr.

Perf. Part. hror-en.
Ind. Indef. ic hreós-e he hrýs-t.
— *Perf.* ic hreás ṭhú hrur-e we hrur-on.
Sub. — ic hryr-e.

§ 298. "hreówan," *to rue.*

3 Con. 3 Cl.

Perf. Part. hrow-en.
Ind. Indef. ic hreów-e he hrýw-th.
— *Perf.* ic hreáw we hruw-on.

§ 299. "hrépan," *to cry, call out.*

2 Con. 2 Cl.

Perf. Part. hrép-en.
Ind. Indef. ic hrép-e.
— *Perf.* ic hreop.

§ 300. "hrínan," *to touch.*

3 Con. 2 Cl.

Perf. Part. hrin-en.
Ind. Indef. ic hrín-e he hrín-th.
— *Perf.* ic hrán we hrin-on.

---

[1] *Hón,* hangan;—*hó,* hóh;—*hóth,* hóhth;—*heng,* hong.
[1] *Hreósan,* reósan, reósian;—*hreás:* also, hrýsede.

§ 301. "hweorfan,"[1] *to return.*

3 Con. 1 Cl.

Perf. Part. hworf-en.
Ind. Indef. ic hweorf-e, ṭẹhú hweorf-est, he hwyrf-th.
— *Perf.* ic hwearf we hwurf-on.

§ 302. "Leán,"[1] *to blame, reprove.*

2 Con. 3 Cl.

Perf. Part. laeg-en.
Ind. Indef. ic leá he lýh-th.
— *Perf.* ic lóh we lóg-on.

§ 303. "leógan,"[1] *to lie, deceive,* LIG.

3 Con. 3 Cl.

Perf. Part. log-en.
Ind. Indef. ic leóg-e he lýh-th.
— *Perf.* ic leág we lug-on.

§ 304. "lesan," *to gather, choose, lease.*

2 Con. 1 Cl.

Perf. Part. les-en.
Ind. Indef. ic les-e he lis-t.
— *Perf.* ic láes we láes-on.

§ 305. "licgan,"[1] *to lie, lie down, lie along.*

2 Con. 1 Cl.

Perf. Part. leg-en.
Ind. Indef. ic licg-e ṭẹhú li-st he li-th.
— *Perf.* ic láeg ṭẹhú lág-e we láeg-on.

[1] *Hweorfan,* hwyrfan, hwerfan ;—*hwyrfth,* hwerfth —*hwearf,* hwaerf.

[1] *Leán,* leáhan ;—*leá,* leáh.

[1] *Leógan,* lígan, lýgnian ;—*leág,* leáh, leóh.

[1] *Licgan,* licgean, licggan, lycgan, ligan, liggan ;—*lith,* ligth, lihth ; —*láegon,* lágon.

§ 306. "líhan," *to lend.*

3 Con. 2 Cl.

Perf. Part. lig-en.
Ind. Indef. ic líh-e.
— *Perf.* ic láh.

§ 307. "líthan,"[1] *to sail.*

3 Con. 2 Cl.

Perf. Part. lith-en.
Ind. Indef. ic líth-e
— *Perf.* ic láth ṭḥú lid-e we lith-on.

§ 308. "lútan,"[1] *to bow,* LOUT, *incline, lurk.*

3 Con. 3 Cl.

Perf. Part. lot-en.
Ind. Indef. ic lút-e he lýt.
— *Perf.* ic leát we lut-on.

§ 309. "Melcan,"[1] *to milk.*

3 Con. 1 Cl.

Perf. Part. molc-en.
Ind. Indef. ic melc-e.
— *Perf.* ic mealc we mulc-on.

§ 310. "meltan,"[1] *to melt.*

3 Con. 1 Cl.

Perf. Part. molt-en.
Ind. Indef. ic melt-e.
— *Perf.* ic mealt we mult-on.

---

[1] *Líthan,* leóthan ;—*lithen,* geliden ;—*lithon,* lithan, lidon.
[1] *Lútan,* lútian, hlútan, leótan ;—*leát,* hleát.
[1] *Melcan,* melcian, meolcian.
[1] *Meltan,* miltan, myltan.

§ 311. "metan,"[1] *to measure, mete.*

2 Con. 1 Cl.

Perf. Part. met-en.
Ind. Indef. ic met-e he mit.
— *Perf.* ic mǽt we mǽt-on.

§ 312. "mígan,"[1] *to make water*, MINGE.

3 Con. 2 Cl.

Perf. Part. mig-en.
Ind. Indef. ic míg-e he míh-th.
— *Perf.* ic máh we mig-on.

§ 313. "míthan," *to hide, dissemble.*

3 Con. 2 Cl.

Perf. Part. mith-en.
Ind. Indef. ic míth-e.
— *Perf.* ic máth.

§ 314. "murnan," *to mourn, care for.*

3 Con. 1 Cl.

Perf. Part. morn-en.
Ind. Indef. ic murn-e he myrn-th.
— *Perf.* ic mearn we murn-on.

§ 315. "Neótan,"[1] *to enjoy.*

3 Con. 3 Cl.

Perf. Part. not-en.
Ind. Indef. ic neót-e he nýt.
— *Perf.* ic neát we nut-on.

---

[1] Metan, *to paint, adorn,* has the *p.* mette and the *pp.* metod.
[1] *Mígan,* mícgan, mengan;—*míge,* míhe;—máh, mág.
[1] *Neótan,* nîótan.

§ 316. "niman,"[1] *to take.*

2 Con. 1 Cl.

Perf. Part. num-en.
Ind. Indef. ic nim-e he nim-th.
— *Perf.* ic nam we nam-on.

§ 317. "Ondráedan,"[1] *to dread.*

2 Con. 2 Cl.

Perf. Part. ondráed-en.
Ind. Indef. ic ondráed-e, ṭḥú ondráet-st, he ondráet.
— *Perf.* ic ondred we ondred-on.

§ 318. "onginnan,"[1] *to begin, attempt.*

3 Con. 1 Cl.

Perf. Part. ongunn-en.
Ind. Indef. ic onginn-e he ongin-th.
— *Perf.* ic ongan, ṭḥú ongunn-e we ongunn-on.

§ 319. "ongitan,"[1] *to understand, get.*

2 Con. 1 Cl.

Perf. Part. ongit-en.
Ind. Indef. ic ongit-e he ongit.
— *Perf.* ic ongeat we ongeat-on.

---

[1] *Niman*, neman, nioman ;—*nam*, nom, naem.

[1] *Ondráedan*, ondrédan, ondreárdan.

[1] *Onginnan*, ongynnan, beginnan ;—*onginth*, onginneth ;—*ongan* ongean.

[1] *Ongitan*, ongytan, ongetan, ongeotan, ongietan, getan, geatan, gytan ;—*ongit*, ongyt ;—*ongeat*, onget.

§ 320. "onlígan,"[1] *to grant, bestow.*

3 Con. 2 Cl.

Perf. Part. onlig-en.
Ind. Indef. ic onlíg-e.
— *Perf.* ic onláh we onlig-on.

§ 321. "Rennan,"[1] *to run, flow.*

3 Con. 1 Cl.

Perf. Part. —
Ind. Indef. ic renn-e.
— *Perf.* ic ran.

§ 322. "reócan,"[1] *to reek.*

3 Con. 3 Cl.

Perf. Part. roc-en.
Ind. Indef. ic reóc-e he rýc-th.
— *Perf.* ic reác we ruc-on.

§ 323. "rídan," *to move, ride.*

3 Con. 2 Cl.

Perf. Part. rid-en.
Ind. Indef. ic ríd-e he rít.[1]
— *Perf.* ic rád we rid-on.

§ 324. "rówan," *to row.*

2 Con. 2 Cl.

Perf. Part. rów-en.
Ind. Indef. ic rów-e he réw-th we réw-ath.
— *Perf.* ic reow we reow-un.

---

[1] *Onlígan*, onlíhan;—*onláh*, onleáh, onlág;—*onligon:* onlehton, but from "onlígan," "onlégan," *to kindle, irritate.*

[1] *Rennan*, reonan, rinnan. See also § 195.

[1] *Reócan*, récan, réccan.

[1] *Rít*, rídeth.

§ 325. "Sáwan," *to sow.*

2 Con. 2 Cl.

Perf. Part. sáw-en.
Ind. Indef. ic sáw-e he sǽw-th.
— *Perf.* ic seow[1] we seow-un.

§ 326. "scacan,"[1] *to shake, evade,* SHACK.

2 Con. 3 Cl.

Perf. Part. scac-en.
Ind. Indef. ic scac-e.
— *Perf.* ic scóc we scóc-on.

§ 327. "scafan," *to shave.*

2 Con. 3 Cl.

Perf. Part. scaf-en.
Ind. Indef. ic scaf-e he scaef-th.
— *Perf.* ic scóf we scóf-on.

§ 328. "sceádan,"[1] *to divide, shade.*

2 Con. 2 Cl.

Perf. Part. sceád-en.
Ind. Indef. ic sceád-e.
— *Perf.* ic sceod we sceod-on.

§ 329. "sceran,"[1] *to shear, shave, allot.*

2 Con. 1 Cl.

Perf. Part. scor-en.
Ind. Indef. ic scer-e he scyr-th.
— *Perf.* ic scǽr we scǽr-on.

---

[1] *Seow,* sew.

[1] *Scacan,* sceacan ;—*scace,* sceace ;—*scóc,* sceóc.

NOTE.—We doubt whether *to shake,* and *to shack,* can be referred to the same root in Saxon.

[1] *Sceádan,* scádan, scǽdan.

[1] *Sceran,* sciran, scyran, scieran, scirian ;—*scǽr,* sceár ;—*scǽron,* sceáron.

§ 330. "scínan," *to shine.*

3 Con. 2 Cl.

Perf. Part. scin-en.
Ind. Indef. ic scín-e he scín-th.[1]
— *Perf.* ic scán we scin-on.

§ 331. "scríthan," *to wander.*

3 Con. 2 Cl.

Perf. Part. scrid-en.
Ind. Indef. ic scríth-e.
— *Perf.* ic scráth we scrid-on.

§ 332. "scúfan,"[1] *to shove.*

3 Con. 3 Cl.

Perf. Part. scof-en.
Ind. Indef. ic scúf-e he scýf-th.
— *Perf.* ic sceáf we scuf-on.

§ 333. "scyppan,"[1] *to create, form, shape.*

2 Con. 3 Cl.

Perf. Part. sceap-en.
Ind. Indef. ic scypp-e.
— *Perf.* ic scóp we scóp-on.

§ 334. "seóthan," *to boil, seethe.*

3 Con. 3 Cl.

Perf. Part. sod-en.
Ind. Indef. ic seóth-e.
— *Perf.* ic seáth ṭḥú sud-e we sud-on.

[1] *Scínth,* scíneth ;—*scán,* sceán.

[1] *Scúfan,* sceófan ;—*scofen,* scofan.

[1] *Scyppan,* sceppan, sceapan, scipan ;—*sceapen,* scapen, gesceapen ;—*scóp,* sceóp ;—*scópon,* sceópon.

§ 335. "sígan," *to fall, fail.*

3 Con. 2 Cl.

Perf. Part.	sig-en.			
Ind. Indef.	ic síg-e		he síh-th.	
— *Perf.*	ic sáh			we sig-on.

§ 336. "síhan,"[1] *to strain,* SILE, SIE.

3 Con. 2 Cl.

Perf. Part.	sih-en.			
Ind. Indef.	ic síh-e.			
— *Perf.*	ic sáh			we sih-on.

§ 337. "sincan,"[1] *to sink.*

3 Con. 1 Cl.

Perf. Part.	sunc-en.			
Ind. Indef.	ic sinc-e.			
— *Perf.*	ic sanc			we sunc-on.

§ 338. "singan,"[1] *to sing.*

3 Con. 1 Cl.

Perf. Part.	sung-en.			
Ind. Indef.	ic sing-e		he sing-th.	
— *Perf.*	ic sang			we sung-on.

§ 339. "sittan," *to sit.*

2 Con. 1 Cl.

Perf. Part.	set-en.			
Ind. Indef.	ic sitt-e	ṭḥú sit-st	he sitt[1]	we sitt-ath.
— *Perf.*	ic sǽt			we sǽt-on.

---

[1] *Síhan,* seóhan, seón;—*sihen,* sigen, seowen;—*síhe,* seó;—*sáh,* seáh;—*sihon,* sigon, seowon, sugon.

[1] *Sincan:* besincan, very common.

[1] *Singan,* syngan;—*sungen,* asungen;—*sang,* sanc, song.

[1] *Sitt,* sit.

§ 340. "slápan,"[1] *to sleep.*

2 Con. 2 Cl.

Perf. Part.	sláp-en.		
Ind. Indef.	ic sláp-e	he slǽp-th.	
— *Perf.*	ic slep		we slep-on.

§ 341. "sleán,"[1] *to slay.*

2 Con. 3 Cl.

Perf. Part.	sleg-en.		
Ind. Indef.	ic sleá	he slýh-th.	
— *Perf.*	ic slóh	ṭḥú slóg-e	we slóg-on.
Imp.	sléh ṭḥú.		

§ 342. "slífan," *to split.*

3 Con. 2 Cl.

Perf. Part.	slif-en.		
Ind. Indef.	ic slíf-e	he slíf-th.	
— *Perf.*	ic sláf		we slif-on.

§ 343. "slítan," *to tear, slit.*

3 Con. 2 Cl.

Perf. Part.	slit-en.		
Ind. Indef.	ic slít-e	he slít.	
— *Perf.*	ic slát		we slit-on.

§ 344. "smeócan,"[1] *to smoke.*

3 Con. 3 Cl.

Perf. Part.	smoc-en.		
Ind. Indef.	ic smeóc-e	smýc-th.	
— *Perf.*	ic smeác		we smuc-on.

[1] *Slápan*, slǽpan, slépan;—*slápen*, slǽpen.

[1] *Sleán*, slán, slágan;—*slegen*, slagen, slaegen;—*sleá*, sleáh;—*slýhth*, slíhth;—*slóh*, slóg;—*sléh*, slýh ṭḥú.

[1] *Smeócan*, smécan, smeógan, smócian.

§ 345. "smítan," *to smite.*

3 Con. 2 Cl.

Perf. Part. smit-en.
Ind. Indef. ic smít-e he smít.
— *Perf.* ic smát we smit-on.

§ 346. "sníthan," *to cut, slay.*

3 Con. 2 Cl.

Perf. Part. snid-en.
Ind. Indef. ic sníth-e ṭẖú snít-st.
— *Perf.* ic snáth we snith-on.[1]

§ 347. "spanan,"[1] *to allure, persuade.*

2 Con. 3 Cl.

Perf. Part. span-en.
Ind. Indef. ic span-e, ṭẖú spaen-st, he spaen-th.
— *Perf.* ic spón we spón-on.

§ 348. "spannan," *to span, measure, join.*

2 Con. 2 Cl.

Perf. Part. spann-en.
Ind. Indef. ic spann-e.
— *Perf.* ic spenn.[1]

§ 349. "spinnan," *to spin.*

3 Con. 1 Cl.

Perf. Part. spunn-en.
Ind. Indef. ic spinn-e he spin-th.
— *Perf.* ic span we spunn-on.

---

[1] *Snithon*, sneddun.

[1] *Spanan*, spenan ;—*spanen*, asponen, gesponnen ;—*spón*, speón ;—*spónon*, speónon.

[1] *Spenn*, spen.

§ 350. "spíwan,"[1] *to spit, vomit, spew.*

3 Con. 2 Cl.

Perf. Part. spiw-en.
Ind. Indef. ic spíw-e he spíw-th.
— *Perf.* ic spáw we spiw-on.

§ 351. "spówan," *to succeed.*

2 Con. 2 Cl.

Perf. Part. —
Ind. Indef. ic spów-e.
— *Perf.* ic speow we speow-un.

§ 352. "sprecan,"[1] *to speak.*

2 Con. 1 Cl.

Perf. Part. gesprec-en.
Ind. Indef. ic sprec-e, ṭḥú spryc-st, he spric-th.
— *Perf.* ic spraéc we spraéc-on.

§ 353. "springan,"[1] *to spring, spread.*

3 Con. 1 Cl.

Perf. Part. sprung-en.
Ind. Indef. ic spring-e he spring-th.
— *Perf.* ic sprang we sprung-on.

§ 354. "spurnan," *to spurn.*

3 Con. 1 Cl.

Perf. Part. sporn-en.
Ind. Indef. ic spurn-e he spyrn-th.
— *Perf.* ic spearn we spurn-on.

---

[1] ***Spíwan***, speówian;—***spiwen***, speowen, spigen;—***spáw***, spáu;—***spiwon***, speowen, spigon.

[1] ***Sprecan***, sprcocan, specan, spaecan, speacan;—***sprycst***, spricst, spricest;—***spricth***, sprycth, spreceth, spycth.

[1] ***Springan***, spryngan, sprincan;—***springth***, spryngth;—***sprang***, spranc.

§ 355. "standan,"[1] *to stand.*

2 Con. 3 Cl.

Perf. Part. gestand-en.
Ind. Indef. ic stand-e, ṭhú stent-st, he stent.
— *Perf.* ic stód we stód-on.

§ 356. "stelan,"[1] *to steal.*

2 Con. 1 Cl.

Perf. Part. stol-en.
Ind. Indef. ic stel-e he styl-th.
— *Perf.* ic stǽl we stǽl-on.

§ 357. "steorfan," *to die, starve.*

3 Con. 1 Cl.

Perf. Part. storf-en.
Ind. Indef. ic steorf-e he styrf-th.
— *Perf.* ic stearf[1] we sturf-on.

§ 358. "steppan,"[1] *to step.*

2 Con. 3 Cl.

Perf. Part. stap-en.
Ind. Indef. ic stepp-e he step-th.
— *Perf.* ic stóp we stóp-on.

§ 359. "stígan,"[1] *to ascend.*

3 Con. 2 Cl.

Perf. Part. stig-en.
Ind. Indef. ic stíg-e he stíh-th.
— *Perf.* ic stáh we stig-on.

---

[1] *Standan,* stondan;—*stentst,* standest;—*stent,* stynt; also "stadath," for "standath."

[1] *Stelan,* staelan.

[1] *Stearf,* staerf.

[1] *Steppan,* staepan, stapan.

[1] *Stígan,* stýgan.

§ 360. "stincan,"[1] *to smell, perfume, stink.*

3 Con. 1 Cl.

Perf. Part. stunc-en.
Ind. Indef. ic stinc-e he stinc-th.
— *Perf.* ic stanc we stunc-on.

§ 361. "stingan,"[1] *to sting.*

3 Con. 1 Cl.

Perf. Part. stung-en.
Ind. Indef. he sting-th.
— *Perf.* ic stang we stung-on.

§ 362. "súcan,"[1] *to suck.*

3 Con. 3 Cl.

Perf. Part. soc-en.
Ind. Indef. ic súc-e he sýc-th.
— *Perf.* ic seác we suc-on.

§ 363. "swápan," *to sweep, brush.*

2 Con. 2 Cl.

Perf. Part. swáp-en.
Ind. Indef. ic swáp-e he swǽp-th.[1]
— *Perf.* ic sweop we sweop-on.

§ 364. "swefan," *to sleep, go to sleep.*

2 Con. 1 Cl.

Perf. Part. swef-en.
Ind. Indef. ic swef-e he swef-th.
— *Perf.* ic swǽf[1] we swǽf-on.

---

[1] *Stincan,* stencan.
[1] *Stingan,* styngan, ofstingan.
[1] *Súcan,* sýcan, súgan.
[1] *Swǽpth,* swápeth.
[1] *Swǽf,* swáf.

§ 365. "swelgan,"[1] *to swallow.*

3 Con. 1 Cl.

Perf. Part. swolg-en.
Ind. Indef. ic swelg-e he swylg-th.
— *Perf.* ic swealg we swulg-on.

§ 366. "swellan," *to swell.*

3 Con. 1 Cl.

Perf. Part. swoll-en.
Ind. Indef. ic swell-e he swil-th.
— *Perf.* ic sweoll we swull-on.

§ 367. "sweltan," *to die.*

3 Con. 1 Cl.

Perf. Part. swolt-en[1]
Ind. Indef. ic swelt-e he swylt.
— *Perf.* ic swealt we swult-on.

§ 368. "sweorcan," *to dim, darken.*

3 Con. 1 Cl.

Perf. Part. sworc-en.
Ind. Indef. ic sweorc-e.
— *Perf.* ic swearc we swurc-on.

§ 369. "swícan,"[1] *to deceive, wander, offend.*

3 Con. 2 Cl.

Perf. Part. swic-en.
Ind. Indef. ic swíc-e.
— *Perf.* ic swác we swic-on.

---

[1] *Swelgan,* swilgan, swylgan;—*swylgth,* swilgth, swelgth;—*swealg,* swealh.

[1] *Swolten,* swulten;—*swealt,* sweolt.

[1] *Swícan;* beswícan, *to seduce.*

§ 370. "swífan," *to revolve.*

3 Con. 2 Cl.

Perf. Part. swif-en.
Ind. Indef ic swíf-e.
— *Perf.* ic swáf we swif-on.

§ 371. "swimman," *to swim.*

3 Con. 1 Cl.

Perf. Part. swomm-en.
Ind. Indef. ic swimm-e he swim-th.
— *Perf.* ic swamm we swumm-on.

§ 372. "swincan," *to toil.*

3 Con. 1 Cl.

Perf. Part. swunc-en.
Ind. Indef. ic swinc-e he swinc-th.
— *Perf.* ic swanc we swunc-on.[1]

§ 373. "swindan," *to vanish.*

3 Con. 1 Cl.

Perf. Part. swund-en.
Ind. Indef. ic swind-e he swint.
— *Perf.* ic swand we swund-on.

§ 374. "swingan,"[1] *to scourge, beat.*

3 Con. 1 Cl.

Perf. Part. swung-en.
Ind. Indef. ic swing-e he swing-th.
— *Perf.* ic swang we swung-on.

---

[1] *Swuncon*, swuncgon.
[1] *Swingan*, swyngan ;—*swang*, swong.

§ 375. "Tacan," *to take.*

2 Con. 3 Cl.

Perf. Part.	tac-en.			
Ind. Indef.	ic tac-e.			
— *Perf.*	ic tóc.			

§ 376. "teón,"[1] *to draw, tug, tow, create, accuse.*

3 Con. 3 Cl.

Perf. Part.	tog-en.			
Ind. Indef.	ic teó,	ṭḥú týh-st,	he týh-th,	we teó-th.
— *Perf.*	ic teáh,	ṭḥú tug-e		we tug-on.
Sub. Indef.	ic teó			we teó-th.
— *Perf.*	ic tug-e			we tug-on.
Imp.	teó ṭḥú.			

§ 377. "teran," *to tear.*

2 Con. 1 Cl.

Perf. Part.	tor-en.			
Ind. Indef.	ic ter-e,	ṭḥú tyr-st,	he tyr-th.	
— *Perf.*	ic taér			we taér-on.

§ 378. "to-slípan,"[1] *to dissolve.*

3 Con. 2 Cl.

Perf. Part.	to-slip-en.			
Ind. Indef.	ic to-slíp-e		he to-slíp-th.	
— *Perf.*	ic to-sláp			we to-slip-on.

---

[1] ***Teón***, tión, teógan, teóhan ;—*teó*, teóge ;—*týhth*, tíhth ;—*teóth*, teóhth ;—*teáh*, téh, tróg ;—*tugon*, trugon ;—*teó*, teóh.

[1] ***To-slípan***, slípan ; slippan, *to* SLIP, *relax*.

§ 379. "to-slúpan," *to loosen.*

3 Con. 3 Cl.

Perf. Part. to-slop-en.[1]
Ind. Indef. ic to-slúp-e he to-slýp th.
— *Perf.* ic to-sleáp we to-slup-on.

§ 380. "tredan," *to tread.*

2 Con. 1 Cl.

Perf. Part. tred-en.
Ind. Indef. ic tred-e he trit.
— *Perf.* ic traéd we traéd-on.

§ 381. "Theótan,"[1] *to howl.*

3 Con. 3 Cl.

Perf. Part. thot-en.
Ind. Indef. ic theót-e he thýt.
— *Perf.* ic theát we thut-on.

§ 382. "therscan,"[1] *to thresh.*

3 Con. 1 Cl.

Perf. Part. thorsc-en.
Ind. Indef. ic thersc-e he thyrsc-th.
— *Perf.* ic thaersc we thursc-on.

§ 383. "thráwan," *to throw, cast.*

2 Con. 2 Cl.

Perf. Part. thráw-en.[1]
Ind. Indef. ic thráw-e.
— *Perf.* ic threow.

---

[1] *To-slopen,* slopen.
[1] *Theótan,* thiótan.
[1] *Therscan,* thaerscan.
[1] *Thráwen,* thraéwen.

§ 384. "ṭḥringan," *to crowd, throng, rush on.*

3 Con. 1 Cl.

Perf. Part. geṭḥrung-en.
Ind. Indef. ic ṭḥring-e.
— *Perf.* ic ṭḥrang we ṭḥrung-on.

§ 385. "ṭḥweán," *to wash.*

2 Con. 3 Cl.

Perf. Part. ṭḥweg-en.
Ind. Indef. ic ṭḥweá,[1] ṭḥú ṭḥwýh-st, he ṭḥwíh-th.
— *Perf.* ic ṭḥwóh we ṭḥwóg-on.
Imp. ṭḥweáh ṭḥú.

§ 386. "Wacan," *to arise, awake.*

2 Con. 3 Cl.

Perf. Part. wac-en.
Ind. Indef. ic wac-e he waec-th.
— *Perf.* ic wóc we wóc-on.

§ 387. "wacsan,"[1] *to wash.*

2 Con. 3 Cl.

Perf. Part. waesc-en.
Ind. Indef. ic wacs-e.
— *Perf.* ic wócs we wócs-on.

§ 388. "wadan," *to wade.*

2 Con. 3 Cl.

Perf. Part. waed-en.[1]
Ind. Indef. ic wad-e he waet.
— *Perf.* ic wód we wód-on.

---

[1] *Ṭḥweá,* ṭḥweáh;—*ṭḥwíhth,* ṭḥwéhth;—*ṭḥwóh,* ṭḥwóhg;—*ṭḥweáh,* ṭḥwéh.

[1] *Wacsan,* waxan;—*wócs,* wóx.

[1] *Waeden,* gewod.

§ 389. "wealcan," *to roll, turn from side to side, walk.*

2 Con. 2 Cl.

Perf. Part. —
Ind. Indef. ic wealc-e.
— *Perf.* ic weolc.

§ 390. "wealdan,"[1] *to govern, wield.*

2 Con. 2 Cl.

Perf. Part. weald-en.
Ind. Indef. ic weald, ṭḥú weald-est, he weald.
— *Perf.* ic weold we weold-on.

§ 391. "weallan,"[1] *to boil, well.*

2 Con. 2 Cl.

Perf. Part. weall-en.
Ind. Indef. he wyl-th.
— *Perf.* ic weoll.

§ 392. "weaxan,"[1] *to grow,* WAX.

2 Con. 2 Cl.

Perf. Part. weax-en.
Ind. Indef. ic weax-e ṭḥú wyx-t he wyx-th.
— *Perf.* ic weox we weox-on.

§ 393. "wegan,"[1] *to weigh, bear, carry.*

2 Con. 1 Cl.

Perf. Part. geweg-en.
Ind. Indef. ic weg-e.
— *Perf.* ic wǽg we wǽg-on.

---

[1] *Wealdan*, wyldan;—*wealdest*, weltst, wyldst;—*weald*, wealdeth, wealt, welt, wylt.

[1] *Weallan*, wyllan, welan;—*weallen*, wollen;—*wylth*, wealleth; —*weoll*, weol.

[1] *Weaxan*, wexan;—*wyxth*, weaxath, weahxath, wexth;—*weox* waex, weocs, weohs.

[1] *Wegan*, waegan;—*wǽg*, wǽh.

§ 394. "weorpan,"[1] *to throw.*

3 Con. 1 Cl.

Perf. Part. worp-en.
Ind. Indef. ic weorp-e he wyrp-th.
— *Perf.* ic wearp we wurp-on.

§ 395. "wépan," *to weep.*

2 Con. 2 Cl.

Perf. Part. wép-en.
Ind. Indef. ic wép-e he wép-th.
— *Perf.* ic weop we weop-on.

§ 396. "windan," *to wind.*

3 Con. 1 Cl.

Perf. Part. wunden.
Ind. Indef. ic wind-e he wint.
— *Perf.* ic wand we wund-on.

§ 397. "winnan," *to toil, win.*

3 Con. 1 Cl.

Perf. Part. wunn-en.
Ind. Indef. ic winn-e he win-th.
— *Perf.* ic wan[1] we wunn-on.

§ 398. "withsacan,"[1] *to deny, contradict.*

2 Con. 3 Cl.

Perf. Part. withsac-en.
Ind. Indef. ic withsac-e he withsaec-th.
— *Perf.* ic withsóc we withsóc-on.

---

[1] *Weorpan,* wurpan, wyrpan, werpan.
[1] *Wan,* wann, won, wonn.
[1] *Withsacan,* sacan.

§ 399. "wlítan," *to look.*

3 Con. 2 Cl.

Perf. Part. wlit-en.
Ind. Indef. ic wlít-e he wlít.
— *Perf.* ic wlát we wlit-on.

§ 400. "wrecan," *to revenge, wreak, defend.*

2 Con. 1 Cl.

Perf. Part. wrec-en.
Ind. Indef. ic wrec-e he wric-th.
— *Perf.* ic wrǽc we wrǽc-on.

§ 401. "wreón,"[1] *to cover.*

3 Con. 3 Cl.

Perf. Part. wrog-en.
Ind. Indef. ic wreó he wrýh-th.
— *Perf.* ic wreáh we wrug-on.

§ 402. "wrígan,"[1] *to cover,* RIG.

3 Con. 2 Cl.

Perf. Part. wrig-en.
Ind. Indef. ic wríg-e, ṭḥú wríh-st, he wríh-th.
— *Perf.* ic wráh we wrig-on.

§ 403. "wringan," *to wring.*

3 Con. 1 Cl.

Perf. Part. wrung-en.
Ind. Indef. ic wring-e he wring-th.
— *Perf.* ic wrang we wrung-on.

---

[1] *Wreón,* wrýon, wreóhan;—*wreáh,* wróh.

[1] *Wrígan,* wríhan;—*wrigen,* wregen;—*wríhth,* wrígth;—*wrigon,* wraegon.

§ 404. "wríthan," *to wreathe, writhe.*

3 Con. 2 Cl.

Perf. Part. writh-en.
Ind. Indef. ic wríth-e.
— *Perf.* ic wráth we writh-on.

IMPERFECT VERBS.

§ 405. Besides the Complex verbs which we have classed under their respective conjugations, there are others that present only the Infinitive, or the Infinitive with a single person or more.[1] The same thing also occurs among verbs of the Simple Order.

§ 406. We sometimes meet with words that are evidently participles, although no verbs to which they can be assigned, any longer exist. Such generally have *ge* prefixed to them when they terminate in -ed, -od, etc.

---

[1] Some of these are, acálan; *p.* acól, *to grow cold:* ahnipan; *p.* ahneop, *to pluck, gather, nip:* aretan; *p.* arét; *pp.* aretten, *to restore, invigorate, correct, gladden:* ascreópan; *p.* ascræ´p, *to scrape off, scrape:* athreótan; *p.* athreát, *pp.* athroten, *to loathe, disdain; to tire, fatigue, weary:* ceásan; *p.* ceós; *pp.* ceásen, *to strive, contend, fight:* cínan; *p.* cán; *pp.* cinen, *to split, break into chinks:* cnedan; *p.* cnæ´d; *pp.* cneden, *to knead:* cnídan, *to beat:* deóran, dýran, *to be dear:* dreóran; *p.* dreár; *pp.* droren, *to fall, diminish, become weak:* eácan; *p.* eóc; *pp.* eácen, *to bring forth:* felan, felhan, feolan; *p.* fæ´l, fealh; *pp.* folen, *to devote:* freósan; *p.* freás; *pp.* froren, *to freeze:* hnítan; *p.* hnát; *pp.* hniten, *to butt, gore with the horns:* laecan, lacan; *p.* léc; *pp.* laecen, lacen, *to offer, sacrifice, celebrate religiously:* sinnan; *p.* sann, san, *to think of, be mindful of:* stintan; *p.* stant; *pp.* stunten, *to be blunt, be weak,* or *faint:* streódan, strúdan; *p.* streád; *pp.* stroden, *to spoil, rob, plunder:* suppan, supan; *p.* seap; *pp.* sopen, *to sup, sip, taste:* swelan; *p.* swæ´l; *pp.* swolen, *to burn, burn slowly, sweal.* These can all be arranged under their respective conjugations and classes without any difficulty.

ORIGIN AND FORMATION OF VERBS.

§ 407. In some languages, as in our own, verbs are very often made by the simple employment of nouns with the appropriate signification. This, strictly speaking, is never the case in Anglo-Saxon, though all verbs in that language owe their origin to nouns.[1]

§ 408. Anglo-Saxon verbs are formed from nouns by the addition of the termination -an or -ian; as, "dǽl," *a part,* "dǽl-an," *to divide;* "blót," *a sacrifice,* "blót-an," *to sacrifice;* "bód," *an edict,* "bód-ian," *to proclaim;* "cár," *care,* "cár-ian," *to take heed, to be anxious.* Such forms as "beón," "teón," "wreón," "fón," "hón," and the like, are evidently contracted.[1]

---

[1] Rather, in the majority of cases, to the *idea merely expressed,* which lies at the foundation of every part of speech.—See *Gloss. to Anal. Anglo-Sax., Introd.,* § IV.

[1] The common opinion is, that the terminations which go to form verbs from nouns in Anglo-Saxon, are expressive of *giving* or *bestowing, possession,* and *motion,* being no other than the infinitives "unnan," *to give* or *bestow,* "ágan," *to have* or *possess,* and "gán," *to go.* "An" is generally considered the original form of the first verb, as "unnan" (anan?) may be a double form like "gangan." But are not "ágan" and "gán" themselves made by means of a significant ending? And did none of the verbs, into the composition of which these are said to enter, exist before they themselves were formed?

There can be very little doubt that at one time the infinitives of all Anglo-Saxon verbs had the same forms as the corresponding nouns, and that afterwards one verb, and only one, was employed to distinguish the former part of speech from the latter. We will also say that that verb was "unnan," "geunnan," *ind. indef.* "ic an, gean," signifying *to give either to one's self or to another person, or thing.* Thus, "dǽl-an," *to give a part,* "blót-an," *to give a sacrifice,* "bód-ian," *to give an edict,* "cárian," *to give care.* "Baeth-ian" *to wash,* therefore, is not "'baeth-gán,' *to go to a bath,*" but "baeth-gean," *to give a bath;* and so throughout the vocabulary. See also Appendix D

Sometimes the termination -gean, -gan, or -gian is used; as, "sceawi-gean," "sceawi-gan," *to look;* "geþyld-gian," *to endure.* Indeed, -ian appears to be no other than a softened form of these endings, and to have therefore the same original signification as -an. Thus we have "sceawi-gean," "sceawi-gan," "sceawi-an;" "geþyld-gian," "geþyld-ian;" "forht-gean," "forht-ian." The last verb has the adjective "forht," *timid,* for its root. It not unfrequently happens that we find verbs formed in this way from adjectives, and also from words which have dropped out of the Anglo-Saxon vocabulary, both as nouns and as adjectives, but which are to be met with in many instances as nouns in the cognate languages and dialects. It is very probable, however, that in all such cases the verb preserves the original noun, or the *idea merely expressed* in itself.

§ 409. In a subsequent stage verbs were compounded; as, "geþancmetan," *to deliberate;* from "geþanc," *mind, thought,* and "metan," *to measure, compare;* "út-gán," *to go out,* from "út," *out,* and "gán," *to go.*[1]

---

[1] Some verbs are made by means of another, -laecan; *p.* -láehte; *pp.* -láeht, *to do, perform, cause, bring, bring about, make real,* never found in its simple state, unless "laecan," *to offer an oblation, to sacrifice,* is the same in a modified sense. Its root then might be identified with "laec," "lac," used independently as a noun, and as a termination as given in § 75 Note

CHAPTER VIII.

ADVERBS.

§ 410. The following are the most of the Adverbs in Anglo-Saxon not formed by the termination -lice:—

á,[1] *always, ever, forever*, AYE.

---

[1] The following variations in orthography and etymology will be found, among others, as belonging to the adverbs here given:—

á, aa;—*adún*, adúne, of-dúne;—*aefer*, aefre;—*aeft*, eft, aefter, aeftan;—*aeghwáer*, aeghwár, aeghwér, aghwár, ahwáer, oeghwáer; —*aeghwánon*, aeghwónon, aeghwánun, aeghwánum, aeghwánan, aeghwónane;—*aeghwider*, ahwider;—*aegylde*, agilde;—*áene*, aeene; —*áer*, ár, aar, ér, eár, áeron;—*aet-gaedere*, tó-gaedere;—*aet-somne*, tó-somne;—*ahwár*, ahwáer, ahwér, awér;—*ahwónan*, ahwónon;—*ánunga*, áninga;—*asundran*, asundron;—*áwa*, áwo;—*awég*, anwég, on-wég, on-wáeg.

baeftan, baefta;—*begeondan*, beiundan, begeond;—*benythan*, beneothan, beneoth, beniutha;—*bufan*, bufon, abufan, be-ufan;—*dúneweard*, dúneward.

eall-neg, eall-nig;—*eall-swá*, eal-swá, ael-swá, al-swá;—*eallunga*, eallenga, eallinga, eallnunge;—*ealmáest*, aelmáest;—*efnes*, efenes; —*ellor*, ellicor, aelcor, aelcra;—*éndémes*, áendémes.

feor, feorr, fyr;—*feorran*, feorrene;—*for*, fore;—*fóran*, fóro, fór; see also "fórne;"—*fóre-weard*, fór-weard;—*forhwám*, forhwáem, forhwón;—*forhwý*, forhwí, forhwíg;—*fórne*, fórene;—*furthan*, furthon, furthum;—*furthor*, furthur, forthor.

geá, gáe, iá;—*geára*, gára, gére;—*gefyrn*, gefern;—*gehwáer*, gehwár;—*gen*, gaen, gien, gena, giena, geona;—*genóg*, genóh, nóh, geneóhe, geneóhhe, neóhe, geneáhe, geneáhhe, genéhe, genéhhe;—*geó*, gú, ieó, iú, ió;—*gese*, gyse, ise;—*gyt*, git, giet, get, geot, geta, gieta, iett, iette.

heónon, heónun, heónan, heónone, heónane, heóna, hénan, hénon, hínan;—*hér*, háer, hýr;—*hér-aefter*, hýr-after;—*hider*, hyder, hieder, hither;—*hindan*, hyndan;—*hú*, hwú;—*hwaene*, hwene;—*hwáenne*, hwénne, hwónne, ahwáenne;—*hwáer*, hwár;—*hwý*, hwí, hwíg;—

adún, *down, downward,* ADOWN.
aefer, *ever, always.*
aeft, *after, again, behind, aft, afterward.*
aefteweard, *afterward, after, behind.*
aeghwǽr, *everywhere.*
aeghwánon, *everywhere, every way, on all sides.*
aeghwider, *on every side, every way.*
aegylde, *without amends.*

---

hwider, hwyder, hwaeder ;—*hwon,* hwonn, huon ;—*hwónan,* hwóna, be-hwón.

innan, inne, inn.

lange, longe ;—*litlum,* lytlum, litlon

má, mǽe, már, máre, móre.

ná, nó ;—*naefre,* nefre ;—*ná-hwǽr,* ná-hwár, ná-wár, ná-wér, ná-hwérn ;—*ná-hwánan,* ná-hwónan, ná-hwénan ;—*ná-laes,* ná-les, nállas, náls ;—*nalles,* nallaes ;—*neáh,* néh ;—*neothan,* niothan, nythan, nithan, neothone ;—*nese,* naese ;—*nither,* nyther, nythor, nether ;—*nither-weard,* nither-ward, nither-werd, nither-weardes ;—*nó-wiht,* nó-wuht, nó-hwit, náht, nóht.

ongean, ongen, angean, agean, agen ;—*oth,* oththe.

recene, recone, recine.

sámod, sámad, sómod, sómed ;—*seld,* seldum, seldon, seldan ;—*siththan,* syththan, seththan, siththen, sithen, syththon, sython, siththa ; —*sona,* suna, sones, be-sone ;—*stille,* stylle ;—*sunder,* sundor, synder, syndor ;—*swithe,* swythe ;—*symle,* simle, semle, siemle, symble, simble, symbel, ael-symle.

téla, teála ;—*tó-efenes,* tó-emnes ;—*túwa,* tuua ;—*thá,* thάge ;—*thǽr,* thár, thér ;—*thánon,* thánun, thánan, thánone, thánonne, thónan, thónon, thóna ;—*thónne,* thǽnne, thánne, thǽn, thón ;—*thriwa,* thrywa, thriga ;—*thus,* dus ;—*thyder,* thider, thaeder, thyther ;—*thyder-weard,* thider-weard, thider-weardes

ufan, ufon, ufen, ufane, ufene, ufenan, ufa ;—*up,* upp, uppe ;—*út,* úte.

weald, geald ;—*wel,* well, wael ;—*with-útan,* with-úton, with-úten

NOTE.—The foregoing forms, with others in the sequel of the Indeclinable Parts of Speech, many of which are archaic, will be found to throw no little light upon the early and more intimate structure of the language, as well as upon general grammar See also *Anal. Anglo-Sax.,* Notes, *pass.* with *Glossary.*

áene, *once.*

áer, *ere, before, sooner, earlier, first, heretofore, formerly, already, some time ago, lately, just now, till, until.*

aetgaedere, *together.*

aet-nyhstan, *at last, lastly.*

aet-sithestan, *at length, at last.*

aet-somne, *in a sum, at once, together, also, likewise.*

á-forth, *always, continually, daily, still.*

ahwáer-gen, *everywhere, again, continually.*

ahwár, *somewhere, anywhere, in any wise.*

ahwónan, *from what place, whence, anywhere, somewhere.*

al-geátes, *always, altogether,* ALL GATES.

ánlapum, *from one part, at once, one by one.*

ánunga, *one by one, singly, at once, clearly, plainly, entirely, altogether, necessarily.*

ariht, *aright, right, well, correctly.*

asundran, *asunder, apart, alone, privately.*

athánon, *from thence.*

áwa, *always.*

awég, *away, out.*

awóh, *awry, unjustly, wrongfully, badly.*

baeftan, *after, hereafter, afterward.*

begeondan, *beyond.*

benythan, *beneath, below, under.*

bufan, *above, before, beyond, moreover.*

dúneweard, *downward.*

eall-neg, *always.*

eall-swá, *also, likewise.*

eallunga, *all along, altogether, entirely, quite, indeed, at all, assuredly, utterly, absolutely, excessively.*

ealmáest, *almost.*

eal-symle, *always.*

eáwunga, *openly, publicly.*

efnes, *evenly, plainly.*

eft-sona, *soon after, again,* EFTSOONS.

elles, *else, otherwise, amiss.*
ellor, *elsewhere, besides, otherwise.*
éndémes, *equally, likewise, in like manner, together.*
eonu, *moreover.*
feor, *far, at a distance.*
feorran, *from far.*
for, *notwithstanding, too, very.*
foran, *only.*
fóran, *before.*
fóre-weard, *forward, before, first.*
forhwaega, *at least.*
forhwám, *wherefore, why.*
fórne, *before, sooner.*
forth, *forth, thence, further, directly, forward.*
furthan, *also, too, even, indeed, further.*
furthor, *further.*
geá, *yea, yes.*
geára, *yore, formerly, for a long time; well, certainly, enough.*
gebaec, *aback.*
gefyrn, *formerly, long ago, of old.*
gegnum, *forthwith, immediately, against.*
gegnunga, *directly, certainly, wholly, plainly, altogether.*
gehende, *nigh, near at hand.*
gehwáer, *on every side, everywhere.*
gehwaetheres, *anywhere, on every side, every way.*
gehwánon, *on all sides, round-about.*
gehwider, *whithersoever, anywhere, everywhere.*
gelíce, *likewise, also, as.*
gen, *again, moreover, besides, at length, as yet, hitherto.*
genóg, *sufficiently, abundantly, enough.*
geó, *formerly, of old.*
geond, *yond, yonder, thither, beyond.*
gese, *yes, yea.*
gewel-hwáer, *everywhere.*

gyt, *yet, hitherto, moreover, still, as yet.*

heáh, *high.*

heónon, *hence, from hence;*—heónon-forth, *henceforth.*

hér, *here, now, at this time;*—hér-aefter, *hereafter.*

hider, *hither;*—hider-weard, *hitherward.*

hindan, *behind;*—hindan-weard, *hindward.*

hólenga, *in vain.*

hrathe, *quickly, soon,* RATH.

hú, *how, in what manner.*

hugu, *a little, but a little, scarcely, at least.*

húmeta, *how, in what manner.*

huru, *at least, at all events, yet, only, indeed, especially.*

hwaene, *somewhat, almost, a little, scarcely.*

hwǽnne, *when.*

hwǽr, *where.*

hwaet, *besides, in short, indeed, moreover, but yet.*

hwaethre, *whether.*

hwider, *whither.*

hwon, *a little, a little while, rarely.*

hwónan, *whence, where.*

hwý, *why, wherefore, for what, indeed.*

innan, *within, inwardly;*—innan-weard, *inward.*

laes, *less.*

lange, *long, a long time.*

litlum, *with little, in pieces, by degrees.*

lungre, *immediately, forthwith.*

má, *more; rather, of more value; afterward.*

mǽlum, *in parts,* with its compounds, such as "bit-mǽlum," *in parts, piecemeal, by degrees;* "dǽl-mǽlum," *id.;* "drop-mǽlum," *by drops, drop by drop;* "lim-mǽlum," *limb by limb;* "stycce-mǽlum," *piece by piece, by little and little, by degrees;* and the like.

mǽst, *most, more than.*

middan, *in the midst.*

ná, *no, not.*

naefre, *never.*

naes, *not.*

ná-hwáer, *nowhere.*

ná-hwánan, *never, nowhere, from no time,* or *place.*

ná-laes, *no less, not only.*

nalles, *not at all, not, no.*

náte, *not.*

ne, *not, nay, by no means.*

neáh, *nigh, near, almost.*

neán, *nearly, almost.*

neothan, *beneath, downward;*—neothe-weard, *downward.*

nese, *nay, not, no.*

nin, *not, no.*

nither, *down, downward, below;*—nither-weard, *downward.*

nó-wiht, *by no means, not.*

nú, *now, still, since, then.*

oft, *oft, often.*

on-án, *in one, once for all, continually.*

on-gean, *again.*

on-hinder, *backward, behind.*

oth, *until, even to, as far as.*

recene, *quickly, soon, immediately, speedily.*

sámod, *also, likewise, together.*

sció, *hence.*

seld, *seldom, rarely.*

síde, *far, widely.*

sith, *late, lately, afterward.*

siththan, *afterward, after that, then, thenceforth, since, further, moreover, successively, in order.*

sneome, *suddenly, quickly, immediately, readily.*

sona, *soon, immediately, forthwith.*

stille, *still.*

sum-hwíle, *somewhile, sometime.*

sunder, *asunder, apart.*

swá, *so, thus.*
swithe, *very, much, very much, greatly.*
symle, *always, ever, constantly, continually.*
téla, *well, rightly.*
tó, *too, also.*
tó-efenes, *along, evenly, plainly.*
túwa, *twice.*
ṭḥá, *then, until, while, whilst, when, as.*
ṭḥǽr, *there; where, whither.*
ṭḥaes, *of this, for this, so far, so much so, thus, since, that, whereby, whereof.*
ṭḥaet, *from that place, thence, only.*
ṭḥánon, *thence, whence.*
ṭḥónne, *then, immediately, when, since, whilst, afterward.*
ṭḥriwa, *thrice, three times.*
ṭḥus, *thus, so.*
ṭḥyder, *thither;*—ṭḥyder-weard, *thitherward.*
ufan, *above, high, upward, from above.*
up, *up, upward;*—upweardes, *upward.*
út, *out, without, abroad;*—úte-weard, *outward.*
útan, *outward, without, outwardly.*
weald, *perhaps.*
weás, *by chance, accidentally.*
wel, *well, much, enough, truly, plainly.*
with-ufan, *above, from above.*
with-útan, *without.*

COMPARISON OF ADVERBS.

§ 411. Many Adverbs, especially those which end in -e and -lice, admit of comparison. In that case, the final vowel of the positive is cut off, and the syllables -or and -ost are added respectively for the comparative and superlative; as, "raeth-e," *soon,* "rath-or,"[1] *sooner,* "rath-ost," *soonest;*

[1] ***rathor,*** **rathur.**

"riht-lice," *justly*, "rihtlic-or," *more justly*, "rihtlic-ost," *most justly*.

§ 412. Some are irregular in forming the comparative and superlative degrees; as, "wel," *well*, "bet,"[1] *better*, "betst," *best*; "yfele," *badly*, "wyrs,"[2] *worse*, "wyrrest," *worst*.

CHAPTER IX.

PREPOSITIONS.

§ 413. Prepositions in Anglo-Saxon govern different cases, and some of them two or more. They govern, 1. The Dative; 2. The Accusative; 3. The Genitive, or the Dative;[1] 4. The Dative, or the Accusative; and, 5. The Genitive, the Dative, or the Accusative.

1. The Prepositions which govern the Dative are:—

Aefter,[2] *after, for, on account of, according to, through, over.*
efter.
Aer, *ere, before.*
Aet, *at, to, next, with, against, in; of, from.*
actt.

---

[1] *bet*, bett, abet.

[2] *wyrs*, wirs. Perhaps no other than the Genitive of the Old Positive "weor," sc. "weores," changed, in the lapse of time, to the comparative signification, like "bet," and "laes." See § 93, Note 1.

[1] Those which govern the Dative, or the Genitive, may also be found with the Old Ablative.

[2] We have thought it better, in giving the different forms of the Prepositions, to deviate from our common rule in placing such by themselves.

Baeftan, *after, behind; without.*
be-aeftan.
beftan.
aeftan.
eftan.
Be, *of, from, about, touching, concerning; for, because of,*
bi. *after, according to; besides, out of.*
big.
by.
Be-eástan, *to,* or *on the east of.*
Beheónan, *on this side, close by.*
behiónan.
Be-láste, *in the footsteps of, behind.*
Be-northan, *to,* or *on the north of.*
Be-súthan, *to,* or *on the south of.*
Betwýnan, *between, among.*
betweónan.
betweónum.
betwínan.
Be-westan, *to,* or *on the west of.*
Bí,[3] *by, near to, at, to, in, upon, with.*
bii.
bý.
bé.
Binnan, *within.*
binnon.
be-innan.
Bufan, *above.*
bufon.
Feor, *far from, far off from.*
feorr.

[3] Some would make no distinction between "bí" and "be," but they evidently have a different origin. "Be," as appearing in compound prepositions, is used for "bé."

Gehende, *nigh.*
hende.
Mith, *with.*
Neáh, *near, nigh.*
néh.
geneáhe.
genéhe.
On-fóran, *before.*
On-innan, *within.*
On-ufan, *above, upon.*
on-ufon.
on-uppan.
on-uppon.
Tó-eácan, *besides.*
Tó-fóran, *before.*
tó-fóron.
tó-fóren.
tó-fóre.
tó-fór.
Unfeor, *nigh, near, not far from.*
un-feorr.
With-northan, *to the north of.*

2. Those governing the Accusative are:[4]—

Abútan, *about, around, round-about.*
abúton.
onbútan.
onbúton.
Begeond, *beyond.*
begeondan.
begiondan.
beiundan.

---

[4] Some of these, as investigations are made in the language, will be found also to govern the Dative. The composition and forms of several of them require that case.

Behindan, *behind.*
Geond, *through, over, as far as, after, beyond.*
  geonda.
  gynd.
  eond.
Míl, *among, at, amid, in.*
Ongean, *against, opposite, opposite to, towards.*
  ongen.
  angean.
  agen.
Siththan, *after, since.*
  siththon.
Ṭḥurh, *through, by, by means of.*
  ṭḥorh.
  ṭḥerh.
  ṭḥurch.
With-aeftan, *behind, after.*
With-fóran, *before.*
With-geondan, *about, throughout.*
With-innan, *within.*
With-útan, *without.*
Ymb, *round, about.*
  ymbe.
  emb.
  embe.
  imb.
Ymb-útan, *round-about, without, beyond, except.*
  ymbe-útan.
  emb-útan.
  embe-útan.

3. Those which govern the Genitive, or the Dative are:—

Of, *of, from, out of, concerning.*
  af.
Tó, *to, towards, for, under, from.*

Tó-emnes, *along.*
Tó-middes, *in the middle, in the midst, among.*
Tóweard, *towards.*
 tóward.
 tówerd.
 tó-weardes.
 tó-wardes.

4. Those governing the Dative, or the Accusative, are:—

Aet-fóran, *close before, close by, before, at.*
 befóran.
 befóre.
 befeóre.
Betwúh, *bewixt, among.*
 betúh.
 betwý.
 betwíh.
 betwýh.
 betweóh.
 betweohs.
 betux.
 betweox.
 betwux.
 betwuxt.
 betwyx.
 betwixt.
Butan,[5] *without, except, but.*
 buton.
 butun.
 buta.
 bute.
For, *for, on account of, because of, according to, as.*

[5] "Butan" is also found with the Genitive.

Gemang, *among.*
gemong.
amang.
onmang.
on-gemang.
on-gemong.
Innan, *in, into, within.*
innon.
Intó, *into, in.*
Mid, *with, by means of, among.*
myd.
Ofer, *over, above, upon, beside, beyond.*
ouer.
On, *in, into, with, among, on, upon, a-,* or *a.*
in.
an.
en.
o', oo.
Oth, *to, unto, till.*
Under, *under.*
Uppan, *upon ; beyond, after, against, from.*
uppon.
Utan, *without, beyond*
úton.

5. Those which govern the Genitive, the Dative, or the Accusative, are:—

Andlang, *along, by the side of; through, during*
andlong.
ondlong.
andlangne
ondlongne
anlangne.
onlongne.
lang.

gelang.
gelong.
Fram, *from.*
fra.
from.
Nymþe, *except, save, unless.*
nimþe.
nemþe.
Tó-geanes, *towards, against, to meet, in the way of.*
tó-genes.
tó-gaegnes.
tó-gegnes.
tó-geaegn.
Tó-yppan, *before, in the presence of.*
yppan.
With, *against, opposite; near, about, by, before, by the side of, along; towards, with, for, instead of, through.*

§ 414. A Preposition is sometimes separated from the word which it governs, and in that case it is placed before the verb in the sentence. Several of the compound prepositions are also elegantly divided by the nouns or pronouns depending upon them.

§ 415. Some Prepositions are of an inseparable nature, and much used in the composition of Anglo-Saxon words. These will be found among the Prefixes given under § 75.

CHAPTER X.

CONJUNCTIONS.

§ 416. Conjunctions in Anglo-Saxon are either single words or phrases. The principal are contained in the following list:—

ac,[1] *but, whether.*

ah, *whether, but*; ahne, *whether or not.*

and, *and.*

andhwaether, *notwithstanding, but yet.*

áthor-oththe . . . . oththe, *either . . . . or.*

á-thý, á-the, *therefore, so far as, so much as*

butan, *but, unless, except.*

eác, *also, likewise, and, moreover.*

eornostlice, *therefore, but.*

forthá, *because.*

forthám, *for the reason that, because, for that cause, for, therefore.*

forthý, *therefore, wherefore, for, because*; forthý thónne, *therefore then, wherefore then.*

ge, *and, also*; ge . . . . ge, aeghwaether-ge . . . . ge, aegther-ge . . . . ge, *both . . . . and, as well . . . . as, so . . . . as.*

gif, *if, when, though.*

hwaet, *moreover, but, wherefore, because.*

---

[1] The following, among others, are the various forms of the conjunctions here given:—

ac, oc;—*and*, aend, end, ond.

áthor in the former clause of "áthor-oththe . . . . oththe," áther, auther, outher.

butan, buton, butun, bute.

eác, aéc, éc, ge-ác, ge-eác.

forthám, forthán, forthón;—*forthý*, forthí, forthíg.

gif, gyf, gef.

hwý, hwí, hwíg.

náthor, náther, náthaer, nawther, nauther;—*nymthe*, nimthe, nemthe, nymne, nimne, nemne.

oththe, oththon.

sám, sóm;—*swá*, swáe, suáe, (swáe, suáe, (?);)—*swilce*, swylce.

thaet, that, and thaette, contracted from "thaet the;"—*theáh*, théh, tháeh, thóth;—*thónne*, thánne, tháenne;—*thonne*, thanne, thaenne.

witodlice, witedlice, witudlice.

hwaethre, *whether, nevertheless, yet, but, if;* hwaether-ṭḥe . . . . ṭḥe, *whether . . . . or.*

hwý, *wherefore, indeed.*

laes-hwon, ṭḥe-laes, ṭḥe-laes-ṭḥe, ṭḥý-laes, ṭḥý-laes-ṭḥe, las-ṭḥe, *lest, lest that.*

naes ná, naes ne, *neither.*

náṭḥeles, *nevertheless natheless.*

náthor, *neither, nor;* náthor-ne . . . . ne, *neither . . . . nor.*

ne, *neither, nor;* ne-ne, *neither;* ne . . . . ne, *neither . . . . nor.*

nymṭḥe, *except, save, unless, but.*

ono, *if;* onó hwaet, *but;* ono nú, *if now;* ono gif, *but if.*

oththe, *or, either;* oththe . . . . oththe, *either . . . . or.*

other-twéga, *or* other-ṭḥára, *either of the two,* often in the first clause for "oththe."

sám, *whether;* sám . . . . sám, *whether . . . . or.*

set, *therefore, on that account.*

sóthlice, *but, wherefore, therefore.*

swá, swá-swá, *as, so as, as if;* swá-sáme, swá-sóme, *so, also;* swá-sáme-swá, *the same as, as. even as;* sáme-ylce-swá, *in such wise as, so as;* eall-swá, *also;* swá-eác, *so as, also;* swá-ṭḥeáh, *yet, but for all that, nevertheless, however;* swá . . . . swá, swá . . . . swá-swá, *so . . . . as, that,* swá-wel-swá, *so well as;* swá-ṭḥaet, *so that.*

swilce, *as if, as it were, so that, also, moreover, seeing.*

ṭḥaet, *that;* tó-ṭḥón-ṭḥaet, *in order that.*

ṭḥe, *than, whether, either, or, whether . . . . or.*

ṭḥeáh, *though, although, yet, still, however;* ṭḥeáh-ṭḥe, *although;* ṭḥeáh-hwaethere, *yet, nevertheless, moreover, but yet, but.*

ṭḥónne, *therefore, wherefore, then;* gif ṭḥónne, *if indeed.*

ṭḥonne, *than, but.*

ṭḥý, *for, because, therefore;* ṭḥý . . . . ṭḥý, ṭḥý . . . . ṭḥe, *therefore, because;* also, for-ṭḥý . . . . for-ṭḥý, for-ṭḥý . . . .

ṭẖe, for-ṭẖý . . . . for-ṭẖám, for-ṭẖí . . . . for-ṭẖám-ṭẖe, for-ṭẖám-ṭẖe . . . . for-ṭẖý, *therefore . . . . because.*

wénre, *except, saving, but.*

with-ṭẖón-ṭẖaet, *so that, provided that.*

witodlice, *but, for, therefore, wherefore.*

CHAPTER XI.

INTERJECTIONS

§ 417. The following are the most of the Anglo-Saxon Interjections:—

á-faest-lá, *Oh certainly! Oh assuredly!*

eálá, *Oh! alas! Oh!* eálá eálá, *very well!* eálá gif, *Oh if; I wish;* eálá ṭẖaet, *Oh that!* eálá hú, *Oh how.*

efne, *lo! behold! truly!* al-efne, *behold all!*

eów, *wo! alas!*

heno, *behold!*

híg, *Oh!* hí lá hí, *alas!*

hiú, *ha!*

huí, *ho!*

hwaet, *what! lo! behold!*

lá, *Oh! lo! behold!*

taeg, *tush! pish!*

wá, *wo! alas!* wá lá, *Oh! Oh if!* wá lá wá, *well-a-way! well-a-day! alas!*

wei, *wo! alas!*

wel-lá wel, *well well!* wel lá,[1] *well alas!*

---

[1] The various forms of some of these are:—
eálá, aeálá, eáwlá, hélá;—*efne*, aefne, eofne.
heno, heonu;—*huí*, huíg.

ORIGIN AND FORMATION OF THE INDECLINABLE PARTS OF SPEECH.

§ 418. Admitting the view which we have taken of the formation of the Anglo-Saxon verb to be correct, it cannot be considered in any case as the direct source of the adverb, preposition, conjunction, and interjection. These must therefore have some other origin assigned them.

The indeclinable parts of speech are either derived from words which still exist in the language as nouns, adjectives, or pronouns, or they are themselves primitive words, and, as such, were once used as nouns. In proof of our assertion we will give a few examples.

1. With regard to Adverbs, as:—

"Hwílum," *awhile, now,* the Dative, or Ablative plural of "hwíl," *time, space.*

"Ṭḥances," *freely, gratefully,* the Genitive singular of "ṭḥanc," *favor, will, thanks.*

"Gyt," *yet,* from "giht," "geht," "gyte," *time, staying.* This noun in the sense of *time* is still found united with another word; as, "gebed-giht," *bed-time.* "Gyt," in its old forms "gyta," "gieta," and the like, would seem to be the noun in the Ablative.

"Lange," *a long time,* is probably no other than the Accusative feminine of "lang," *long,* "hwíle," *time* being understood.

Adverbs ending in -lice, and many others, are really adjectives in the Old Ablative masculine or neuter agreeing with a noun understood; as, "hraedlice," *quickly;* i. e. *in a quick manner,* or the like.

2. With regard to Prepositions, as:—

"Bý," "bí," *by, near,* is the same as the root of "býe," *a habitation.*

"Gemang," *among*, taking away the prefix ge-, differs but little from "menge," *a crowd, multitude.* "Menge" exists as one of the numerous forms of "maenigeo."

"Ṭhurh," "ṭhuruh," *through, thorough*, are the same as "ṭhuru," "ṭhuruh," "duru," *a door*, or *passage of any kind.*

3. With respect to Conjunctions, as:—

"Eác," *also, and, moreover*, and "eáca," *an addition*, are one and the same. "Eác" is evidently the radical and independent form of the noun.

"Gif," *if*, and the verb "gifan," *to give*, if related, must both be referred to a noun no longer in existence, but of which the conjunction may preserve the radical form. It is evident that the particle was needed in the language as soon as the verb.[1]

4. With respect to Interjections, as:—

"Wá," *wo! alas!* which is the noun "wá," *wo, sorrow, affliction.*

5. Many of the indeclinable parts of speech in the language are compounds; as, "ná-hwáer," *nowhere;* "be-hindan," *behind;* "and-hwaether," *notwithstanding;* "á-faest-lá," *Oh certainly!*[2]

---

[1] We may say that the adverb, preposition, and conjunction, have preserved, in many cases, the root of the noun and of the verb unchanged. But more of this view of the subject elsewhere.

[2] See further, *Anal. Anglo-Sax.*, Notes, *passim*, with *Glossary* in both which works the real nature and full powers of the parts of speech under consideration will be found clearly exhibited.

PART III.—SYNTAX.

CONSTRUCTION OF SENTENCES.

§ 419. Syntax, which is divided into Concord and Government, is the arrangement of words in a sentence according to certain rules established by usage.

1. CONCORD.

§ 420. The verb agrees with its Nominative in number and person, as:—

Ic lufige	*I love.*
Thú wrítst	*Thou writest.*
He wáes rihtwís	*He was righteous.*
We standath	*We stand.*
Ge etath	*Ye,* or *you eat.*
Wagas burston	*Waves burst.*

NOTE.—The subject usually stands before the verb, but when "thá" or "thónne," *then*, is introduced before a consequent proposition, it is commonly placed after it; although, as in English, the particle in most cases is omitted, and the subject maintains its natural position in the sentence. Negation, in some instances, has also the effect of throwing it after the verb.

§ 421. A noun of multitude may have the verb either in the singular or the plural number, or two verbs of different numbers even in the same sentence, as:—

Eall thaet folc arás and stódon.	*All the people arose and stood.*

§ 422. Two or more Nominatives in the singular connected by "and," *and*, either expressed or understood, have the verb in the plural, as:—

Synderlice hine Pétrus and Iácobus and Ióhannes and Andréas acsodon	*Peter and James and John and Andrew asked him privately.*

NOTE.—The verb may be in the singular when the two Nominatives are closely connected in sense.

§ 423. The verbs of *existence* may have a Nominative both before and after them, as:—

God wáes ṭḥaet Word	*God was the Word.*
Ṭḥaet bíth Godes weorc	*That is God's work.*
Híg wurdon gefrýnd	*They became friends.*

§ 424. The first of the two Nominatives may be one of the singular neuters, "ṭḥis" and "ṭḥaet," belonging to the verb, and referring to a noun, both in the plural, as:—

Ne synd ná ṭḥis wódes mannes word	*These* (*this*) *are not the words of a madman.*
Ṭḥaet synd ṭḥá woruld-sorga	*Those* (*that*) *are the worldly cares.*

§ 425. The article agrees with the noun which it defines, in gender, number, and case, as:—

Se anwealda	*The governor.*
Ṭḥá háethenan	*The heathen.*
Ṭḥaes líc-haman	*Of the body.*

§ 426. It also is frequently used before proper names, and after possessive and other pronouns, as:—

Se Jóhannes	*The* (said) *John.*
On ṭḥínum ṭḥám hálgum naman	*In thy* (*the*) *holy name.*

§ 427. All adjectives, including all other words having the nature of adjectives, agree with the nouns to which they belong, in gender, number, and case, as:—

Lengran dagas	*Longer days.*
Ṭḥeós stow	*This place.*
Twégen englas	*Two angels.*
Lócigende ge geseóth	*Looking ye shall see.*

NOTE.—In such cases as the example given under § 432, "anlícnys" being feminine, "ṭḥis" must be supposed to agree with "ṭḥing," *a thing*, understood. So also if "ṭḥaet" were used.

§ 428. The perfect participle with "habban," *to have*, as we have seen, § 179, Note 1, does not always agree with the Nominative, or help to constitute a compound tense, but is frequently inflected and made to agree with the governed word, as:—

Aenne haefde he swá swithne geworhtne	*One had he made so strong.*

§ 429. The relative agrees with its antecedent in gender and number, but its case depends upon some other word in the sentence, as:—

Sum faemne seó haefde	*A certain virgin who had.*
Ṭḥú ṭḥe eart	*Thou who art.*
Se mann, se-ṭḥe	*The man, he who.*
Se bé ṭḥám	*He by whom.*

NOTE.—"Wíf," *a woman*, though neuter, sometimes takes the relative in the feminine.

§ 430. The relative is frequently omitted, as:—

Ṭḥá wáes sum consul Boetíus wáes háten	*Then was there a certain consul* (who) *was named Boethius.*

§ 431. The relative is sometimes elegantly expressed through "the" and the personal pronoun, as:—

The thurh his willan	*Through whose will.*
The thurh hine	*Through whom.*

§ 432. The interrogative and the word that answers to it, must be in the same case, as:—

Hwaes anlícnys ys this? Thaes Cáseres	*Whose image is this? (The) Cæsar's.*
Hwám sealde he hit? Thám scíre-geréfan	*To whom did he give it? To the sheriff.*

§ 433. Nouns signifying the same thing agree in case, as:—

Aelfred, Cyning	*King Alfred.*
Jóhannes se Fulluhtere	*John the Baptizer.*

NOTE.—We not unfrequently find two pronouns in the like agreement with each other; as, "hí ealle," *they all:* or a pronoun and a numeral; as, "sume nigon," *some nine.*

§ 434. Sometimes a noun defined by the article is repeated after the pronoun which expresses it, agreeing with it in the same case, as:—

He se biscop	*He the bishop.*
Heó seó meowle	*She the virgin.*

2. GOVERNMENT.

§ 435. One noun governs another, when a different person, or thing is signified, in the Genitive case, as:—

Mannes líf	*Man's life.*
Thaes cildes faeder	*The child's father.*
Waeteru sǽs	*Waters of a sea.*

NOTE.—The personal pronoun as representing the noun, can take its place in the Genitive; as, "his modor," *his mother.*

§ 436. A noun united with an adjective, which expresses either *a good* or *a bad quality*, or which denotes *condition*, and the like, is put in the Genitive, as:—

This folc is heardes módes   *This people is of hard mind.*
He wǽs aethelre strýnde   *He was of a noble race.*
Aegtheres hádes   *Of either sex.*

NOTE 1.—The adjective occasionally appears in agreement with the subject; as, "fugel úrig fethera," *a bird hoary of wings*, unless all such cases can be explained under § 444.

NOTE 2.—We sometimes find the article agreeing with the qualitative Genitive, instead of the noun on which this depends; as, "thǽre eádigre gemynde mann," but more commonly, "se mann eádigre gemynde," *the man of blessed memory.*

§ 437. Nouns denoting *measure, value, age,* and the like, are put in the Genitive, as:—

Threóra míla brád   *Three miles broad.*
Sex peninga wyrthe   *Sixpence worth.*
Anes geáres lamb   *A yearling lamb.*

NOTE.—The *measure of extent* is put independently in the Accusative, unless we suppose a preposition understood in every instance of the kind, and that preposition answering to the Latin "quoad," *as to*, if the same is not "ymbe."

§ 438. Nouns answering the question *when?* are found in the Genitive, the Dative, or the Old Ablative; but *how long?* or *how often?* in the Accusative, as:—

This wǽs feórthes geáres   *This was in the fourth year.*
Thám monthe   *In that month.*
Thý daege   *On that day.*
Thǽr híg wǽron seofon dagas fulle   *They were there seven entire days.*
Fíf sithas   *Five times.*

NOTE.—*Circumstances of time and place united* are put in the Accusative, a rule preserved only in adverbial construction.

§ 439. A noun answering the question *where?* may be put in the Genitive, or the Dative, as:—

Eorthan getenge	*Prostrate on the ground.*
Ṭḥǽre stowe	*In that place.*

NOTE.—*Whence?* when standing independently in the sentence, is expressed through the Old Ablative, and preserved mostly, if not altogether, in adverbial terms.

§ 440. "Hám," *home,* when the question is made by *whither?* is put in the Accusative, a rule also applicable to other words, as:—

Ṭḥá he hám cóm	*When he came home.*

§ 441. The *cause, manner,* and *instrument,* in relation to a thing, are found in the Dative, or the Old Ablative, and sometimes in the Genitive, as:—

His ágenum willum	*Of his own will.*
Micelre stefne	*With a loud voice.*
Billum abreótan	*With bills to destroy.*
Ealde swurde	*With an old sword.*
Ealles his maegnes	*With all his power.*

§ 442. Nouns are used absolutely in the Dative, or the Ablative, with participles, as:—

Gebigedum cneówum	*Knees being bent.*
Him ṭḥencendum	*He thinking.*

§ 443. A pronoun in the neuter gender sometimes governs the Genitive case singular, as:—

Nánṭḥing grénes	*Nothing green.*
Hwaet aetheles	*Something noble.*

§ 444. Adjectives denoting *plenty, want, desert, likeness, dignity, care* or *desire, knowledge, ignorance, etc.,* govern the Dative, the Ablative, or the Genitive, as:—

Full Hálgum Gáste *Full of the Holy Spirit.*
Fugel fetherum deál *A bird deficient in feathers.*
Deathes scyldig *Deserving death.*
Gelíc witegan *Like unto a prophet.*

§ 445. *Partitives, superlatives, interrogatives,* and *numerals,* usually employ the Genitive plural, but with a noun of multitude, the same case singular, as:—

Náenig ṭḥinga *No one of things.*
Scipío, se betsta Rómana witena *Scipio, the best of the Roman senators.*
Twentig wintra *Twenty years.*
Feala folces *Many a one of the people.*

Note.—Under this rule may fall "sum" and its government of numerals in the Genitive plural; as, "sum hund-nigontigra," *some,* or *about ninety.*

§ 446. The comparative degree governs nouns and pronouns in the Dative, or the Ablative, when it can be translated by *than,* as:—

Hefigran ṭḥáere áe *Weightier than the law.*

§ 447. Verbs for the most part govern the Accusative, when a direct object is implied, as:—

Ṭḥisne mann ic lufige *I love this man.*
Hí hine ondredon *They feared him.*

Note.—The object is commonly placed before the verb; deviations from this rule, though, are frequent.

§ 448. Verbs of *governing, wanting, enjoying,* and the like, require the Genitive case, as:—

He wealt ealles *He governs all.*
Ne ṭḥearf he nánes ṭḥinges *Nor needs he any thing.*
Gif hí ṭḥaes wuda benugon *If they have enjoyment of the woods.*

§ 449. Verbs of *serving, listening, answering, fearing for, etc.*, govern the Dative case, as:—

We ṭẖeowiath blíthelice ṭẖám cynge	*We will serve the king with joy.*
Sunu mín, hlyste mínre láre	*My son, listen to my counsel.*
Ṭẖá ne mihton híg him andswarian	*Then were they not able to answer him.*
Hí him ondredon	*They feared for themselves.*

NOTE.—We will here observe that some verbs are found either with the Dative, or the Accusative; as, "onfón him, *or* hine," *to receive him;* while others, it is said, may govern both cases, when united with a conjunction.

§ 450. A verb of *existence* usually governs the Dative, but when *property,* or *possession* is implied, it requires the Genitive, as:—

Wes us fáele freónd	*Be unto us a faithful friend.*
Hit ṭẖaes cildes wáes	*It was the child's.*

NOTE.—"Wesan" is sometimes elegantly used for "habban;" as, "hí me sind ealle on maegne," *I have them all in my power,* lit. *they are all unto me in power.*

§ 451. An impersonal verb governs the Dative, but is sometimes found with the Accusative, as:—

Me ṭẖúhte	*It seemed to me.*
Hine hyngrade	*It hungered him.*

§ 452. Reflexive verbs govern the pronoun in the Accusative, as:—

Ic me reste	*I rest myself.*

NOTE 1.—Verbs having an active-intransitive sense are also found accompanied with the personal pronoun in an oblique case, but in the Dative, if not in the Old Ablative; as, "hí gewiton him," *they departed.*

NOTE 2.—Reflexive and impersonal verbs generally follow both the subject and the object.

§ 453. Verbs of *thanking, admonishing, etc.,* govern either the Dative or the Accusative of the person with the Genitive of the thing, as:—

Sceolde his Drihtne ṭḥancian ṭḥaes leánes	*Should thank his Lord for the favor.*
Mana ṭḥone ṭḥaes angyldes	*Admonish that one of the recompense.*

NOTE.—Under this rule may be classed some verbs having an impersonal nature; as, "mec hreóweth ṭḥaes," *it rueth me of that.*

§ 454. Verbs of *ordering, giving, doing, providing,* and the like, govern the Accusative with the Dative, as:—

Ṭḥás ṭḥing ic eow beóde	*These things I order you.*
Hwaet gifst ṭḥú me	*What givest thou me?*
Dó ge him ṭḥaet sylfe	*Do ye the same unto them.*

NOTE.—Sometimes the Old Ablative is found in the place of the Dative, indicating its general use at one time, when peculiarly required by the import of the verb.

§ 455. Verbs of *asking, teaching, etc.,* govern the Accusative both of the person and the thing, but when the question is made *concerning* the one or the other, or implies *a portion,* or *fragment* of any object, we find the Accusative with the Genitive, as:—

Hine axodon ṭḥá bígspell	*They asked of him parables.*
Ic ṭḥé maeg taecan other ṭḥing	*I can teach thee another thing.*
Ic thé axige his	*I ask thee about it.*
Heó hine axode hláfes	*She asked him for a piece of bread.*

§ 456. Verbs of *naming,* or *terming,* govern both the object and the appellation in the Accusative, as:—

God het ṭhá faestnisse heofenan	*God called the firmament heaven.*
Nemnde hine Drihten	*Termed him Lord.*

§ 457. Sometimes, however, we find the appellation in the Nominative, as:—

Ṭhá waés sum consul ṭhaet we *heretoha* hátath	*Then was there a certain consul that we call* heretoha.

§ 458. But "hátan" signifying *to be called,* or *named,* takes a Nominative both before and after it, as:—

Se hátte Lúcifer	*Who was called Lucifer.*

§ 459. A verb in the Infinitive is usually governed by another verb, but sometimes by an adjective, as:—

Hwaet sceal ic singan	*What shall,* or *ought I to sing?*
Eáthig laéran	*Easy to teach,* or *to be taught.*

§ 460. The Infinitive mood may be preceded by the Accusative, as:—

Swá ge geseóth me habban	*As ye see me have.*

§ 461. The gerund is always governed by the preposition TÓ which precedes it, as:—

Ic dó eow tó witanne	*I do you to wit.*

§ 462. Participles and gerunds have the same government as the verbs to which they belong, as:—

Cwethende ṭhaet ylce gebed	*Uttering the same prayer.*
Hearran tó habbanne	*A lord to have.*

§ 463. The Perfect participle of a verb which governs two cases, when united with a verb of existence, retains only the latter of them, as:—

Wǽs him nama sceapen	*A name was given him.*

§ 464. Adverbs qualify other words, and some of them may be defined by the article, as:—

Wíslice ic sprece	*I speak wisely.*
Tó micel	*Too much.*
Neáh fíf thúsenda wera	*Almost five thousand men.*
Swithe wel	*Very well.*
The laes	*The less.*
Thý má	*The more.*

§ 465. Two or more negatives strengthen the negation, as:—

Ne geseáh naefre nán mann God	*No man ever (never) saw (not) God.*

§ 466. Some adverbs govern the Genitive, and others the Dative, as:—

Forth nihtes	*Far in the night.*
Laes worda	*Less words.*
Nehst thǽre eaxe	*Nearest the axel.*

NOTE.—Adverbs are, for the most part, placed arbitrarily in the sentence, but "ne" always stands before the verb which it qualifies. Words compounded with this particle do not express a complete negation unless it is also added in its simple state, and occupies its proper position. When "ná" having the sense of *not*, is used in connection with it, the verb is placed between them. *Nor* and *not* are expressed by "ne ne" when one "ne" already precedes, or after "náther," *neither*, by only a single "ne" in each member.

§ 467. Prepositions govern different cases as specified in § 418. Thus:—

Tó-middes hyra	*In the midst of them.*
Of aelcum treowe	*Of every tree.*
Ṭḥurh me-sylfne	*By myself.*
Mid ṭḥý earme	*With the arm.*

Note 1.—"On," and some other prepositions governing the Dative or Ablative, and the Accusative, usually govern the latter when *motion to*, or *toward* is denoted, and the former, when *rest*, or *continuance* is signified.

Note 2. Sometimes, especially in phrases, we find the Accusative following "aet," "tó," and "on," when we would expect the Dative, or Ablative.

Note 3.—A preposition when compounded with a verb, may have the same government as in its ordinary construction in the sentence.

§ 468. Conjunctions connect sentences and parts of sentences, as well as words of the same kind, as:—

Ic eom wín-eard, and ge synd twigu	*I am a vine, and ye are branches.*
Gesceóp God heofenan and eorthan	*God created heaven and earth.*
Oth ṭḥone án and twentugothan daeg ṭḥaes ylcan monthes	*Until the one-and-twentieth day of the same month.*

§ 469. The conjunctions "gif," *if*, "ṭḥaet," *that*, "sám," *whether*, "ṭḥeáh," *though*, "swilce," *as if*, etc., are followed by the Subjunctive mood when any thing doubtful or contingent is implied, as:—

Gif he wille and cunne his dǽda andettan	*If he will and can confess his deeds.*
Hwaet dó ic ṭḥaet ic éce líf áge	*What shall I do that I may have eternal life?*
Sám hit monnum gód ṭḥince	*Whether it may seem good to men.*

§ 470. But when a simple declaration is made, the Indicative follows, as:—

Gif we secgath	*If we say.*

§ 471. The verbal conjunction "utan," "uton," "utun," *let us*, governs the Infinitive, as:—

Utan biddan God	*Let us beseech God.*
Uton gán heónon	*Let us go hence.*
Utun faran tó Bethleem	*Let us go to Bethlehem.*

§ 472. Some Interjections are followed by the Nominative, and others by the Dative case, as:—

Lá ṭḥú liccetere	*Oh thou hypocrite!*
Wá ṭḥám men	*Wo to the man!*
Wá eow, bóceras	*Wo unto you, scribes!*

§ 473. The Indefinite form of the adjective is used with common nouns, when the interjection is either expressed or understood, as:—

Eálá, leóf hláford	*Alas! dear lord.*
Awyrgede woruld-sorga	*Accursed worldly cares!*

§ 474. But with pronouns of the first and second persons, the Definite form usually occurs, as:—

Ic wrecca	*Wretched me!*
Ṭḥú stunta	*Foolish thou!*

PART IV.—PROSODY.

OF ANGLO-SAXON POETRY IN GENERAL.

§ 475. Anglo-Saxon poetry in its nature resembles the abrupt, nervous expressions of man in his uncultivated state. Its leading characteristic is periphrasis, which is always mingled with metaphor, and sometimes in great abundance, while artificial inversions of words and phrases are not uncommon. In its constitution, it is precisely such as we would expect to meet with in an age when bards sung the praises of heroes, taking up and arranging the epithets showered upon them by the applauding multitude, interspersed with any ideas that might occur to their own minds. And this feature appears as well when sacred subjects are the poet's theme as any others. The praises of the Deity and of the warrior chieftain are celebrated in like strains.[1]

[1] Upon this subject we quote the words of Mr. Wright, as contained in his *Biographia Britannica Literaria—Anglo-Saxon Period*, pp. 8, 9: "The Anglo-Saxon poetry," he observes, "has come down to us in its own native dress. In unskilful hands it sometimes became little more than alliterative prose; but as far as it is yet known to us, it never admitted any adventitious ornaments. Having been formed in a simple state of society, it admits, by its character, no great variety of style, but generally marches on in one continued strain of pomp and grandeur, to which the Anglo-Saxon language itself was in its perfect state peculiarly adapted. The principal characteristic of this poetry is an endless variety of epithet and metaphor, which are in general very expressive, although their beauty sometimes depends so much on

§ 476 The poetry of the Anglo-Saxons is of two kinds, *native* or *vernacular*, and *Latin*. The latter originated from the Roman, and follows the same laws. It is the construction of the former that requires a brief consideration in this place.

§ 477. The only rule which they appear to have observed in the composition of their native verses was that of pleasing the ear, and this they effected by combining their words into a rhythmical cadence. "'Rhythmus,' says Bede, 'is a modulated composition of words, not according to the laws of meter, but *adapted in the number of its syllables to the judgment of the ear*, as are *the verses of our vulgar* (or *native*) *poets*. Rhythm may exist without meter, but there cannot be meter without rhythm, which is thus more clearly defined.

"'Meter is an artificial rule with modulation: rhythmus is the modulation without the rule. Yet, for the most part, you may find, by a sort of chance, some rule in rhythm, but this is not from an artificial government of the syllables. It arises because the sound and the modulation lead to it. The vulgar poets effect this rustically: the skilful attain it by their skill.'"[1]

§ 478. This *rhythmus* "the skilful" produced by such a choice and arrangement of their words, not disregarding accent, that a proper modulation was maintained in giving utterance to any two or more corresponding lines in a

---

the feelings and manners of the people for whom they were made, that they appear to us rather fanciful. As, however, these poets drew their pictures from nature, the manner in which they apply their epithets, like the rich coloring of the painter, produces a brilliant and powerful impression on the mind. They are, moreover, exceedingly valuable to the modern reader, for they make him acquainted with the form, color, material, and every other attribute of the things which are mentioned."

[1] Sharon Turner—*Hist. of the Anglo-Saxons*, Vol. III, B. IX, Ch. I

poem, although one of them might contain fewer syllables, or even a less number of words themselves, than the other. But in general they were satisfied with a near approach to the proper cadence. The following examples will illustrate the principle. Thus, in a *Riddle* from the *Codex Exoniensis* :—

"Ic eom máre
Thonne thes middan-geard,
Laesse thonne land-wyrm,[1]
Leohtre thonne mona,
Swiftre thonne sunne ;
Saés me sind ealle,
Flódas, on faethmum,
And thás foldan bearm,
Gréne wongas.
Grundum ic hríne,
Helle under-hníge,
Heofonas ofer-stíge,
Wuldres éthel
Wíde raéce,
Ofer engla eard ;
Eorthan gefylle,
Ealne middan-geard,
And mére-streámas,
Síde mid me-sylfum.
Saga hwaet ic hátte."

I am greater
Than this middle region,
Less than an *earth-worm,*
Lighter than the *moon,*

---

[1] "Land-wyrm" we have substituted in the place of "hand-wyrm," which is evidently an error. In favor of the change compare the principle contained in § 479.

Swifter than the *sun;*
I have all the *seas,*
The *floods, in embrace,*
And this lap of earth,
The *green plains.*
The *abysses I touch,*
Under hell descend,
The *heavens mount over,*
The *clime of glory*
Widely compass,
Beyond the *abode of angels;*
The *earth* I *fill,*
All the *middle-region,*
And the *mere-streams,*
On all sides with myself.
Say what I am called.

Again, in the *Seafarer:—*

. . . . "Thǽr ic ne gehýrde
Butan hlimman sǽ,
Is-caldne waeg.
Hwílum ylfetes sang
Dyde ic me tó gámene,
Ganates hleothor,
And hú-ilpan sweg;
Fore hleahtor wera,
Mǽw singende;
Fore médo-drince,
Stormas thǽr stán-clifu beotan,
Thǽr him stearn oncwǽth,
Isig fethera" . . . . .

. . . . *Where I heard naught*
Save the *sea roaring,*
The *ice-cold wave.*

At times the *swan's song*[2]
Made I to me for pastime,
The *ganet's cry,*
And the '*hu-ilpe's*' *scream;*
In lieu of the *laughter of men,*
The *mew* was *singing;*
Instead of the joyousness of *mead-drinking,*
Storms there beat the *stone-cliffs,*
Where them the *starling answered,*
Icy of wings . . . . .

Also, in a *Poem on the Day of Judgment*:—

. . . . "Ṭḥá mec ongan hreówan,
Ṭḥaet mín hand-geweorc
On feónda geweald
Feran sceolde,
Man-cynnes tuddor
Mán-cwealm seón;
Sceolde uncuthne
Eard cunnian,
Sáre sithas.
Ṭḥá ic-sylf gestág,
Maga in modor,
Ṭḥeáh wǽs hyre maegden-hád
Aeghwaes onwalg.
Wearth ic ána geboren
Folcum tó frófre.
Mec man folmum bewand,
Beṭḥeáhte mid ṭḥearfan wǽdum,

[2] We have read "ylfetes" the Gen. for "ylfete," but retaining the word in the Nom., the construction would be,

At times the *swan sang;*
I made to me for pastime,
etc., *etc.*

And mec ṭḥá on ṭḥeostre alegde,
Bewundenne mid wonnum cláthum.
Hwaet, ic ṭḥaet for worulde geṭḥólade;
Lytel ṭḥúhte ic leóda bearnum;
Láeg on heardum stáne,
Cild geong on crybbe,
Mid-ṭḥý ic ṭḥó wolde cwealm afyrran,
Hat helle beálu;
Ṭḥaet ṭḥú móste hálig scínan,
Eádig on ṭḥám écan life,
For-ṭḥón ic ṭḥá earfothe wann."

. . . . *Then began* it *to rue me,*
That my hand-work
Into the *power of fiends*
Should go,
That the *offspring of mankind*
Sin-death should *see;*
Should an *unknown*
Dwelling prove,
Sore fortunes.
Then I my*self descended,*
A *son into* his *mother,*
Although her maidenhood was
In every thing inviolate.
I alone was born
For a *comfort to* the *nations.*
They with hands inwrapped me,
Covered me *with poor garments,*
And then in darkness laid me,
Wrapped about with dusky clothes.
Indeed, did I suffer that for the *world;*
Little seemed I to the *sons of men;*
I *lay on* a *hard stone,*
A *young child in* a *crib,*

Because I would put death afar from thee,
Hell's hot misery;
That thou mightest holy shine,
Blessed in the eternal life,
Therefore did I that hardship suffer.

In the last illustration we have an instance of the employment of long lines in regular series. Such were very often introduced by the poet when the dignity, or the importance of the subject required it. The practice will be exemplified more fully in the following lines from *Caedmon*:—

.... "Haefde se Eal-walda
Engel-cynna,
Ṭḥurh hand-maegen,
Hálig Drihten,
Tyne getrymede,
Tháem he getrúwode wel
Ṭḥaet híe his giongorscipe
Fyligan wolden,
Wyrcean his willan;
Forṭḥón he him gewit forgeáf,
And mid his handum gesceóp,
Hálig Drihten.
Gesette haefde he híe swá gesaeliglice,
Aenne haefde he swá swithne geworhtne,
Swá mihtigne on his mód-geṭḥóhte,
He let hine swá micles wealdan,
Hehstne tó him on heofona ríce.
Haefde he hine swá hwítne gewrhtne,
Swá wynlic wáes his waestm on heofonum,
Ṭḥaet him cóm from weroda Drihtne,
Gelíc wáes he ṭḥám leohtum steorrum.
Lóf sceolde he Drihtnes wyrcean,

Dyran sceolde he his dreámas on heofonum,
And sceolde his Drihtne thancian
Thaes leánes the he him on thám leohte gescérede;
Thónne lete he his hine lange wealdan:
Ac he awende hit him tó wyrsan thinge,
Ongan him winn up-ahebban,
With thone hehstan heofnes Wealdend,
The siteth on thám hálgan stóle" . . . . .

The All-powerful had
Angel-kinds,
Through might of *hand,*
The *holy Lord,*
Ten established,
In whom he trusted well
That they his service
Would follow,
Would *work his will;*
Therefore gave he them intellect,
And shaped them *with his hands,*
The *holy Lord.*
So happily had he placed them,
One had he made so powerful,
So mighty in his mental capacity,
He let him rule over so much,
*Highest after him*self *in* the *kingdom of* the *heavens.*
He had made him so fair,
So beauteous was his form in the *heavens,*
That came unto him from the *Lord of hosts,*
He was like unto the light stars.
The *praise of* the *Lord should he have wrought,*
Dear should he have held his joys in the *heavens,*
And should have thanked his Lord
For the favor which he had allotted him in that light;
Then would he have let him long have sway:

*But he turned it unto him*self *for* a *worse thing,*
Began to raise up war upon him,
Against the highest Ruler of heaven,
Who sitteth upon the holy throne . . . .

§ 479. *Alliteration,* or *alliterative rime,* though sometimes neglected, was a fundamental principle in Anglo-Saxon poetry. It consists, as will have been perceived, in the employment of three words beginning with the same letter, if a consonant, in two adjacent and connected lines of verse.[1] The most important alliterative letter, termed the *chief letter,* always stands in the second line, while the two others, which are called *assistants,* or *sub-letters,* occupy places in the first. In short lines, however, there usually occurs but one assistant, especially if the chief letter appears in such combination as *sc, st, sw,* and the like, through which a difficulty would not unfrequently be experienced in finding proper words to carry out the original principle in full.

In prefixed words, the alliterative letter is the one that comes after the prefix, if unemphatic;[2] and whenever the *chief letter* is a vowel, the *assistants* are also vowels, but not necessarily the same. The initial of an unemphatic particle is never considered, but such with all other words not receiving the emphasis or tone, constitute the *complement* of the verse, even when they may contain the alliterative letter. The reader must not expect, however, to find an alliteration in every case regularly constituted.

In the following selections, the first from *Caedmon,* and

---

[1] Not necessarily connected in sense, as in the Icelandic poetry. "Their separation in sense," says Prof. Rask, "seems rather to have been sought after, and regarded as a kind of *caesura.*" Sometimes we find this *caesura* at a paragraphical division of the subject.

[2] ge-, be-, a-, and the like, which never receiving the tone, are not considered in the alliteration.

the second from the *Menologium Saxonicum*, of which it forms the conclusion, we have italicized the alliterative letters:—

1.

. . . . "Ne wǽs *h*ér ṭẉá-gyt,
Nymṭẉe *h*eolster-sceado,
*W*iht ge*w*orden;
Ac ṭẉes *w*ída grund
Stód *d*eóp and *d*im,
*D*rihtne fremde,
*I*del and *u*nnýt;
On ṭẉám *e*águm wlát
*St*ith-frith Cyning,
And ṭẉá *st*owe beheold
*D*reáma leáse;
Geseáh *d*eorc gesweorc
*S*emian *s*innihte,
*S*weart under roderum,
*W*ann and *w*éste,
Oth-ṭẉaet ṭẉeós *w*oruld-gesceaft
Ṭẉurh *w*ord ge*w*earth
*W*uldor-cyninges" . . . .

There *had not here as yet,*
Save cavern-shade,
Aught been;
But this wide abyss
Stood deep and dim,
Unto the *Lord strange,*
Empty and useless;
On which with his *eyes looked*
The *firm-souled King,*
And beheld the place
Void of joys;

Saw a *dark cloud*
Lower with perpetual night,
Swart under the *skies,*
Wan and waste,
Until this worldly creation
Through the *word existed*
Of the *King* of *Glory.*

2.

. . . . "Meotod ána wát
Hwyder seó *s*awul *s*ceal
*S*yththan hweorfan;[3]
And ealle ṭḥá *g*ástas,
Ṭḥe for *G*ode hweorfath[4]
Aefter *d*eath-*d*aege,
*D*ómas bídath.
On *F*aeder *f*aethme
Is seó *f*orth-gesceaft
*D*igol and *d*yrne;
*D*rihten ána wat,
*N*ergende Faeder.
*N*ǽnig eft cymeth
*H*ider under *h*rófas,
Ṭḥe ṭḥaet *h*ér for sóth
*M*annum secge,

---

[3] It is possible that the alliterative letters in these two lines may be the compound *hw*, (§ 1, Note 6,) contained in "hwyder" and "hweorfan."

[4] As the *e* in "ealle" may have had the sound of *y* given it in the enunciation of this line, a sound to which the Saxon *g* approximated in certain connections, (§ 1, Notes 3 and 5,) it would form a *quasi* alliteration with this letter in "gástas" and "Gode." We also not unfrequently find *c* and *g* in alliteration with each other, from the relationship of the two letters in their original sounds. In this case, we might write "ge-alle," (§ 107, Note 2.)

Hwylc sý *M*eotodes gesceaft,
*S*ige-folca geseta,
Thǽr he *s*ylfa wunath."

The *Creator alone knoweth*
Whither the soul shall
Afterwards depart;
And all the spirits,
Who for God depart[5]
After the *death-day,*
Their *dooms await.*
In the *bosom of* the *Father*
Is the future state
Hidden and concealed;
The *Lord alone knoweth* it,
The *preserving Father.*
No one again cometh
Hither under our *roofs,*
Who that here in sooth
Unto men may say,
What is the *Creator's condition,*
The *seats of* the *victor-people,*
Where he him*self dwelleth.*[6]

---

[5] Mr. Thorpe renders this line, "That wander *before* God," taking "for" for "fóre." But the meaning which we have assigned the word as it stands, is one preserved in the same preposition in English.

[6] Alliteration was not confined to one or more of the ancient Teutonic tongues, but is found to have been a principle pervading all of them, so far as specimens of poetry in the different dialects of the family have come down to us. It will be perceived in the following extracts from the Old-Saxon *Harmonia Evangelica,* as quoted by Rask, who drew the first from *Hickes,* and the second from *Docen,* the latter being derived from the *Bamberg* MS., and the former from one in the *Cottonian Library.* Thus in Peter's Confession:—

§ 480. *Line-rime* and *final-rime* are both met with in Anglo-Saxon poetry, and although not to any great extent,

---

... "Thú bíst thie *w*aro (quat Pétrus)	*Thou art the true (quoth Peter)*
*W*aldendes suno,	*Son of* the *ruling* One,
*L*ibbiandes Godes,	*Of* the *living God,*
The thit *l*joht giscóp,	*Who this light created,*
*C*ríst *C*uning éwig;	*Christ* the *eternal King;*
So welliat wi *q*uethan alla,	*So will we all say,*
Jungron *th*ína,	*Thy disciples,*
That *th*ú sis God selbo"...	*That thou art God* him*self*. ..

And in Christ's reply to his disciples, upon their inquiry, *When shall these things be?* alluding to his coming in judgment to the Jewish nation, commonly supposed to have reference also to a winding up of the affairs of this world :—

...."That habad so bi*d*ernid (qvad he)	*That hath so hidden (quoth he)*
*D*rohtin the Gódo,	The *Lord the Good,*
Jac so *h*ardo far*h*olen,	*And so firmly concealed,*
*H*imiríkjes Fader,	The *Father of* the *heavenly kingdom,*
*W*aldand thesaro *w*eroldes,	The *Ruler of this world,*
So that *w*iten ni mag	*As that to know is not able*
Enig *m*annisc barn,	*Any human child,*
Hván thjú *m*arje tíd	*When the eventful time*
Ge*w*irdid an thesaru *w*eroldi:	*Shall come upon this world:*
Ne it ok te *w*aran ni kunnun	*Yea, nor it for certain know*
*G*odes engilos;	*God's angels;*
Thie fór imu ge*g*inwarde	*Though* they *present before him*
*S*imlun *s*indun,	*Always are,*
Sie it ok giseggian ni mugun"....	*They cannot indeed say it ....*

We also find it obtaining in Britain after the Anglo-Saxon period, and disappearing only upon the general cultivation of final rime as a feature of poetic harmony. Thus in the following selections made by the same author, the first from a poem belonging to the transition state of the language, of which this with other fragments will be found in *Hickes*, and the second from Robert Langland's *Vision of Peirce Plowman*, A. D. 1350 :—

still in instances enough to show that they were known and cultivated from the earliest times, especially as some

---

1.

38 "He (God) *w*ot[1] hwet thenceth and hwet dóth
Alle quike *w*ihte,
Nis no louerd swich is *C*ríst,
Ne no *k*ing swich is Drihte.
39 *H*euene and erthe and all that is,
Biloken is on his *h*onde,
He déth *a*ll thaet his wille is,
On seá and *é*c on londe.
40 He *w*iteth and *w*ialdeth alle thing,
He is*c*óp alle *s*ceafte,
He wróhte *f*isc on thér sáe
And *f*ogeles on thár lefte.
41 He is *ó*rd abúten *ó*rde,
And *e*nde abúten *e*nde;
He is *a*fre on *e*che stéde,
*W*ende (thé) wér thú *w*ende."[2]

2.

"I *l*ooked on my *l*eft halfe[3]
As the *l*ady me taught,
And was *w*are of a *w*oman
*W*orthlyith clothed;
Pur*f*iled with pelure,
The *f*inest upon erthe,
*C*rowned with a *c*rowne
The *k*ing hath no better;

1 "Wot," *Anglo-Saxon* "wat;" "wihte"—"wihta," plur. of "wiht;" "quike"—"cwice;" "louerd"—"hláford;" "swich"—"swilc;" "Drihte" —"Drihten;" "heuene"—"heofon;" "erthe"—"eorthe;" "biloken"—"belocen," or "bilocen;" "honde"—"handa," or "honda;" "wialdeth"—"wealdeth;" "iscóp"—"gescóp;" "sceafte"—"sceafta," or "gesceafta;" "thér" and "thár"—"tháere;" "fogeles"—"fugelas," or "fuglas;" "lefte" —"lyfte;" "afre"—"aefre;" "eche"—"aelcere;" "wér"—"hwáer."

2 But see Hickes's *Thesaurus*, 3 vols., London, 1705, and Docen's *Miscellaneen*, 2 vols., Munich, 1809.

3 "Halfe," *A. S.* "healfe," the Dat.; "worthlyith," for "worthily;" "purfiled," from the *Norman-French, bordered;* "pelure," ("*f*elure," i. e. "veloure,' *velvet*" (?)) from *Id.*, "*furs;*" "fetislich," *Norman-Saxon, handsomely;* "glede, *A. S.* "gléd."

of the specimens which have reached us, appear to be very ancient. Of *final-rime* it is unnecessary here to speak. *Line-rime* takes place when two syllables in the same line of verse have their vowels alike, and likewise the consonants which follow them, forming in that case *perfect rime*, but *imperfect rime*, when the consonants being alike, the vowels are unlike. The following selections from the *Riming Poem* in the *Codex Exoniensis*, will illustrate the two sorts of verse with both peculiarities of the latter species:—

. . . . "Scealcas wǽron scearpe,
Scyl[1] wǽs hearpe;
Hlúde hlynede,
Hleothor dynede;
Swegl-rád swinsade,
Swithe ne minsade;
Burg-séle beofode,
Beorht hlifade;[2]
Ellen eácnade,
Eád beácnade;

---

*F*etislich her *f*ingers
Were *f*retted with gold wiers,
And thereon *r*ed *r*ubies,
As *r*ed as any glede,
And *d*iamonds of *d*earest price,
And *d*ouble maner saphirs" . . . .

In the former piece, the alliteration is not complete, the deficiency in that respect being probably made up in the poet's mind by the partial rime. The latter cannot be charged with the same fault, and would not have been unpleasing to the ear of a '*Scóp*' *Laureate.*

[1] As *Scyl* would appear to have been the father of *Scilling* mentioned in the *Scóp's Excursion*, (*v. Anal. Anglo-Sax.*, Vol. II., Art. XXI., l. 205,) the antiquity of this poem may be readily surmised.

[2] Perhaps a form "hleofode" belongs here in the place of "hlifade." The completeness of the alliteration in this extract will be observed.

Freáum fródade,
Frómum gódade;
Mód maegnade,
Míne faegnade;
Treow telgade
Tír welgade" . . . .

My *attendants were skilful,*
Scyl was my *harper;*
Loudly he *sounded,*
The *tone re-echoed;*
The *plectrum*[3] *modulated,*
Nor much did it *lessen* the vibration;
The *castle-hall trembled,*
Bright towered it.
Valor increased,
Happiness beckoned;
I *counseled lords,*
To the *brave was bounteous;*
I *strengthened* my *mind,*
Rejoiced my subjects;
My *tree branched,*
My *glory waxed abundant* . . . .

2.

. . . . "Fláh máh flíteth,
Flán man hwíteth;
Burg sorg bíteth,
Bald ald ṭḥwíteth"[4] . . . .

---

[3] We have adopted Mr. Thorpe's rendering of "swegl-rád."

[4] Mr. Wright alluding to this poem, (*Biographia Britannica Literaria—Anglo-Saxon Period,* p. 80,) says: "The whole of these verses are extremely obscure and difficult to understand, a proof that rhime was a great trial of the ingenuity of the writer, and by no means congenial to the language." But we think that rime was less prac-

Among other lines the most of which are difficult of translation.

Sometimes another species of *line-rime* is met with, as in the following verses from a *Riddle* which we have introduced in the *Analecta Anglo-Saxonica*:—

. . . . " Corfen sworfen,
Cyrred thyrred,
Bunden wunden,
Bláeced wáeced,
Fraetwed geatwed,
Feorran laeded" . . . .

. . . . *Cut* and *swathed,*
Turned and *dried,*
Bound and *twisted,*
Bleached and *'wakened,*
Decked and *poured out,*
Carried from far . . . .

§ 481. All the poetry of the Anglo-Saxons may be arranged under three heads, *songs* or *ballads, narrative poems* or *romances,* and *lyrics.* By the last term we must understand their productions of a miscellaneous kind. Only a few specimens of their ballads and romances in the vernacular language have come down to us.[1]

tised by the Anglo-Saxons, because alliteration being an essential characteristic of their poetry, it was exceedingly difficult to unite both features in the choice of words, and at the same time to give a proper expression to sentiment, as well as introduce any requisite ideas. To have done both to any extent would have required a copiousness which very few, if any, languages possess. We may readily conceive the difficulty, not to say the almost utter impracticability, of even complete alliteration with certain letters in particular combinations, except in rare instances.

[1] See *Analecta Anglo-Saxonica,* Vol. II., in which specimens of the vernacular poetry will be found in full.

A LIST OF ANGLO-SAXON PHRASES.

THE following phrases, which comprise the most of those in common use not already given, or expressed differently, under other heads, are written as they are generally found in Anglo-Saxon MSS. Some of them, as will be perceived, are adverbial and conjunctional, and others prepositional. The syntactical order of each member in any case will be observed.

A forth, *ever forth, from thence, evermore.*

A of tide, *on a sudden, forthwith.*

A tó aldre, *forever and ever.*

A world, *forever,* lit. *world always.*

A ṭḥý bet, *ever the better.*

A ṭḥý má, *ever the more.*

Aefre tó aldre, *forever and ever.*

Aefterran sithe, *secondly.*

Aefter burgum, *openly, publicly,* lit. *through cities.*

Aefter faece, *after a space, afterward.*

Aefter rihte, *according to right, rightly, justly.*

Aefter ṭḥám ṭḥe, aefter ṭḥón ṭḥe, *after that, after, afterward.*

Aeghwilce wísan, *in every manner, all manner of ways.*

Aegṭḥer ge heónan ge ṭḥánan, *both here and there, on this side and that.*

Aelce healfe, aelce wise, *in all ways,* or *in every manner.*

Aelces cynnes, *of each sort,* or *of all sorts.*

Aer ṭḥe, áer ṭḥám ṭḥe, áer ṭḥám ṭḥaet, *before that, ere that, before.*

Aerest sona, áerest ṭḥinga, aet áerestan, *at first, first of all.*

Aet fruman, *in the beginning.*

Aet handa, *at hand.*

Aet hwega, aet hwegu, *somewhat, about, in some measure.*

Aet neáhestan, aet nyhstan, *at last.*

Aet rihtost, *by-and-by, presently.*

Aet sithestan, aet sithemestan, *at length, at last.*

Agenes ṭḥances, *of his own accord, freely.*

Ahwónan útan, *anywhere without, outwardly, extrinsically.*

An eágan beorht, *in the glance of an eye, in a twinkling.*

And gehú elles, *and the like.*

And swá forth, *and so forth.*

Anes hwaet, *at all, in any degree, anything, anywhat.*

Awa tó aldre, *forever and ever.*

Bé ánfealdum, *singly.*

Bé dáele, *in part, partly.*

Bé hwón, *whence.*

Bé swilcum and bé swilcum, *by such means and the like.*

Bé twífealdon, *doubly.*

Bé ṭḥám máestan, *at the most.*

Be ṭḥám ṭḥe, *as, according as.*

Betwýh ṭḥás ṭḥing, *between these things, in the mean while, whilst.*

Bí ṭḥisse wísan, *for this cause, hence, therefore.*

Eác swá, eác swilce, *so also, also, moreover, very like, even so.*

Eall swá oft, *so often, quite so oft.*

Eall swá micles, *for so much, at that price.*

Ealle aetsomne, *in like manner, at once, altogether.*

Ealle gemete, eallum gemetum, *by all means, altogether.*

Ealle wáega, *of all, fully, altogether, in all ways.*

Ealne wég, *always.*

Eást inne, *in the east.*
Eást rihte, *due east, towards the east.*
Eáthe maeg, *easily can, perhaps, it is possible.*
Eft sona, efter sona, *soon after, soon.*
Eft syththan, *after that, furthermore.*
Eft ṭḥá ymbe lytel, *after a little then.*
Elles hwǽr, *elsewhere.*
Elles mǽst, *chiefly.*
Elles ofer, *from some other place.*
Emne swá, *equally so, even so.*

For hwaega, *at least.*
For hwám, for hwón, for hwí, *wherefore, why.*
For sóth, *forsooth, truly, certainly.*
For ṭḥǽre wísan, *for that reason, wherefore.*
For ṭḥearle, *very much, exceedingly.*
For ṭḥón ṭḥe, *because.*
For ṭḥý, *for that, wherefore.*
For ṭḥý ṭḥe, *for that which, since, because.*
For ṭḥysse wísan, *for this cause, hence, therefore.*
Fóran ongean, *opposite.*
Forth daeges, *far in the day.*
Forth nihtes, *far in the night.*

Gemang ṭḥám, *in the mean time, meanwhile.*
Geneáh ge feor, *both far and near.*
Geó ǽer, geó geára, geó dagum, geó hwílum, *heretofore, long ago.*
Gyt beheónan, git behiónan, *yet nearer.*

Hidres ṭḥidres, *hither and thither.*
Hú geáres, *however.*
Hú hugu, hú hwego, *about, almost, nearly.*
Hú ne, *not, whether or not.*
Hugu dǽl, *a little, but a little, at least.*

Huru ṭḥinga, *at least, at all events, yet, only, indeed, especially.*

Hwaene áer, hwone áer, *a little before, just before.*

Hwaene laes, *a little less.*

Hwaet hugu, *somewhat, almost, nearly.*

Hwaet hwaega, hwaet hwega, hwaet hweg, hwaet hwugu, hwaet hwygu, *about, a little, somewhat.*

Hwaet hwára, *somewhere.*

Hwaet lytles, *some little, somewhat.*

Hwaet ṭḥá, *wherefore then, what then, but.*

Hwider wéga, *somewhere.*

Hwílon áer, *sometime before.*

Hwílon án, hwílon twá, *now one, now two.*

Hwylce hugu, *how little, as little as.*

Hyder geond, *yonder.*

In aldre, *forever.*

In stéde, *in the place, instead.*

Litlum and litlum, *by little and little.*

Má ṭḥe, *more than.*

Máest ealle, *almost all, almost wholly,* or *entirely.*

Micle má, *much more.*

Mid áer daege, *at the early day,* or *first dawn.*

Mid ealle, *with all, altogether, entirely.*

Mid rihte, *with justice, rightly, really.*

Mid ṭḥám ṭḥe, mid ṭḥón ṭḥe, mid ṭḥón, *with that, while, when, whereas, inasmuch as, forasmuch as, seeing that.*

Mid ṭḥý, mid ṭḥý ṭḥá, mid ṭḥý ṭḥe, *when, whilst, thereupon, as soon as, after that, when therefore.*

Ná elles, ná hú elles, *not otherwise.*

Ná hwónan útane, *nowhere without.*

Ná ṭḥe laes, nó ṭḥý laes, *nevertheless.*

Naénige gemete, *in no wise, by no means.*

Naénige ṭḥinga, *not at all,* lit. *in no one of things.*

Naes ná, naes ne, *neither.*

Náte ṭḥaes hwón, *or contracted,* nátes-hwón, nátes-tó-hwí, *by no means, not at all.*

Ne on aldre, *never at all.*

Neáh and efene, *almost, well-nigh.*

Neán and feorran, *from far and near.*

Nese, nese, *no, no, by no means.*

Nóhtes hwón, *without doubt.*

Nó wiht elles, *nothing else.*

Nú gyt, *hitherto, as yet.*

Nú hwaene aér, *just now, a little while before.*

Nú hwónne, *now and then, sometimes.*

Nú nú, *now now, immediately, right off.*

Nú rihte, *straightway.*

Nú tó morgen, *by to-morrow.*

Nú ṭḥá, *just now, now then.*

Of ansýne tó ansýne, *face to face.*

Of dúne, *down, downward,* lit. *from the mountain.*

Of hwylcere wísan, *from which cause, whence.*

On aefteweard, *behind.*

On aegṭḥere hand, on aegṭḥere healfe, *on either hand, on either half,* or *side, on both sides.*

On aegṭḥre healfe weard, *toward both sides.*

On aelcere tíde, *at all times.*

On aér daege, *at the first dawn.*

On aéron, on aéran, on aér daegum, *formerly.*

On aewiscnesse, *openly,* (as not being ashamed to be seen.)

On án, *in one, continually.*

On baec, *behind, afterward.*

On daeg, *in the day, by day, day by day.*

On diglum, *in secret.*

On écnysse, *forever.*

On ell-ṭḥeóde, on ell-ṭḥeódignesse, on ael-ṭḥeóde, on ael-ṭḥeódignesse, *abroad, in foreign parts, from abroad, from afar.*

On emn, *opposite, over-against.*

On eorneste, on eornust, *in earnest.*

On fóre-weard, *forward.*

On fruman, *in the beginning.*

On gemang ṭḥám, *in the mean time, then.*

On hóh, *behind*, lit. *on*, or *at the heel.*

On hwón, *how little.*

On hlote, on hlyte, *by lot, freely.*

On ídel, *in vain.*

On lande, *in the country.*

On láste, *at last, at length, finally, after, behind.*

On morgen, *in the morning, early.*

On othre wísan, *in another manner, otherwise.*

On sundron, on sundran, *in a separate body, separately, apart, asunder.*

On symbol, *at all times.*

On ṭḥanc, on ṭḥonce, *with gratitude, gratefully, thankfully, gratis, freely.*

On ṭḥón ṭḥaet, *for the reason that.*

On uppan, *against.*

Oth on, *even unto, as far as.*

Oth ṭḥaes, *until this, hitherto.*

Oth ṭḥaet, *until that, until, thitherto.*

Othre hwíle, *sometimes.*

Oththe furthum, *or further, also, moreover*

Oththe hwíle, *until*, lit. *or awhile.*

Oththe ṭḥis, *even until now*, lit. *or this.*

Sáme ylce swá, *in such wise as, so as.*

Seldon hwónne, *seldom when, seldom.*

Sona aefter, *soon after, again.*

Sona hrathe, *immediately, right off.*

Sona instaepe, *at once*, lit. *in the very step*, or *place.*

Sona swá, sona ṭhaes ṭhe, *immediately.*

Sume dǽle, *in some part*, or *measure, partly, partially.*

Swá efne, *even so.*

Swá forth oththe, *thenceforth, until.*

Swá gerade, *in such manner.*

Swá hwǽer-swá, *wheresoever, wherever.*

Swá hwider swá, *whithersoever.*

Swá leng, *the longer.*

Swá micle swithor, swá mycle má, *so much the more.*

Swá sáme, *likewise, also.*

Swá sáme swá, *the same as, as, even as.*

Swá swithe, *so long as, in the mean time.*

Swá swithor . . . . swá swithor, *the more . . . . the more.*

Swá swithost, *as best.*

Swá ṭhearle, *very exceeding*, or *exceedingly, as much as vossible.*

Swilce swilce, *such as;* swilce . . . . swilce, *such . . . . as.*

Ṭhá . . . . ṭhá, *then . . . . when, when . . . . then.*

Ṭhá gyt, *as yet, moreover.*

Ṭhá hwíle, ṭhá hwíle ṭhe, *the while that, the while, while.*

Ṭhá sona, *as soon, immediately.*

Ṭhá sona ṭhá, *as soon as.*

Ṭhá swithor, *the rather.*

Ṭhǽer ṭhǽer, *there where, where;* ṭhǽer . . . . ṭhǽer, *where . . . there, there . . . . where.*

Ṭhǽer of, *thereof.*

Ṭhǽer on, *thereon.*

Ṭhǽer rihte, *directly there, instantly, immediately, just.*

Ṭhǽer tó, *thereto.*

Ṭhaes longa ṭhaes, *the time*, or *period that.*

Ṭhaes ṭhe, *since that, after, for that, because that, that.*

Ṭhaes ṭhe má, *or* máre, *so much the more.*

Ṭḥaet is ǽerost, *that is first, in the first place.*
Ṭḥám mycle má, *by so much the more.*
Ṭḥe laes hwǽnne, *lest at any time.*
Ṭḥe má ṭḥe, *the more than.*
Ṭḥeáh gita, *as yet, hitherto.*
Ṭḥeáh hwaethere, *yet nevertheless, moreover, but yet, but.*
Ṭḥeáh ṭḥe, *although.*
Ṭḥónan ṭḥe .... ṭḥónan, *whence .... thence.*
Ṭḥurh syndrige dagas, *one day after another, day by day,* lit. *through sundry days.*
Tó ánum tó ánum, *from one to another, only.*
Tó bóte, *to boot, with advantage, besides, moreover.*
Tó daeg, *to-day.*
Tó eáçan, *besides, moreover.*
Tó emnes, *opposite to, opposite, over against.*
Tó hwón, *how little.*
Tó morgen, *to-morrow.*
Tó niht, *to-night.*
Tó ṭḥám, *for that reason, therefore.*
Tó ṭḥám ǽer daege, *just before day.*
Tó ṭḥám ánum, *for this end, only.*
Tó ṭḥám swithe, *so that, so far, to that degree.*
Tó ṭḥám ṭḥaet, *to the end that, furthermore.*
Tó ṭḥaes ṭḥe, *to such an extent.*
Tó ṭḥance, tó ṭḥonce, *thankfully, gratis.*
Tó ṭḥón, *so.*
Tó ṭḥón ṭḥaet, tó ṭḥý ṭḥaet, *to the end that.*
Tó ṭḥý, tó ṭḥí, *for that cause.*

Under baec, *behind, backward.*
Under lyfte, *in the open air.*

Wel hwǽr, wel gehwǽr, *for the most part, everywhere.*

Ymbe lytel, *after a little.*

POSTSCRIPT.

Many of the various forms of words which are continually met with in the monuments of the Anglo-Saxon language, must be attributed not so much to uncertainty of orthography on the part of writers as to dialectic differences, dating not from the emigration to Britain, but from earlier periods in the history of the peoples composing the confederacy, while many of them, indeed, can be referred to other divisions of the common family. This is a consideration of some importance, and should be borne in mind by every student. It is a feature which appears in the earlier monuments of the Greek, Latin, and other languages, and in the case of the two specified, would be exhibited to a much greater extent, if the pens of ancient copyists had not reduced diversity in the majority of instances to uniformity, or if the plastic power of the rhapsodist had not often molded the antique into the contemporary. For an example of such commingling of dialectic variations in Greek, the Homeric poems will readily suggest themselves to the mind of every one conversant with that tongue.

The diversity to which we have reference will be found to obtain not only in initial, or medial forms, as different modifications of the same root, which time and accident bring about, either singly or through conjoint operation, but also in what, in all the Indo-Germanic languages, constitutes the peculiar grammatical features of words, the inflections as denoted by terminations.

Without doubt, many of the forms which inflected words in Anglo-Saxon present in their terminations, are archaic, but others evidently owe their origin to a difference of dialect, it being almost impossible in many cases, except through strict comparison, to ascertain the real nature of the form in question.

Omitting to say any thing about variations which are merely orthographical, of which examples have been given in full,[1] we will refer to a few inflections and other peculiarities to be met with, not strictly and undoubtedly archaic, but perhaps owing their origin to earlier sectional and other influences within the Teutonic range in general.

1. The termination -ys for -es in the Gen. of the 1st declension.

2. That of -a for -e in the Dat. and Abl. of the same, as obtaining in a few words.

3. That of -a for -an in the same cases, especially of the 2d declension, but also found in all the others having the same termination, and obtaining as well in the definite state of adjectives as in nouns.

4. That of -ana for -ena in the Gen. plural of the same. The former, indeed, appears to be the more analogical termination.

5. That of -a for -e in the Dat. and Abl. of the 3d declension. It is possible, however, that this termination, which is also found in the Gen. of some words, is one belonging to a declension lost from the language. Such would appear to be the case, as it is the peculiar feature of many adverbs which are evidently Ablatives of nouns,

[1] We will not forbear noticing, however, the varied use of the *edh* (ð) for the *the*, (þ,) and *vice versa*, undoubtedly assignable to the same causes as for diversity of orthography, and antecedently, of pronunciation in general. Hence also the interchange of other letters, both vowels and consonants. We do not deny that many such originated among the distinct settlements in Britain.

now only met with as falling under that division of grammar, and the generality of the feature in question is one savoring strongly of archaism.

6. That of -u, especially in the Acc. of the same, and of -o mostly, in the other cases singular, as well as of both and of -e, for -a in the Nom. and Acc. plural.

7. That of -en, and perhaps of -un, for -um, and the archaisms -on and -an, in the Dat. and Abl. plural.

8. The inflection of the same noun in some instances according to two different declensions, and not unfrequently, the omission of a termination distinguishing the Nom. from the independent form of the word, applicable also to adjectives.

9. The difference of gender for the same noun, giving rise to a difference of declension, or *vice versa.*

10. The diversity which is met with for pronouns, especially in the oblique cases of those of a personal nature, when the forms are not strictly archaic.

11. The diversity obtaining generally for the terminations which enter into the composition of words belonging to the different parts of speech, as well as the various phases which the prefixes assume.

12. The use of -en, -a, and -e, for -an, in the Inf. of verbs.

13. The termination -a for -ige in the 1st Pers. sing. of verbs belonging to the 1st Conj., 1st Cl., and that of -o or -u in others.

14. That of -s for -st, in the 2d Pers. sing., and those of -as, -es, and -s, in the 3d, while all the persons of the plural end in -ias, or -as, instead of -iath and -ath. Hence also the use of -ias and -as for -ige and -e, in the 2d Pers. plur. of the Imperative.

15. That of -en, and perhaps also those of -un and -an for -on.

16. That of -enne for -anne in many cases in the Gerund,

not to speak of the different forms which the endings of perfect participles assume, and which belong to those of terminations in general. We might also mention here the termination -ende of indefinite participles for the more analogical one -ande, and hence -end for -and in nouns.[2]

17. The diversity which obtains in the syntax of the language, and which in a corresponding and analogical measure will be found in all the Indo-Germanic group, like effects from like causes operating in the ante-literary period of each one.

---

[2] Many of these peculiarities have been called *Northumbrian*, but although they prevailed to a greater extent in the northern part of the island, as they are found also in some of the southern Germanic dialects, the evidence is clear that they did not originate in Britain. The Danish invasions setting mostly in that direction, *disturbed* rather than *changed* the language of the native population, although leading to a marked difference of speech in the following ages.

APPENDIX A.

"ON THE ALPHABET OF THE ANGLO-SAXONS."

"It has been much doubted whether the Anglo-Saxons had the use of *letters* when they possessed themselves of England. It is certain that no specimen of any Saxon writing, anterior to their conversion to Christianity, can be produced. It cannot, therefore, be proved that they had letters by any direct evidence, and yet some reasons may be stated which make it not altogether safe to assert too positively, that our ancestors were ignorant of the art of writing in their pagan state.

"1st. Alphabetical characters were used by the Northern nations on the Baltic before they received Christianity,[1] and the origin of these is ascribed to Odin, who heads the genealogies of the ancient Saxon chieftains as well as those of Sweden, Norway, and Denmark: and who is stated to have settled in Saxony before he advanced to the North. Either the pagan Saxons were acquainted with the Runic characters, or they were introduced in the North after the fifth century, when the Saxons came to Britain, and before the middle of the sixth, when they are mentioned by Fortunatus, which is contrary to the history and traditions of the Scandinavian nations, and to probability. We may remark,

[1] "I would not attribute to the Runic letters an extravagant antiquity, but the inscriptions on rocks, etc., copied by Wormius, in his *Literaturæ Runicæ*, and by Stephanius, in his notes on *Saxo*, proved that the Northerns used them before they received Christianity."

that 'rún'* is used in Anglo-Saxon[2] as 'rúnar' in the Icelandic, to express *letters* or *characters*. It is true that Odin used the 'rúnar' for the purpose of magic, and that in Saxon 'rún-craeftig,' *skilled in runæ*, signifies *a magician*;[3] but the magical application of characters is no argument against their alphabetical nature, because many of the foolish charms which our ancestors and other nations have respected, have consisted, not merely of alphabetical characters, but even of words.[4]

"2d. The passage of Venantius Fortunatus, written in the middle of the sixth century, attests that the Runic was used for the purpose of writing in his time. He says:—

> The barbarous Runæ is painted on ashen tablets,
> And what the papyrus says, a smooth rod effects.

"Now as the Anglo-Saxons were not inferior in civilization to any of the barbarous nations of the North, it cannot

---

* In this and the following extracts, we have taken the liberty of quoting all foreign words, and of italicizing their meanings in English, as in the body of our work. We have also accented Saxon words introduced by Mr. Turner, when requiring the accent, as well as corrected his orthography of the same in some few instances.—*K.*

[2] "So Cedmon uses the word, 'rún bíth gerecenod,' p. 73; 'hwaet seó rún bude,' p. 86; that he to him the letters should read and explain, 'hwaet seó rún bude,' p. 99; he had before said, in his account of Daniel and Belshazzar, that the angel of the Lord 'wrát thá in wage worda gerýnu, baswe bóc-stafas,' p. 90."

[3] "Thus Cedmon says, 'the 'rún-craeftige' men could not read the handwriting till Daniel came,' p. 90."

[4] "One passage in a Saxon MS. confirms this idea: 'Then asked the 'ealdorman' the 'heftling,' whether through 'drý-craeft,' or through 'rýn-stafas,' he had broken his bonds; and he answered that he knew nothing of this *craft*.' *Vesp.* D. 14, p. 132. Now 'rýn-stafas' means literally *ryn-letters*. We may remark that the Welsh word for *alphabet* is 'coel bren,' which literally means *the tree* or *wood of Omen*; and see the Saxon description of the Northern Runæ, in Hickes's *Gram. Ang. Sax.*, p. 135."

be easily supposed that they were ignorant of Runic characters,[5] if their neighbors used them.

"3d. Though it cannot be doubted that the letters of our Saxon MSS., written after their conversion, are of Roman origin, except only two, ꝥ, and ƿ, the '*thorn*' and the '*wen*,' yet these two characters are all allowed by the best critics to be of Runic parentage; and if this be true, it will show that the Anglo-Saxons were acquainted with Runic as well as with Roman characters when they commenced the handwriting that prevails in their MSS.

"4th. If the Saxons had derived the use of letters from the Roman ecclesiastics, it is probable that they would have taken from the Latin language the words they used to express them. Other nations so indebted, have done this. To instance from the Erse language:—

For *book*, they have	leabhar, from	liber.
letter	liter[6]	litera.
to write	scriobham	scribere.
	grafam	γραφω.
writing	scriobhadh	scriptura.
to read	leagham	legere.
	leabham	

But nations who had known letters before they became acquainted with Roman literature, would have indigenous terms to express them.

"The Saxons have such terms. The most common word by which the Anglo-Saxons denoted *alphabetical*

---

[5] "There are various alphabets of the Runæ, but their differences are not very great. I consider those characters to be most interesting which have been taken from the ancient inscriptions remaining in the North. Wormius gives these, *Lit. Run.*, p. 58. Hickes, in his *Gram. Anglo-Isl.*, c. 1, gives several Runic alphabets."

[6] "In the Erse Testament, *Greek letters* are expressed by 'litrichibh Greigis.' Luke xxiii. 38."

letters was 'staef;' plural 'stafas,'—Elfric, in his Saxon Grammar, so uses it. The copy of the Saxon coronation oath begins with, 'This writing is written, 'staef bé staefe' (*letter by letter*) from that writing which Dunstan, archbishop, gave to our lord at Kingston.' In the same sense the word is used in Alfred's translation of Bede, and in the Saxon Gospels. It is curious to find the same word so applied in the Runic mythology. In the *Vafprúthnis-mál*, one of the odes of the ancient Edda of Semund, it occurs in the speech of Odin, who says, 'fornum stavfom,' *in the ancient letters.*[7]

"The numerous compound words derived from 'staef,' *a letter*, show it to have been a radical term in the language, and of general application:—

Staef-craeft,	*the art of letters.*
Staefen-row,	*the alphabet.*
Staef-gefeg,	*a syllable.*
Staeflic,	*learned.*
Staefnian,	*to teach letters.*
Staef-plega,	*a game at letters.*
Staef-wís,	*wise in letters.*
Stafa-heáfod,	*the head of the letters.*
Stafa-naman,	*the names of the letters.*

"The same word was also used like the Latin 'litera, to signify *an epistle.*[8]

---

[7] "Edda Semund, p. 3. In the Icelandic Gospels, for '*in Latin and in Hebrew letters*' we have 'Latiniskum and Ebreskum bókstefum.' Luke xxiii. 38. The Franco-Theotisc, for *letters*, has a similar compound word, 'bók-staven.'"

[8] "When a letter or authoritative document is mentioned in Saxon, the expressions applied to it are not borrowed from the Latin, as 'scriptum,' 'mandatum,' 'epistola,' and such like; but it is said, 'Honorius sent the Scot a 'ge-writ,'' *Sax. Ch.* 39; desired the Pope with

"*The art of using letters*, or *writing*, is also expressed in Saxon by a verb not of Roman origin. The Saxon term for the verb *to write*, is not like the Erse expression, from the Latin 'scribere,' but is 'awrítan,' or 'gewrítan.' This verb is formed from a similar noun of the same meaning as 'staef.' The noun is preserved in the Moeso-Gothic, where 'writs' signifies *a letter*.

"In like manner the Saxons did not derive their word for *book* from the Latin 'liber;' they expressed it by their own term, 'bóc,' as the Northerns called it 'bóg.'

"I do not mean to assert indiscriminately, that whenever a word indigenous to a language is used to express *writing*, it is therefore to be inferred that the people using that language have also letters; because it may so happen that the word may not have been an indigenous term for *letters*, but for something else; and may have been applied to express *letters* only analogically or metaphorically. To give an instance: the Indians of New England expressed *letters*, or *writing*, by the terms 'wussukwhonk,' or 'wussukwheg.' But the Indians had no letters nor writing among them: whence then had they these words? The answer is, that they were in the habit of painting their faces and their garments, and when we made them acquainted with writing, they applied to it their word for *painting*.[9] But though they could figuratively apply their term for *painting* to express *writing*, they had nothing to signify

---

his 'ge-writ' to confirm it, *ib.* 38. So Alfred, translating Bede, says, 'The Pope sent to Augustine 'pallium and ge-writ;'' here borrowing from the Latin the 'pallium,' a thing known to them from the Romans, but using a native Saxon term to express the word *epistle*."

[9] "Thus 'wussukhosu' was *a painted coat*. Williams' *Key to the Language of America*, p. 184, ed. 1643, and see his remark, p. 61. The Malays, who have borrowed their letters from other nations, have used the same analogy. Their word *to write*, is 'toolis,' which also signifies *to paint*, See Howison's *Malay Dictionary*."

a book, and therefore it was necessary to ingraft our English word *book* into their language for that purpose.

"On the whole, I am induced to believe that the Anglo-Saxons were not unacquainted with alphabetical characters when they came into England. However this may be, it is certain that if they had ancient letters, they ceased to use them after their conversion. It was the invariable policy of the Roman ecclesiastics to discourage the use of the Runic characters, because they were of pagan origin, and had been much connected with idolatrous superstitions.[10] Hence, as soon as the Christian clergy acquired influence in the Saxon octarchy, all that appeared in their literature was in the character which they had formed from the Romans.

"We know nothing of the compositions of the Anglo-Saxons in their pagan state. Tacitus mentions generally of the Germans that they had ancient songs, and therefore we may believe that the Anglo-Saxons were not without them. Indeed, Dunstan is said to have learned the vain songs of his countrymen in their pagan state; and we may suppose that if such compositions had not been in existence at that period, Edgar would not have forbidden men, on festivals, to sing heathen songs. But none of these had survived to us. If they were ever committed to writing it was on wood or stones; indeed, their word for *book*, 'bóc,' expresses *a beech-tree*, and seems to allude to the matter of which their earliest books were made.[11] The

---

[10] "The Swedes were persuaded by the Pope, in 1001, to lay aside the Runic letters, and to adopt the Roman in their stead. They were gradually abolished in Denmark, and afterwards in Iceland."

[11] "Wormius infers, that pieces of wood cut from the beech-tree were the ancient northern books, *Lit. Run.* p. 6. Saxo-Grammaticus mentions, that Fengo's Ambassadors took with them 'literas ligno insculptas,' 'because,' adds Saxo, 'that was formerly a celebrated kind of material to write upon,' lib. iii. p. 52. Besides the passage formerly

poets of barbarous ages usually confide the little effusions of their genius to the care of tradition. They are seldom preserved in writing till literature becomes a serious study; and therefore we may easily believe, that if the Anglo-Saxons had alphabetical characters, they were much more used for divinations, charms, and funeral inscriptions, than for literary compositions."—SHARON TURNER—*Hist. of the Anglo-Saxons, Vol. I., B. II., App., Chap. IV.*

---

cited from Fortunatus, we may notice another, in which he speaks of the bark as used to contain characters. See *Worm.*, p. 9, who says that no wood more abounds in Denmark than the beech, nor is any more adapted to receive impressions, *ib.* p. 7. In Welsh, 'gwydd, *a tree*, or *wood*, is used to denote *a book*. So Gwilym Tew talks of reading the gwydd.' Owen's *Dict. voc.* 'gwydd.'"

APPENDIX B.

"ON THE COPIOUSNESS OF THE ANGLO-SAXON LANGUAGE."

"THIS language has been thought to be a very rude and barren tongue, incapable of expressing any thing but the most simple and barbarous ideas. The truth, however, is, that it is a very copious language, and is capable of expressing any subject of human thought. In the technical terms of those arts and sciences which have been discovered, or much improved, since the Norman Conquest, it must of course be deficient. But books of history, *belles-lettres*, and poetry, may be now written in it, with considerable precision and correctness, and even with much discrimination, and some elegance of expression.

"The Saxon abounds with synonyms. I will give a few instances of those which my memory can supply."

Our author here introduces a number of words as synonyms, but which rather express the same objects under different relations.

"They had a great number of words for *a ship*, and to express *the Supreme*, they used more words and phrases than I can recollect to have seen in any other language.

"Indeed, the copiousness of their language was receiving perpetual additions from the lays of their poets. I have already mentioned that the great features of their poetry were metaphor and periphrasis. On these they prided themselves. To be fluent in these was the great object of their emulation, and the great test of their merit. Hence, Cedmon, in his account of the deluge, uses near thirty synonymous words and phrases to express *the ark*. They could not attain this desired end without making new words and phrases by new compounds, and most of these became naturalized in the language. The same zeal for novelty of expression led them to borrow words from every other language which came within their reach."*

* * * * * * * * *

"But the great proof of the copiousness and power of the Anglo-Saxon language may be had from considering our own English, which is principally Saxon. It may be interesting to show this by taking some lines of our principal authors, and marking in *italics* the Saxon words they contain.

SHAKSPEARE.

To be or not to be, that is the question;
Whether 'tis nobler *in the mind to* suffer
The slings and arrows of outrageous fortune,
Or to take arms *against a sea of* troubles,
And by opposing *end them? To die, to sleep;*
No more! and by a sleep to say we end
The heart-ach, and the thousand natural *shocks*
The flesh is heir *to! 'twere a* consummation
Devoutly *to be wished. To die, to sleep;*
To sleep? perchance *to dream!*

MILTON.

With thee conversing *I forget all time,*
All seasons, *and their* change; *all* please *alike.*
Sweet is the breath of morn, her rising sweet,
With charm *of earliest birds;* pleasant *the sun*
When first on this delightful *land he spreads*

---

* We must here observe that a word strictly foreign, or not belonging to the Teutonic family, is rarely met with in any Anglo-Saxon writer, and those introduced from the Latin and the Greek are usually found modified in orthography to suit the genius of the tongue.—*K.*

His orient *beams on* herb, *tree*, fruit, *and* flower,
Glistening with dew; fragrant *the* fertile *earth*
After soft showers; and sweet the coming on
Of grateful *evening mild; then* silent *night*
With this her solemn *bird, and this fair moon,*
And these the gems *of heaven, her starry train.*

COWLEY.

Mark that swift arrow; how it cuts *the air!*
How it outruns the following eye!
Use *all* persuasions *now and try*
If thou canst call *it back, or* stay *it there.*
That way it went; but thou shalt find
No track *is left behind.*
Fool! 'tis thy life, and the fond archer *thou.*
Of all the time thou'st shot away
I'll bid thee fetch but yesterday,
And it shall be too hard a task *to do.*

TRANSLATORS OF THE BIBLE.

And they made ready the present *against* Joseph *came at noon: for they heard that they should eat bread there. And when* Joseph *came home, they brought him the* present *which was in their hand into the house, and bowed themselves to him to the earth. And he asked them of their welfare, and said, Is your father well, the old man of whom ye spake? Is he yet alive? And they answered, Thy* servant *our father is in good health, he is yet alive. And they bowed down their heads, and made* obeisance. *And he lifted up his eyes, and saw his brother* Benjamin, *his mother's son, and said, Is this your younger brother, of whom ye spake unto me? And he said, God be* gracious *unto thee, my son.* Gen. xliii. 25–29.

Then when Mary *was come where* Jesus *was, and saw him, she fell down at his feet, saying unto him, Lord, if thou hadst been here, my brother had not died. When* Jesus *therefore saw her weeping, and the* Jews *also weeping which came with her, he groaned in the* spirit, *and was* troubled. *And said, Where have ye laid him? They said unto him, Lord, come and see.* Jesus *wept. Then said the* Jews *Behold how he loved him.* John xi. 32–36

THOMSON.

These as they change, *Almighty Father, these*
Are but the varied *God. The* rolling *year*
Is full of thee. Full in the pleasing *spring*
Thy beauty walks, thy tenderness *and love.*
Wide flush the fields; the soft'ning air is balm;
Echo *the mountains round; the forest smiles;*
And every sense *and every heart is* joy.
Then comes thy glory *in the summer months,*
With light and heat refulgent. *Then thy sun*
Shoots full perfection *through the swelling year.*

ADDISON.

I was yesterday, about sunset, walking in the open fields, till the night insensibly *fell upon me. I at first* amused *myself with all the richness and* variety *of* colors *which* appeared *in the western parts of heaven. In* proportion *as they* faded *away and went out,* several *stars and* planets appeared, *one after another, till the whole* firmament *was in a glow. The blueness of the* æther *was* exceedingly *heightened and enlivened by the* season *of the year.*

SPENSER.

Hard is the doubt, *and* difficult *to deem,*
When all three kinds of love together meet,
And do dispart *the heart with* power extreme,
Whether shall weigh the balance *down; to weet*
The dear affection *unto kindred sweet,*
Or raging *fire of love to woman kind,*
Or zeal *of friends* combined *with* virtues *meet:*
But of them all the band of virtuous *mind*
Me seems the gentle *heart should most* assured *bend.*

Book 4, C. 9.

LOCKE.

Every man, being conscious *to himself, that he thinks, and that, which his mind is* applied *about whilst thinking, being the* ideas *that are there; it is* past doubt, *that men have in their minds* several ideas. *Such are those* expressed *by the words, whiteness, hardness, sweetness, thinking,* motion, *man,* elephant, army, *drunkenness, and others. It is in the first* place, *then, to be* inquired, *How he comes by them? I know it is a* received doctrine *that men have* native *ideas, and* original characters stamped *upon their minds in their very first being* Locke's Essay, Book 11, Ch. 1.

POPE.

How happy is the blameless vestal's *lot!*
The world forgetting, by the world forgot;
Eternal *sunshine of the spotless mind!*
Each pray'r accepted, *and each wish* resign'd;
Labor *and rest that* equal periods *keep;*
Obedient *slumbers that can wake and weep;*
Desires composed, affections *ever even;*
Tears that delight, *and sighs that waft to heaven,*
Grace *shines around her with* serenest *beams,*
And whispering angels prompt *her golden dreams.*
For her th' unfading *rose of* Eden *blooms,*
And wings of seraphs *shed* divine perfumes.

YOUNG.

Let Indians, *and the gay, like* Indians, *fond*
Of feather'd fopperies, *the sun* adore;
Darkness has more divinity *for me;*
It strikes thought inward, it drives back the soul
To settle on herself, our point supreme.
There lies our theatre: *there sits our* judge.
Darkness the curtain *drops o'er life's dull* scene;
'Tis the kind hand of Providence *stretch'd out*
'Twixt man and vanity; *'tis* reason's reign,
And virtue's *too; these* tutelary *shades*
Are man's asylum *from the* tainted *throng.*
Night is the good man's friend and guardian too.
It no less rescues virtue, *than* inspires.

SWIFT.

Wisdom is a fox, who, after long hunting, will at last cost you the pains *to dig out. 'Tis a cheese, which by how much the richer has the thicker, the homelier, and the* coarser coat; *and whereof, to a* judicious palate, *the maggots are the best. 'Tis a sack* posset, *wherein the deeper you go, you will find it the sweeter. But then, lastly, 'tis a nut, which, unless you choose with* judgment, *may cost you a tooth, and* pay *you with nothing but a worm.*

ROBERTSON.

This great emperor, *in the* plenitude *of his* power, *and in* possession *of all the* honors *which can* flatter *the heart of man, took the* extraordinary resolution *to* resign *his kingdom; and to withdraw* entirely *from any* concern *in business, or the* affairs *of this world, in* order *that he might spend the* remainder *of his days in* retirement *and* solitude. Dioclesian *is,* perhaps, *the only* prince capable *of holding the* reins *of* government, *who ever* resigned *them from* deliberate *choice, and who* continued during *many years to* enjoy *the* tranquillity *of* retirement, *without fetching one* penitent *sigh, or casting back one look of* desire *towards the* power *or* dignity *which he had* abandoned.—Charles V

HUME.

The beauties *of her* person, *and* graces *of her* air, combined *to make her the most* amiable *of women; and the* charms *of her* address *and* conversation aided *the* impression *which her lovely* figure *made on the heart of all beholders.* Ambitious *and* active *in her* temper, *yet* inclined *to* cheerfulness *and* society; *of a lofty* spirit, constant, *and even* vehement *in her* purpose, *yet* politic, gentle, *and* affable *in her* demeanor, *she* seemed *to* partake *only so much of the* male virtues *as to* render *her* estimable *without* relinquishing *those soft* graces *which* compose *the* proper ornament *of her* sex.

GIBBON.

In the second century *of the* Christian era *the* empire *of* Rome comprehended *the fairest* part *of the earth, and the most* civilized portion *of mankind. The* frontiers *of that* extensive monarchy *were guarded by* ancient renown *and* disciplined valor. *The* gentle *but* powerful influence *of laws and manners had* gradually cemented *the* union *of the* provinces. *Their peaceful* inhabitants enjoyed *and* abused *the* advantages *of wealth and* luxury. *The* image *of a free* constitution *was* preserved *with* decent reverence.

JOHNSON.

Of genius, *that* power, *which* constitutes *a* poet; *that* quality, *without which* judgment *is cold and knowledge is* inert; *that* energy *which* collects, combines, amplifies, *and* animates, *the* superiority *must, with some* hesitation, *be* allowed *to* Dryden. *It is not to be* inferred *that of this* poetical vigor Pope *had only a little, because* Dryden *had more; for every other writer since* Milton *must give* place *to* Pope; *and even of* Dryden *it must be said, that if he has brighter* paragraphs, *he has not better* poems.

"From the preceding instances we may form an idea of the power of the Saxon language, but by no means a just idea; for we must not conclude that the words which are not Saxon could not be supplied by Saxon words. On the contrary, Saxon terms might be substituted for all the words not marked as Saxon.

"To impress this sufficiently on the mind of the reader, it will be necessary to show how much of our ancient language we have laid aside, and have suffered to become obsolete; because all our writers, from Chaucer to our own times, have used words of foreign origin rather than our own. In three pages of Alfred's Orosius, I found 78 words which have become obsolete, out of 548, or about one-seventh. In three pages of his Boetius I found 143 obsolete out of 666, or about one-fifth. In three pages of his Bede, I found 230 obsolete out of 969, or about one-fifth. The difference in the proportion between these and the Orosius proceeds from the latter containing many historical names. Perhaps we shall be near the truth if we say, as a general principle, that one-fifth of the Anglo-Saxon language has ceased to be used in modern English. This loss must of course be taken into account when we estimate the copiousness of our ancient language, by considering how much of it our English authors exhibit."—SHARON TURNER—*Hist. of the Anglo-Saxons, Vol. I., App. I., Chap. III.*

APPENDIX C.

"THE Greeks and Romans, counting only by tens, composed their numbers from ten to twenty, with 'δεκα,' 'decem,' *ten;* 'ἑνδεκα,' 'undecim,' *eleven;* 'δυωδεκα,' 'duodecim,' *twelve.* The German tribes formed the same numerals in a similar manner, except *eleven* and *twelve,* which were composed with *Ger.* 'lif;' *A. S.* 'laéfan;' 'lif,' 'lef,' 'l'f,' in other dialects. But as this anomaly entered our numeral system in a period anterior to the history of our tongues, and is common to all the Germanic languages, the analogy between the kindred dialects is not disturbed by these irregularities, but rather advanced.

"18. The cause of this disturbance lies in the old practice of using both *ten* and *twelve* as fundamental numbers.

"The advance was by ten, thus 'ṭhrittig,' *Country Friesic* 'tritich;' 'feowertig,' *Ab.* 2, &c.; but on arriving at sixty the series was finished, and another begun, denoted by prefixing 'hund.' This second series proceeded to one hundred and twenty, thus: 'hund-nigontig,' *ninety;* 'hund-teontig,' *a hundred;* 'hund-enlufontig,' *a hundred and ten;* 'hund-twelftig,' *a hundred and twenty:* here the second series concluded. It thus appears that the Anglo-Saxons did not know our hundred = 100, as the chief division of numbers; and though they counted from ten to ten, they, at the same time, chose the number *twelve* as the basis of the chief divisions. As we say, $5 \times 10 = 50$; $10 \times 10 = 100$; they multiplied 5 and 10 by 12, and produced 60 and 120. When the Scandinavians adopted a hundred as a chief division—$100 = 10 \times 10$—they still retained one hundred and twenty; and calling both these numbers ***hundred,*** they distinguished them by the epithets *little* or ten hundred, 'lill-hundrad' or 'hundrad tiraed,' and *great* or the twelve number hundred, 'stor-hundrad,' or 'hundrad tólfraed.' The Danes count to forty by tens, thus: 'tredive,' *thirty;* 'fyrretyve,' *forty;* and then commence by twenties, thus: 'halvtrediesindstyve,' literally in *A. S.* 'ṭḥridda healf sithon twentig'*—*two twenties*—and the *third twenty half,* i. e. *fifty.* The Icelanders call 2500 'half ṭḥridie ṭḥusand,' —*Dut.* 'derdehalfduizend,' i. e. *two thousand,* and *the third thousand half;* 'firesindtyve'—*four times twenty—eighty,* and so on to a hundred. The Francs being a mixture of kindred nations from the middle of Germany, when they entered Gallia, partly adopted the Anglo-Saxon mode of numeration, and partly that of the Danes, and they afterwards translated verbally their vernacular names of the numerals by Latin words. From twenty to fifty it proceeds in the usual manner, 'vingt,' 'trente,' 'quarante,' 'cinquante,' 'soixante;' but having arrived at seventy, the same place where the Anglo-Saxons commenced with 'hund,' 'hundseofontig,' it uses 'soixante-dix,' 'quatre-vingt,' just as the Danes express eighty by 'firesindstyve,' *four times twenty.* As it appears that the old Germans had two fundamental numbers, *ten* and *twelve,* it follows that *eleven* and *twelve* are the *last two* numerals of the twelve series, and the *first two* in the ten series; hence perhaps the same use of the termination 'lif' or 'lef' in *eleven* and *twelve.*"—BOSWORTH, *Origin and Connection of the Germanic Tongues.* London, 1838.

* "The ellipsis of the *two twenties* is supplied in the expression 'twá geáre and ṭḥridde healf,' *two years and half the third year,* literally in *Frs. c.* 'twa jier in t' tredde heal,' but custom contracts it to 'tredde heal jier.' Hickes compares this ellipsis with the Scotch expression, *half ten,* which is also the *Dut.* 'half tien,' but in this he is not accurate. The country Friesians not having this ellipsis, proves that it must be supplied in another way. They say, 'healwei tsjienen,' *half way of the present hour to ten o'clock.* Dr. Dorow has also fallen into the same mistake, p. 127, *Denkmäler,* I., 2 and 3."

APPENDIX D.

"ON THE STRUCTURE AND MECHANISM OF THE ANGLO-SAXON LANGUAGE."

"To explain the history of any language is a task peculiarly difficult at this period of the world, in which we are so very remote from the era of its original construction.

"We have, as yet, witnessed no people in the act of forming their language, and cannot, therefore, from experience, demonstrate the simple elements from which a language begins, nor the additional organization which it gradually receives. The languages of highly civilized people, which are those that we are most conversant with, are in a state very unlike their ancient tongues. Many words have been added to them from other languages; many have deviated into meanings very different from their primitive significations; many have been so altered by the change of pronunciation and orthography, as scarcely to bear any resemblance to their ancient forms. The abbreviations of language, which have been usually called its articles, pronouns, conjunctions, prepositions, and interjections; the inflections of its verbs, the declensions of its nouns, and the very form of its syntax, have also undergone so many alterations from the caprice of human usage, that it is impossible to discern any thing of the mechanism of a language, but by ascending from its present state to its more ancient form.

"The Anglo-Saxon is one of those ancient languages to

which we may successfully refer, in our inquiries how language has been constructed.

"As we have not had the experience of any people forming a language, we cannot attain to a knowledge of its mechanism in any other way than by analyzing it; by arranging its words into their classes, and by tracing these to their elementary sources. We shall perhaps be unable to discover the original words with which the language began, but we may hope to trace the progress of its formation, and some of the principles on which that progress has been made. In this inquiry I shall follow the steps of the author of the *Diversions of Purley,* and build upon his foundation, because I think that his book has presented to us the key to that mechanism which we have so long admired, so fruitlessly examined, and so little understood.

"Words have been divided into nine classes: the article, the substantive or noun, the pronoun, the adjective, the verb, the adverb, the preposition, the conjunction, and the interjection.

"Under these classes all the Saxon words may be arranged, although not with that scientific precision with which the classifications of natural history have been made. Mr. Tooke has asserted, that in all languages there are only two sorts of words necessary for the communication of our thoughts, and therefore only two parts of speech, the noun and the verb, and that the others are the abbreviations of these.

"But if the noun and the verb be only used, they will serve not so much to impart our meaning, as to indicate it. These will suffice to express simple substances or facts, and simple motions of nature or man; but will do by themselves little else. All the connections, references, distinctions, limitations, applications, contrasts, relations, and refinements of thought and feeling—and therefore most of what a cultivated people wish to express by language, cannot be conveyed without the other essential abbreviations—and therefore all nations have been compelled, as occasions occurred, as wants increased, and as thought evolved, to invent or adopt them, till all that were necessary became naturalized in the language.

"That nouns and verbs are the most essential and primitive words of language, and that all others have been formed from them, are universal facts, which after reading the *Diversions of Purley*, and tracing in other languages the application of the principles there maintained, no enlightened philologist will now deny. But though this is true as to the origin of these parts of speech, it may be questioned whether the names established by conventional use may not be still properly retained, because the words now classed as conjunctions, prepositions, etc., though originally verbs, are not verbs at present, but have been long separated from their verbal parents, and have become distinct parts of our grammatical syntax.

"That the conjunctions, the prepositions, the adverbs, and the interjections of our language, have been made from our verbs and nouns, Mr. Tooke has satisfactorily shown; and with equal truth he has affirmed, that articles and pronouns have proceeded from the same source. I have pursued his inquiries through the Saxon and other languages, and am satisfied that the same may be affirmed of adjectives. Nouns and verbs are the parents of all the rest of language; and it can be proved in the Anglo-Saxon, as in other tongues, that of these the nouns are the ancient and primitive stock from which all other words have branched and vegetated."

* * * * * * * * *

"The Anglo-Saxon VERBS have essentially contributed to form those parts of speech which Mr. Tooke has denominated the abbreviations of language. The verbs, however, are not themselves the primitive words of our language. They are all in a state of composition. They are like the secondary mountains of the earth—they have been formed posterior to the ancient bulwarks of human speech, which are the nouns—I mean of course those nouns which are in their elementary state.

"In some languages, as in the Hebrew, the verbs are very often the nouns applied unaltered to a verbal signification. We have examples of this sort of verbs in our English words, *love, hate, fear, hope, dream, sleep,* etc. These words are nouns, and are also used as verbs. Of verbs thus made by the simple application of nouns in a verbal form, the Anglo-Saxon gives few examples.

"Almost all its other verbs are nouns with a final syllable added, and this final syllable is a word expressive of *motion,* or *action,* or *possession.*

"To show this fact, we will take some of the Anglo-Saxon verbs:—

Bád, *a pledge.*	bád-ian, *to pledge.*
baer, *a bier.*	baer-an, *to carry.*
baeth, *a bath.*	baeth-ian, *to wash.*
bat, *a club.*	beát-an, *to beat.*
bebod, *a command.*	bebod-an, *to command.*
bidd, *a prayer.*	bidd-an, *to pray.*
bíg, *a crown.*	bíg-an, *to bend.*
bliss, *joy.*	bliss-ian, *to rejoice.*
blostm, *a flower.*	blostm-ian, *to blossom.*
blót, *a sacrifice.*	blót-an, *to sacrifice.*
bód, *an edict.*	bód-ian, *to proclaim.*
borg, *a loan.*	borg-ian, *to lend.*
brídl, *a bridle.*	brídl-ian, *to bridle.*
bróc, *misery.*	bróc-ian, *to afflict.*
býe, *a habitation.*	bý-an, *to inhabit.*
byseg, *business.*	bysg-ian, *to be busy.*
bysmr, *contumely*	bysmr-ian, *to deride.*

bytla, *a builder.*	bytl-ian, *to build.*
cár, *care.*	cár-ian, *to be anxious.*
ceáp, *cattle.*	ceáp-ian, *to buy.*
céle, *cold.*	cél-an, *to cool.*
cerre, *a bending*	cerr-an, *to return.*
cid, *strife.*	cíd-an, *to quarrel.*
cnyt, *a knot.*	cnytt-an, *to tie.*
comp, *a battle.*	comp-ian, *to fight.*
craeft, *art.*	craeft-an, *to build.*
curs, *a curse.*	curs-ian, *to curse.*
cwid, *a saying.*	cwydd-ian, *to say.*
cyrm, *a noise.*	cyrm-an, *to cry out.*
cyth, *knowledge*	cyth-an, *to make known.*
cos, *a kiss.*	coss-an, *to kiss.*
dǽl, *a part.*	dǽl-an, *to divide.*
daeg, *day.*	daeg-ian, *to shine.*
deág, *color.*	deág-an, *to tinge.*

"If we go through all the alphabet, we shall find that most of the verbs are composed of a noun, and the syllables -an, -ian, or -gan. Of these additional syllables, -gan is the verb of motion, *to go,* or the verb 'ágan,' *to possess;* and -an seems sometimes the abbreviation of 'anan,' *to give,* and sometimes of the verbs 'gán' and 'ágan.' Thus 'deágan,' *to tinge,* appears to me 'deág-an,' *to give a color;* 'dǽlan,' *to divide,* 'dǽl-an,' *to give a part;* 'cossan,' *to kiss,* 'cos-an,' *to give a kiss;* 'cursian,' *to curse,* 'curs-an,' *to give a curse;* while we may presume that 'cárian,' *to be anxious,* is 'cár-ágan,' *to have care;* 'blostmian,' *to blossom,* is 'blostm-ágan,' *to have a flower;* 'býan,' *to inhabit,* is 'bý-ágan,' *to have a habitation.* We may also say that 'cídan,' *to quarrel,* is the abbreviation of 'cíd-gán,' *to go to quarrel;* 'baethian,' *to wash,* is 'baeth-gán,' *to go to a bath;* 'biddan,' *to pray,* is 'bidd-gán,' *to go to pray.* The Gothic *to pray,* is 'bidgan.'

"That the words 'gán,' and 'ágan,' have been abbreviated or softened into -an, or -ian, can be proved from several verbs. Thus 'fylgan,' or 'filigian,' *to follow*, is also 'filian. Thus 'fleógan,' *to fly*, becomes 'fleón' and 'flión.' So 'forhtigan,' *to be afraid*, has become also 'forhtian.' So 'fundigan' has become 'fundian;' 'gethyldgian,' 'gethyldian;' 'fengan,' 'fóan,' and 'fón;' and 'teógan,' 'teón.' The examples of this change are innumerable.

"This abbreviation is also proved by many of the participles of the abbreviated verbs ending in -gend, thus showing the original infinitive to have been -gen; as 'fréfrian,' *to comfort*, has its participle 'fréfergend;' 'fremian,' *to profit*, 'freomigend;' 'fúlian,' has 'fúligend;' 'gǽmnian,' 'gǽmnigend,' etc.

"Many verbs are composed of the terminations above mentioned, and of words which exist in the Anglo-Saxon, not as nouns, but as adjectives, and of some words which are not to be met with in the Anglo-Saxon, either as nouns or adjectives. But so true is the principle, that nouns were the primitive words of these verbs, and that verbs are but the nouns with the additional final syllables, that we shall very frequently find the noun we search for existing in the state of a noun in some of those languages which have a close affinity with the Anglo-Saxon. This language meets our eye in a very advanced state, and therefore, when we decompose it, we cannot expect to meet in itself all its elements. Many of its elements had dropped out of its vocabulary at that period wherein we find it, just as in modern English we have dropped a great number of words of our Anglo-Saxon ancestors. In this treatise, which the necessary limits of my publication compel me to make very concise, I can only be expected to give a few instances.

"'Beran,' is *to bring forth*, or *produce;* there is no primitive noun answering to this verb in the Anglo-Saxon, but there is in the Franco-Theotisc, where we find 'bar' is *fruit*, or *whatever the earth produces;* 'ber-an' is therefore *to give fruit*, or *to produce*. So 'maérsian,' *to celebrate*, is from 'segan,' *to speak*, and some noun from which the adjective 'maéra,' *illustrious*, had been formed. The noun is not in the Saxon, but it is in the Franco-Theotisc, where 'maéra' is *fame*, or *rumor;* therefore, 'maérsian,' *to celebrate a person*, is 'maéra-segan,' *to speak his fame*. I have observed many examples of this sort.

"In searching for the original nouns from which verbs have been formed, we must always consider if the verb we are inquiring about be a primitive verb or a secondary verb, containing either of the prefixes a-, be-, ge-, for-, in-, on-, to-, with-, etc. In these cases we must strip the verb of its prefix, and examine its derivation under its earlier form. The verbs with a prefix are obviously of later origin than the verbs to which the prefix has not been applied.

"Sometimes the verb consists of two verbs put together, as 'gán-gán,' *to go;* so 'for-laétan,' *to dismiss* or *leave*, is composed of two verbs, 'faran,' *to go*, 'laétan,' *to let* or *suffer*, and is literally, *to let go*.

"The Anglo-Saxon NOUNS are not all of the same antiquity; some are the primitive words of the language from which every other has branched, but some are of later date."

* * * * * * * * *

"The primitive nouns expressing sensible objects, having been formed, they were multiplied by combinations with each other. They were then applied to express ideas more abstracted. By adding to them a few expressive syllables, the numerous classes of verbs and adjectives arose; and from these again other nouns and adjectives were formed. The nouns and verbs were then abbreviated and adapted into conjunctions, prepositions, adverbs, and interjections. The pronouns were soon made from a sense of their convenience; and out of them came the articles. To illustrate these principles, from the various languages which I have examined, would expand these few pages into a volume, and would be therefore improper; but I can recommend the subject to the attention of the philological student, with every assurance of a successful research.

"The multiplication of language by the metaphorical application of nouns to express other nouns, or to signify adjectives, may be observed in all languages. Thus, 'beorht,' *light*, was applied to express *bright, shining*, and *illustrious*. So 'deóp,' *the sea*, was applied to express *depth*.

"As a specimen how the Anglo-Saxon language has been formed from the multiplication of simple words, I will show the long train of words which have been formed from a few primitive words. I select four of the words applicable to the mind. The numerous terms formed from them will illustrate the preceding observations on the mechanism of the language.

ANCIENT NOUN :—

Hyge, *or* hige, *mind*, or *thought*.

Secondary meaning: *care, diligence, study.*

Hoga, *care*,

Hogu, *care, industry, effort.*

Adjectives, being the noun so applied:—

Hige, *diligent, studious, attentive*,

Hoga, *prudent, solicitous.*

Verbs from the noun:—

Hogian. *to meditate, to study, to think, to be wise, to be anxious:* and hence, *to groan.*

Hygian, } *to study, to be solicitous, to endeavor.*
Hyggan, }

The verb, by use, having gained new shades of meaning and applications, we meet with it again, as :—

Hicgan, } *to study, to explore, to seek vehemently, to endeavor, to struggle.*
Hycgan, }

Secondary noun derived from this verb :—

Hogung, *care, effort, endeavor.*

Secondary nouns, compounded of the ancient noun and another :—

Hige-craeft, *acuteness of mind.*
Higeleást, *negligence, carelessness.*
Hige-sorga, *anxieties, mental griefs.*
Hogascipe, } *prudence.*
Hogoscipe, }
Hygeleást,* *folly, madness, scurrility.*
Hygesceaft, *the mind,* or *thought.*

Adjectives composed of the ancient noun and a meaning word :—

Hygèleás, *void of mind, foolish.*
Hyge-róf, } *magnanimous, excellent in mind.*
Hige-róf, }
Hogfast, } *prudent.*
Hogofast, }
Hogfull, *anxious, full of care.*
Hige-fród, *wise, prudent in mind.*
Higeleás,† *negligent, incurious.*

---

* The same as "higeleast."—*K.*
† No other than "hygeleás."—*K.*

Hige-strang, *strong in mind.*
Hige-thancol, *cautious, provident, thoughtful.*

Adverbs from the adjective :—

Higeleáslice, *negligently, incuriously.*
Hogfullice, *anxiously.*

ANCIENT NOUN :—

Mód, *the mind;* also, *passion,* and *irritability.*

Verbs :—

Módian, } *to be high minded,*
Módigan, } *to rage,*
Módgian, } *to swell.*

Adjectives composed of the noun and another word or syllable :—

Módig, } *irritable,*
Módeg, } *angry, proud.*
Módful, *full of mind, irritable.*
Módga,* *elated, proud, distinguished.*
Mód-hwat, *fervent in mind.*
Módilic, *magnanimous.*
Módleás, *meek-minded, pusillanimous.*
Mód-stathol, *firm-minded.*
Mód-thwaer, *patient in mind, meek, mild.*

Secondary nouns composed of the ancient noun and some other :—

Mód-gethanc, *thoughts of the mind, council.*
Mód-gethóht, *strength of mind, reasoning.*

---

* Rather, the definite state masculine of "módig," or "módeg," contracted.—*K.*

Mód-gewinn, *conflicts of mind.*
Módes-mynla, *the affections of the mind, the inclinations.*
Mód-héte, *heat of mind—anger.*
Módleást, *folly, pusillanimity, slothfulness.*
Módnes, *pride.*
Mód-sefa, *the intellect, sensation, intelligence.*
Mód-sorg, *grief of mind.*

Secondary nouns of still later origin, having been formed after the adjectives, and composed of an adjective and another noun :—

Módignes, } *moodiness, pride, animosity.*
Módines, }
Mód-seocnes, *sickness of mind.*
Mód-statholnys, *firmness of mind, fortitude.*
Mód-sumnes, *concord.*
Mód-thwaernes, *patience, meekness.*

Adverb formed from the adjective :—

Módiglice, *proudly, angrily.*

ANCIENT NOUN :—

Wit, } *the mind, genius, the intellect, the sense.*
Gewit, }
Secondary meaning : *wisdom, prudence.*

Noun applied as an adjective :—

Wita, } *wise, skilful.*
Wite, }
Gewita, *conscious ;* hence, *a witness.*

Verbs formed from the noun :—

Witan, *to know, to perceive.*
Gewitan, *to understand.*
Witegian, *to prophesy.*

Adjectives composed of the ancient noun, and an additional syllable, or word:—

Witig, *wise, skilled, ingenious, prudent.*
Gewitig, *knowing, wise, intelligent.*
Gewitleás, *ignorant, foolish.*
Gewittig,* *intelligent, conscious.*
Gewit-seoc, *ill in mind, demoniac.*
Witol, wittol, *wise, knowing.*

Secondary nouns formed of the ancient noun and another noun:—

Witedóm, *the knowledge of judgment, prediction.*
Witega, *a prophet.*
Witegung, *prophecy.*
Wite-saga, *a prophet.*
Gewitleást, *folly, madness.*
Gewit-loca, *the mind.*
Gewitnes, *witness.*
Gewitscipe, *witness.*
Wite-clófe, *a trifler.*
Wit-word, *the answer of the wise.*

Nouns of more recent date, having been formed out of the adjectives:—

Gewit-seocnes, *insanity.*
Witigdóm, *knowledge, wisdom, prescience.*
Witolnes, *knowledge, wisdom.*

Secondary adjective, or one formed upon the secondary noun:—

Witedómlic, *prophetical.*

---

* **No other than an orthographic variation of "gewitig."—*K***

Conjunctions :—

Witedlic,
Witodlic, } *indeed, for, but, to-wit.*

Adverbs formed from participles and adjectives :—

Witendlice,
Wittiglice, } *knowingly.*

ANCIENT NOUN :—

Geṭḥanc,
Geṭḥonc, } *the mind, thought, opinion.*

Ṭḥanc,
Ṭḥonc, } *the will, thought.*

Secondary meaning: *an act of the will,* or *thanks.*

Ṭḥing,
Geṭḥing, } *a council.*

And from the consequence conferred by sitting at the council, came—

Geṭḥincth, *honor, dignity.*

Verbs formed from the noun :—

Ṭḥincan,
Ṭḥencan, } *to think, to conceive, to feel, to reason, to consider.*

Geṭḥencan,
Geṭḥengcan, } *to think.*

Ṭḥancian,
Geṭḥancian, } *to thank.*

Ṭḥingan, *to address, to speak, to supplicate.*

Geṭḥanc-metan, *to consider.*

Adjectives formed from the ancient noun :—

Ṭḥancol,
Ṭḥoncol, } *thoughtful, meditating, cautious.*

Geṭḥancol, *mindful.*
Ṭḥancful, *thankful, ingenious, content.*
Ṭḥanc-wurth, *grateful.*
Ṭḥancol-mód, *provident, wise.*

Secondary nouns formed from the verb :—

Ṭḥóht, } *thinking, thought.*
Geṭḥóht, }
Geṭḥeáht, *council.*
Geṭḥeáhtere, *counsellor.*
Ṭḥancung, *thanking.*
Ṭḥanc-metung, *deliberation.*

Secondary verb, from one of these secondary nouns :—

Geṭḥeáhtian, *to consult.*

More recent noun, formed from the secondary verb :—

Geṭḥeáhtung, *council, consultation.*

Another secondary verb :—

Ymbe-ṭḥencan, *to think about any thing.*

Adjective from a secondary verb :—

Geṭḥeátendlic, *consulting.*

Adverb from one of the adjectives :—

Ṭḥanc-wurthlice, *gratefully.*

"These specimens will evince to the observing eye how the Anglo-Saxon language has been formed; and they also indicate that it had become very far removed from a rude state of speech. These derivative compounds imply much cultivation and exercise, and a considerable portion of mental discrimination. It is, indeed, in such an advanced state, that novels, moral essays, dramas, and the poetry of nature and feeling might be written in pure Anglo-Saxon, without any perceptible deficiency of appropriate terms."—SHARON TURNER—*Hist. of the Anglo-Saxons, Vol. II., App. I., Chap.* 1.

We have given these extracts without endorsing, as will have been perceived to a certain extent, all the opinions advanced by the writer, differing, as we do in our philological principles, from the author of the *Diversions of Purley*, and others of the late English school. Our views, so far as called forth by the language with which we have been occupied, will appear more fully, and at the same time be exemplified, in another volume now in press, and also, at some future day, in a less compendious Grammar of the Anglo-Saxon, our expressive and noble ancestral tongue

THE END.